RESISTING THROWAWAY CULTURE

How a Consistent Life Ethic Can Unite a Fractured People

Published by New City Press
202 Comforter Blvd.,
Hyde Park, NY 12538
www.newcitypress.com

Cover design and layout: Miguel Tejerina
Cover photo: Tom Parsons

Resisting Throwaway Culture
How a Consistent Life Ethic Can Unite a Fractured People
Charles C. Camosy

2nd Printing: February 2020

Library of Congress Control Number: 2019930102

ISBN 978-1-56548-687-4 (paperback)
ISBN 978-1-56548-688-1 (e-book)

Printed in the United States of America

RESISTING THROWAWAY CULTURE

How a Consistent Life Ethic Can Unite a Fractured People

CHARLES C. CAMOSY

New City Press
Hyde Park, New York

Camosy diagnoses America's current ills better than anyone and offers the most compelling and hopeful way forward of anybody I've read. Unlike a lot of pro-life activists, he doesn't shy away from the most difficult moral issues of our time. Indeed, he embraces them, even as he dismantles modern America's "throwaway culture." I don't always agree with Charlie on everything, but if you're looking for a coherent argument and compassionate worldview—delivered by someone with the credentials to reach a sophisticated and cynical world—this is the only book of its kind.

Matt Lewis
Senior Columnist at the Daily Beast
CNN Political Commentator

Responding to a climate of political tribalism and cultural fracturing, Dr. Camosy's new book provides a unifying framework for creating a culture of encounter in which mercy, responsibility, and dignity lift up vulnerable populations for special protection and welcome. This framework, a growing edge of the Consistent Life Ethic, challenges us to take a stand against a "throwaway culture" in which vulnerable people are reduced to a product in the marketplace instead of recognized for their inherent and irreducible value. If we allow ourselves to be challenged and moved by Camosy's arguments, we can create a culture of encounter capable of resisting what Pope Francis calls a "globalization of indifference."

Kristin M. Collier, MD FACP
Assistant Professor of Internal Medicine
Director of the Program on Health, Spirituality and Religion
University of Michigan Medical School

This book is a must read, deep dive for anyone with questions about the sanctity and dignity of human life in contemporary society. Conservatives and liberals alike will cheer and loathe various chapters with equal fervor, once again making Professor Camosy impossible to pigeonhole as a partisan of any stripe. Agree or disagree, this work is an important contribution to the national conversation about a consistent life ethic.

Kelly M. Rosati
CEO of KMR Consulting
Former VP of Advocacy for Children at Focus on the Family

Camosy is a principled, smart, faithful, and courageous defender of human life and human dignity. A lot of us talk about the "consistent life ethic," but he articulates, demonstrates, and practices it. If you want to understand how the "throwaway culture" challenges both parties, left and right, and every one of us, read this book.

John Carr
Director, Initiative on Catholic Social Thought and Public Life
Georgetown University

I'm grateful to Charles Camosy for doing the hard work of trying to hash out what Catholic social teaching looks like in practice in the world as it is today. You don't have to agree with every word in this book to be inspired to do the same. This book is an exercise in moral civic responsibility and an act of love.

Kathryn Jean Lopez
Senior Fellow, National Review Institute
Editor-at-Large, *National Review*

Camosy has written a unique, deeply thoughtful book that merits the consideration of anyone who wishes to understand a Catholic approach to the intrinsic value and dignity of every human life. Though I may not agree with all of his conclusions, his arguments are well worth engaging.

Alexandra DeSanctis
Staff Writer, *National Review*

Contents

for my children—Jenie, Jonathan, Gina, and Thaddeus—
who are teaching me how to live out a culture of encounter
and hospitality

Preface

The origins of this book go back to the beginnings of my formation as a Roman Catholic Christian. I've identified as an anti-abortion pro-lifer since I was a fifth grader at St. John the Baptist grade school in Paris, Wisconsin—when I first learned what abortion is. But especially for someone who grew up in a purple Midwestern state, and had family all along the political spectrum, some version of the Consistent Life Ethic has always seemed like common sense. I abhorred abortion on the basis of values that had direct implications for other issues, including social support of women in difficult situations.

I started this book project seven years ago, during a 2012 sabbatical at the McDonald Centre for Theology, Ethics and Public Life at Christ Church, Oxford. This occurred well before the phrase "throwaway culture" was even a thing—and also well before two other books I've published in the meantime. I had trouble finding the right angle; also the right energy, the right press, the right moment in my life, and the right audience. First it was a book for the classroom. Then it was a crossover book. Then it was an academic book. Then it was a crossover book again.

The pro-life ethic of Pope Francis excited me soon after his election and I shifted quickly to make him the "hero" of the project. I must admit to losing a bit of that excitement over time, especially given his self-admitted failures with regard to important aspects of the sex abuse crises, though his vision is still central to the project. Despite the roadblocks, stalls, and twists and turns, a phone call with Jessica Keating, director of the Office of Human Dignity and Life Initiatives in the Institute for Church Life at the University of Notre Dame, convinced me that the time was right for this book and pushed me toward the finish line. I'm so indebted to her, and her boss John Cavadini, for their support of my work. On multiple levels.

Taylor Ott, my theology graduate assistant at Fordham for the 2018-2019 academic year, has been incredibly helpful with research, notes, and the appended charts. Past Fordham theology assistants—including Meg Stapleton Smith, Malik Muhammed, and Pierre Bourgeois—have also been extremely helpful as this project developed. Many colleagues in Catholic moral theology gave me wonderful feedback at earlier stages of this project, especially Patrick Clark, Jana Bennett, Julie Rubio, and Jennifer Beste. I'm particularly grateful for those who looked over what would become the final manuscript and gave me critical feedback: Chris Crawford, Christopher White, Kelly Rosati, Elise Italiano, Alexandra DeSanctis, Kristin Collier, Rachel Metzger, Kim Daniels, and Kate Bryan.

And I'm of course very grateful for the team at New City Press, especially for working to meet stricter-than-usual deadlines in getting this book published. I couldn't be prouder to have worked with them—not least because the Focolare's spirituality of unity is at the very heart of this project. If there is anything that can heal our most profound fractures, that can mitigate our current suffering of Jesus Forsaken, it is the Consistent Life Ethic.

Introduction

A Political Culture on the Brink

Political culture in the United States, at least as we've come to know it over the previous two generations, is collapsing. Congress, now more polarized than at any time since Civil War reconstruction, has an approval rating of 19 per cent.[1] (Notably, the electorate prefers cockroaches to Congress.[2]) Donald Trump was elected to the presidency in 2016 with an electoral college victory, but lost the popular vote by more than three million, and came in with the lowest approval rating in modern history.[3] Significantly, relatively few voters for Clinton or Trump were voting for a good candidate they supported; instead, they were voting against a terrible one they loathed.[4] For some time now, the general consensus has been that the Supreme Court has abandoned its role as a non-partisan interpreter of the law in favor of political warfare poorly disguised with *post hoc* legal arguments. The general consensus could not have been more strongly confirmed by the circus that was the 2018 Senate confirmation hearings for Justice Brett Kavanaugh. After those hearings Elizabeth Bruenig had very good reason to wonder whether our political culture is suffering from a near complete dissolution of the trust required for a democratic republic to function.[5]

There is a deep and growing sense that the whole "public thing" is little more than a rigged game; rigged by a tiny few who have become skilled at disconnecting it from justice and the common good in favor of their own narrow set of interests and/or those of their paymasters. The polarization and disconnect of our national politics have a symbiotic relationship with the polarization and disconnect within the broader culture. In a world dominated by smartphones and social media, many find themselves increasingly disconnected from the physical, the embodied, the real—and especially from authentic encounters with "the other." Given the unprecedented ease of travel and mobility, those with the resources to do so most often choose to live in actual and virtual communities who think pretty much like they do. Whether it is the news we watch, the websites we visit, the people we follow on social media, our physical neighbors, our actual and virtual friends, our churches, or the people with whom we socialize, many of us consume information and engage ideas in ideologically comfortable, largely disconnected communities that rarely force us to examine critically the received wisdom of our ideological community.

The ideas of those with whom we think we disagree are often mediated by journalists, academics, or others who do not take such opposing views seriously. Most who watch MSNBC or Fox News channel—or read the *Drudge Report* or the *Huffington Post*—do not expect a balanced, nuanced approach. Such media are designed to be consumed with the expectation that part of what it means to be a member of an ideological community (or, perhaps better, "tribe") is that we define ourselves by our opposition to "the other side" well before we even engage their ideas and arguments.

It appears that our primary love is not for ourselves and our own political tribe, but more a "love to hate" of our perceived enemies.[6] Far from being motivated by a positive vision of the good, the body politic in the United States is motivated by fear and hatred of people (tribes) assumed to be bad or dangerous. Surely, in the last twenty years the hatred and fear for "the other side" has doubled—not least because politicians and media corporations continuously stoke it for their own benefit.[7]

Especially after the 2016 election, some started to articulate what was happening using the term "tribal epistemology." Depending on a person's place on the political spectrum, "the other side" was often understood to be so hopelessly ideological that they could not distinguish truth from falsehood. A liberal like David Roberts blames right-wing authoritarianism.[8] A conservative like Mark Hemmingway blames left-wing groupthink.[9] Not only can we not agree on what the facts are (though that would be bad enough), but we consider our opponents so biased as to be *incapable* of knowing what the facts are. And it is difficult to see how such people could be worth engaging. They can only be defeated.

In the 1990s a median Democrat and a median Republican were not that far apart, but the politics of defining-by-opposition has pushed those medians further and further apart.[10] For ordinary people, such polarization surfaces most clearly during those increasingly rare times when we have to engage ideas that differ significantly from our own. Perhaps it is over Thanksgiving dinner or other interaction with our family (one of those increasingly few sets of relationships we do not choose), or during a required course in college, or while watching a presidential debate. When confronted with the views of a candidate from "the other" party, have you ever felt so upset that you simply had to change the channel in anger or disgust? Have you ever become profoundly anxious at the prospect of having to engage with your family about politics? Have you ever transferred out of a course because you couldn't handle the ideology of the instructor? Have you avoided or even left a church community because you disagreed with the views of the pastor or most of your fellow worshippers? Many have, and as these trends accelerate it is more evident that many refuse to have their perceived enemies, even thoughtful ones, challenge their safe, comfortable views. We just prefer not to engage.[11]

This disconnect and polarization then leads to an incoherent simplicity in our own ideas and in how we speak about and argue for them in public discourse. The ideological communities to which we belong are (still) almost always viewed through the lens of a narrow liberal/conservative binary—a binary into which all issues, regardless of their complexity, are shoved and made to fit. But in the face of truly complex issues, such simplistic and reductive thinking falls apart.

Polarization, Incoherency, and Christian Communities

We might be tempted to dismiss what has just been described as simply what a pluralistic Western republic has to put up with. After all, in a culture that genuinely tries to welcome multiple and even antagonistic understandings of the good, could there really be another outcome? Especially if we have low expectations for what is possible in an authentically diverse political culture, perhaps we need to put up with significant incoherency as we try to provide freedom and autonomy for individuals and groups with conflicting points of view.

Throughout this book we will critically examine this understanding of pluralism and autonomy. Significantly, the polarization and incoherency. Not only do they shove the complex issues of our day into a simplistic framework, they view their ancient theological tradition through the political lens of the right/left culture wars of the late 1970s in the United States. The result, most often, is that Christian liberals and Christian conservatives often hold views indistinguishable from those of secular liberals and conservatives. In this context, Christianity is at the service of the American secular political tribe with which they identify—and, even more importantly, the defeat of the secular political tribe they perceive as the enemy.

Anyone who prizes critical thinking and authenticity should be skeptical of views that line up neatly with those of a particular political team, but in this regard Christians ought to be particularly sensitive. Authentic attempts to live out the insights and values of scripture and tradition not only provide the chance to lead a more coherent and less idolatrous life (with the God of Jesus Christ and his Body, the Church, as the ultimate concern—not a liberal or conservative tribe's ideology), but they also provide a helpful critique of our secular political culture's incoherency.

Reasons for Hope

Despite this gloomy state of affairs, there are several reasons to be hopeful. US Americans increasingly refuse to accept a lazy liberal/conservative binary. Just ten years ago 34 percent of Americans identified as Independents, but according to Gallup that number today has risen to 44 percent—the highest percentage in seventy-five years of the Pew poll tracking this number.[12] By contrast, the poll found only 27 percent who identify as Democrats and 26 percent as Republicans. Millions who identify as both socially conservative and economically liberal have become increasingly frustrated that they have no one to represent them in US politics.[13] Though if this group could use different language to describe their beliefs, they almost certainly would. A major 2018 study of political affiliation in the United States, "Hidden Tribes," found that most people "do not see their lives through a political lens, and when they have political views the views are far less rigid than those of the highly politically engaged, ideologically orthodox tribes."[14] Two-thirds of US Americans belong to what the study called an "exhausted majority." Their members "share a sense of fatigue with our polarized national conversation, a willingness to be flexible in their political viewpoints, and a lack of voice in the national conversation."[15]

These observations suggest that the simplistic assumptions underlying a two-dimensional right/left, liberal/conservative, model of thinking about politics must be replaced with something that reflects what people actually believe. Post-Trump, forces may well have been set in motion that will lead the old model, finally, to collapse. The current realignment in American politics has been highlighted by dozens and dozens of public figures—everyone from Chuck Todd,[16] to Michael Barone,[17] to Eugene Robinson,[18] to Karl Rove,[19] to Tom Brokaw,[20] to Peggy Noonan.[21] Robinson stated bluntly, "My view is that the traditional left-to-right, progressive-to-conservative, Democratic-to-Republican political axis that we're all so familiar with is no longer a valid schematic of American political opinion. And I believe neither party has the foggiest idea what the new diagram looks like."

The old coalitions do seem to be falling apart. Donald Trump won without being clearly liberal or conservative and has remade the Republican party (if it still exists at all) into a very different thing. At the same time, many Evangelical Christians, whose "moral majority" generated the last iteration of the Republican party in the late 1970s, are increasingly uncomfortable with today's GOP.[22] Southern Baptists have begun to distance themselves from the Republican party, as evidenced by the protests surrounding Mike Pence's speech at the Southern Baptist Convention in 2018.[23] Working class Catholics—once the Democratic base—have now been pushed out by a hyper-secular party driven by sectarian identity politics. Large numbers of Latinos and Latinas, despite the Democratic party's "all-in" stance and purity tests on abortion, strongly identify with the goals of anti-abortion pro-lifers.[24] Democrats once believed in regulating free trade via tariffs, but today 72 percent of Democrats believe new US tariffs will harm the economy in the long run. Eighty percent of Republicans, once the party of free trade, believe either that tariffs will have no effect (18 percent) or will be helpful (62 percent). Perhaps the most-discussed critique of capitalism in 2019 came from—wait for it—conservative Fox News host Tucker Carlson.[25]

Two years after Trump's election many pundits see the trend reflected in the 2018 midterm elections, arguing that the changes in voting reflected not a so-called "blue wave," but the uncertainty and turbulence of a country undergoing a profound political realignment.[26] The ranks that took shape in the 1970s and 1980s left/right culture wars are finally breaking apart. And it may be younger people who finally make them scatter. Consider these facts about the millennial generation:[27]

- Half refuse to identify as Democrat or Republican.

- They are fiercely committed to service and social change.

- They don't see politics or government as a primary way of effecting positive social change.

- Seventy-one percent see a need for a new major third party.[28]

With this new generation rising and the broader political culture disintegrating, we have an opportune moment to change the way we think and talk about politics. As Michael Steele, former head of the Republican National Committee, put it, these young people "are going to destroy the old silos, scatter their elements to the wind, and reassemble them in ways that make sense for them and the new century."[29]

There is no script for replacing a political culture. Some worry that radical moral diversity will leave us so fragmented that we will never find a way to write such a script together. And, indeed, if we plow ahead too quickly in our realignment—if we settle for more politically-motived "ten-point plans" or "contracts with America"—we will miss a rare and important opportunity to do something lasting and significant. This moment of uncertainty offers us a chance to hit the pause button and catch our breath. We can set down the burden of our political anxieties and tend to our deep spiritual wounds. The source of our cultural sickness does not lie in politics or policy. As important as those concerns are, the problem is rooted more deeply in our foundational understandings of the good.

Jonah Goldberg recently said, "Politics cannot fill the holes in our souls."[30] Without doubt, a hyper-focus on politics and policy whips up a superficial froth of anxiety that distracts us from or even blocks our ability to recognize the opportunity for foundational introspection that this cultural moment provides. In speaking recently to pro-life groups, for instance, I've suggested that maybe the most important thing we can do right now is to take a deep, cleansing political shower. Scrub away grime that has built up over years or even decades. Put salve on our neglected wounds and burns. Step away from the anxieties of the news and election cycles and focus instead on fundamental questions. What do we value most in life? What grounds those values? How do those values suggest a way of living together with our neighbors?

This moment gives us an opening where we can explore these questions and thereby help a culture desperate for answers. Having the opportunity to provide them is…well…a reason for hope.

Thesis and Goals of This Book

During the heart of the 2016 Presidential election cycle, Archbishop Gomez of Los Angeles said, "It is clear that we need a new politics—a politics of the heart that emphasizes mercy, love and solidarity."[31] In this book I will show that a revitalized Consistent Life Ethic (CLE)—especially as understood and articulated in the Roman Catholic tradition by Cardinal Bernardin, Pope St. John Paul II, Pope Benedict XVI, and (especially) Pope Francis—could demonstrate how to unify a fractured culture around a vision of the good. As noted above, the disintegrating political culture of the United States is trapped in a simplistic, binary left/right political imagination obsessed with arguments about policy prescriptions and the political maneuvering used to enact them. But through the Church's CLE, rightly understood, a new generation not only can challenge this impoverished and incoherent political imagination but can begin the hard work of laying out the foundational goods and principles upon which whatever comes next can be built.

Some might understandably be skeptical that the Church has the vision to take the lead in this endeavor. Especially in light of the sex abuse crisis (which even to this day has been horrifically mishandled at the highest levels—a failure many people understandably cannot get beyond) do we want to focus our attention on this tradition? It is more than legitimate to point out the flaws of a tradition from where the CLE comes. But this is a tradition that, for all its dramatic faults, has stood the test of centuries. When other political cultures and even entire civilizations have collapsed, the Church has provided a foundation for rebuilding. Significantly, it has been able do this while transcending its own profound failures and deep sinfulness.

And despite a secular discourse that tries to marginalize explicitly religious points of view, a Gallup poll found that the number of people who say they have confidence in the church/organized religion is higher than almost any other US institution.[32] Religion, contrary to what prominent talking heads often presume, is actually a positive, moderating force in politics.[33] Speaking at a Georgetown conference on political polarization, David Brooks, a non-Catholic thinker, suggested that a Catholic social vision is "all we have" to resist the forces that are tearing us apart.[34] And, significantly for this project, millennials of many different religious and political stripes view Pope Francis in positive light.[35]

Although the CLE comes out of the Roman Catholic tradition, Pope Francis's pontificate has demonstrated that the tradition's insights and values are attractive outside Catholicism. Because CLE principles come from the gospel of Jesus Christ as revealed in scripture and other parts of the Christian tradition, biblically-focused Evangelicals will find much that resonates with them.

Furthermore, because the CLE often addresses its arguments to "all people of good will," those who have faith in something other than Christianity (including those who have no explicitly religious faith) will find much to engage as well. Values like the irreducible dignity of the person, nonviolence, hospitality, encounter, mercy, conservation of the ecological world, and giving priority to the most vulnerable are written on the hearts of many kinds of people. And this book will show how those values can provide the basis for unity among a fractured people.

How This Book Will Proceed

Most of this book will focus on applying the central principles of the Consistent Life Ethic to polarizing contemporary moral issues, but the first chapter will focus on the CLE more generally. From where did it come? How did it develop during the pontificates of John Paul II and Benedict XVI? How has this tradition been shaped and revitalized through Pope Francis's call to resist throwaway culture and build up a culture of encounter and hospitality? The tradition is articulated through a somewhat vague and imprecise set of connections between ideas. Can it generate a clear set of moral principles that can be applied to the diverse moral issues and problems our fracturing US political culture faces?

The book will proceed by applying the lessons enumerated in the first chapter to the most difficult moral issues within particular contexts: sex and sex cultures; reproduction and abortion; duties to the poor, immigrants and refugees; ecology and non-human animals; euthanasia and the margins of life; and state-sponsored violence. A readable book, of course, could not make a comprehensive academic argument about each of these topics in a single chapter. But my primary goal is to show how the goods and principles laid out in chapter 1 can and should be applied to the above topics in order to illustrate what a new moral and political vision might look like. Though I try to do this carefully, especially by addressing in each chapter multiple objection to my positions, I will leave it to others to elaborate these issues in a purely academic fashion.

It was frustrating to realize that I could not include other topics. In earlier drafts, for instance, I intended to critique the violence of a throwaway culture in sports like football and ultimate fighting. Editorial decisions, however, led me to set aside that chapter, as well as others: human cloning, (neo)colonialism, police violence, violence directed against gays and lesbians, homelessness, torture, and gun violence. Perhaps others can apply the framework of this book to these and other issues that I do not touch upon.

In its conclusion this book will return to the questions raised above. The book overall, including the conclusion, however, will avoid making arguments for particular policies; doing so would distract us from the opportunity of the present moment. Instead, it will try to show that the seeds of morality necessary to generate a new politics can take root only if we focus first on living out the CLE in our daily life choices. It will make reference to Pope Francis's insistence on a culture of encounter whereby we meet the vulnerable and marginalized personally by disrupting our routines and going to the peripheries of our familiar communities. In the larger scheme of things this may seem small, especially for those who focus on big policy debates. But small seeds produce saplings, then trees, then forests— in this case, the trees and forests necessary to support a new and healthy political ecosystem.

Chapter One

An Ethic That Consistently Protects and Supports Life

Cardinal Bernardin

Though we could go back to much older thinkers—and ultimately to Jesus himself—for the values that underpin the Consistent Life Ethic (CLE), the first person to name and develop the concept was Joseph Bernardin, Cardinal-Archbishop of Chicago.[36] The year was 1981, and for decades Bernardin (along with the rest of the United States) had been dealing with massive threats and acts of violence. The first half-century saw WWI and WWII and their "rivers of blood," but in the early 1980s the protracted war in Vietnam stuck in American social consciousness. Central America saw several bloody revolutions, some supported by the US government. The terrible power of the assassinations of President John Kennedy, presidential candidate and Senator Robert Kennedy, and the Rev. Martin Luther King Jr. cannot be overstated. *Roe v. Wade* unleashed a tidal wave of millions and millions of abortions. Underlying all of these was the dramatic tension and arms race between the United States and the Soviet Union that kept the world on the edge of a nuclear holocaust.

As it became clear that the American tendency to solve problems with violence threatened the very existence of Western culture (and perhaps the human race itself), the US Catholic bishops decided that this tendency needed special critical attention. To craft a response Cardinal Bernardin led an ad hoc commission on war and peace. Two years later the bishops voted 238-9 to approve *The Challenge of Peace: God's Promise and Our Response*, which attempted to balance the Christian presumption of non-violence, the duty to protect vulnerable people, and the overwhelming destructive power of nuclear weapons. That same year the US bishops named Cardinal Bernardin chair of the influential Pro-Life Committee, and (in part because of the influence *The Challenge of Peace* had in public discussions of the nuclear arms race) Fordham University invited Bernardin to New York City to give the 1983 Gannon lecture.

In this speech, "A Consistent Ethic of Life: an American-Catholic Dialogue," the cardinal connected publicly and prophetically a range of "life issues." The reach of his message was certainly extended by a *New York Times* front-page report with the headline "Bernardin Asks Catholics to Fight Both Nuclear Arms and Abortion," describing him as opening "a broad attack on a cluster of issues related to the 'sanctity of life,' among them nuclear arms, abortion, and capital punishment."[37] The intense reactions to and interest in the article, both positive and negative, pushed Bernardin to think through the CLE more thoroughly. He eventually connected issues like poverty, euthanasia, genetics, health care, and pornography.

This idea was unprecedented in US public discourse and understandably needed refinement. In 1986 Bernardin expanded and deepened his thoughts on the CLE in an address to a conference at Seattle University dedicated to this topic.[38] The ethic is founded, he said, upon defense of the human person. She has sacredness as an individual, but her flourishing cannot be understood except in relation to others. The CLE reminds us of our duty to protect the lives of persons at all stages of development (from fertilization until natural death), as well as to give them aid and support. And although Bernardin stated clearly that we should not paper over the real differences between the issues he attempted to connect, he tried to articulate their common characteristics and called for consistent reasoning with respect to such characteristics, regardless of one's professed politics. Those committed to the reason and the authenticity of their values, he argued, must refuse to treat individual issues in an ad hoc manner, in isolation from their relationship to other issues.

Popes St. John Paul II and Benedict XVI

Given his reputation as traditional or conservative, it might be surprising to think of Pope John Paul II as an advocate for the CLE. But anyone who has read his work—especially his pivotal 1995 encyclical *Evangelium vitae*—cannot fail to be impressed by how strongly the CLE influenced his thought. It surprised no one that a pope writing on the "Gospel of Life" would focus particularly on abortion and euthanasia, but his pro-life ethic went well beyond those issues, calling out a number of different-but-interrelated topics that transcend the conservative/liberal binary.

In doing so, the Holy Father invoked "the beginning" of the Church which, "as shown by the Didache, the most ancient non-biblical Christian writing," contrasted the way of life with the way of death. The way of death included those who procure abortion and infanticide (which were thought to be morally similar), but it also included those who "show no compassion for the poor," who "do not suffer with the suffering," and who advocate for "the rich and unjust judges of the poor." In this, the most ancient of Christian traditions, John Paul II saw the Gospel of Life and thus drew attention not only to "the ancient scourges of poverty, hunger, endemic diseases, violence and war" but also "new threats [that] are emerging on an alarmingly vast scale." *Evangelium vitae* echoes the Second Vatican Council in "forcefully condemning" practices that are "opposed to life itself":

> [A]ny type of murder, genocide, abortion, euthanasia, or willful self-destruction, whatever violates the integrity of the human person, such as mutilation, torments inflicted on body or mind, attempts to coerce the will itself; whatever insults human dignity, such as subhuman living conditions, arbitrary imprisonment, deportation, slavery, prostitution, the selling of women and children; as well as disgraceful working conditions, where people are treated as mere instruments of gain rather than as free and responsible persons; all these things and others like them are infamies indeed. They poison human society, and they do more harm

to those who practice them than to those who suffer from the injury.[39]

Pope Benedict XVI's work in this area reflects the views of his predecessor. In the encyclical *Caritas in veritate*, for instance, Benedict says that it is false to distinguish between "pro-life" issues (where the Church is thought to have more conservative views) and "social justice" issues (where the Church is thought to have more liberal views). Abortion, euthanasia, and embryo-destructive research are to be understood as social justice issues—just as global consumerism, ecological concern, and care for the poor are to be understood as life issues. For example, while *Caritas in veritate* (upon which Pope Francis built *Laudato si'*) makes a ground-breaking call for increased ecological concern, in true CLE fashion Benedict refuses to isolate this concern from what he calls "human ecology":

> *[T]he decisive issue is the overall moral tenor of society.* If there is a lack of respect for the right to life and to a natural death, if human conception, gestation and birth are made artificial, if human embryos are sacrificed to research, the conscience of society ends up losing the concept of human ecology and, along with it, that of environmental ecology. It is contradictory to insist that future generations respect the natural environment when our educational systems and laws do not help them to respect themselves. The book of nature is one and indivisible: it takes in not only the environment but

also life, sexuality, marriage, the family, social relations: in a word, integral human development. Our duties towards the environment are linked to our duties towards the human person, considered in himself and in relation to others. It would be wrong to uphold one set of duties while trampling on the other.[40]

The pope goes on to call for "intergenerational solidarity" that respects both human and non-human ecology as we look to those who come after us, and the world that we will pass onto them.

In some contexts, the CLE is thought to be "liberal" or an attempt to conflate or water down the fundamental truths about the Gospel of Life. But as both John Paul II and Benedict XVI clearly show, this is a mistake. The CLE, in affirming the way of life and rejecting the way of death, rests upon the very foundations of the Christian Church. Both of these popes founded their central moral ideas on the CLE tradition, a tradition that the Church ought to conserve with great energy and care if it wants to remain faithful to its originating values.

The Consistent Life Ethic of Pope Francis

Though many have tried to paint Francis as a "liberal pope"—not least because of his deep embrace of the CLE—in his 2017 homily for the feast of Pentecost he explicitly calls out commitments to either liberal or conservative Christianity as problematic.[41] Tellingly for the argument at the heart of this book, when the Holy Father visited the United States he declared that we must "confront every form of polarization which would divide [us] into these two camps."[42] Although the media often distort his record, Francis's actual positions follow the CLE, as do those of his predecessors, Church tradition, and the gospel. This beautiful paragraph from *Laudato si'* resonates deeply with what John Paul II and Benedict XVI have said:

> The culture of relativism is the same disorder which drives one person to take advantage of another, to treat others as mere objects, imposing forced labor on them or enslaving them to pay their debts. The same thinking leads to the sexual exploitation of children and abandonment of the elderly who no longer serve our interests. It is also the mindset of those who say: Let us allow the invisible forces of the market to regulate the economy, and consider their impact on society and nature as collateral damage. In the absence of objective truths or sound principles other than the satisfaction of our own desires and immediate needs, what limits can be placed on human trafficking, organized crime, the drug trade, commerce in blood diamonds and the fur of endangered species? Is it not the same relativistic logic which justifies buying the organs of the poor for resale or use in experimentation, or eliminating children because they are not what their parents wanted?

This same "use and throw away" logic generates so much waste, because of the disordered desire to consume more than what is really necessary. We should not think that political efforts or the force of law will be sufficient to prevent actions which affect the environment because, when the culture itself is corrupt and objective truth and universally valid principles are no longer upheld, then laws can only be seen as arbitrary impositions or obstacles to be avoided. (#123)

In decrying a "culture of relativism" that rejects "objective truth," Pope Francis enumerates a variety of practices bound by the logic of a consumerist "use and throw away" culture—a culture that fills the void left by the lack of "universally valid principles."

In deciding who should lead the Pontifical Academy for Life, Pope Francis selected Italian Archbishop Vincenzo Paglia, a champion of the CLE. Tellingly, Francis gave his pro-life office specific charges:

- care for the dignity of the human person in different ages of existence,

- reciprocal respect between the sexes and among the generations,

- defense of the dignity of every single human being,

- promotion of the quality of human life that integrates material and spiritual values, and

- an authentic human ecology, which can help restore the original balance of creation between the human person and the entire universe.

Pope Francis insists that the Didache's pro-life posture is not one of disdain or judgment, but one of mercy—one that "kneel[s] before the wounds of the human person, in order to understand them, care for them and heal them."[43]

Some may look at Francis's approach and conclude that he wants to put traditional pro-life issues on the back-burner. This likely comes from the intense coverage of an interview the Pope did with *America* magazine in which he said:

> We cannot insist only on issues related to abortion, gay marriage and the use of contraceptive methods. This is not possible. I have not spoken much about these things, and I was reprimanded for that. But when we speak about these issues, we have to talk about them in a context.[44]

Contrary to what has been reported, Francis did not tell Catholics to stop talking about abortion and other traditional life issues. Instead, he joined his predecessors in insisting that opposition to abortion should be understood in the context of commitments to other life issues.

Then, the *very next day* the pope used strong language to condemn abortion in a speech to OB-GYNs in Rome. Although this statement did not get the same media attention, Francis declared, "Every unborn child, though unjustly condemned to be aborted, has the face of the Lord." Significantly, the pope characterized abortion as a product of a "widespread mentality of profit, the 'throwaway culture,' which has today enslaved the hearts and minds of so many."[45] In paragraph #120 of his eco-encyclical *Laudato si'* the pope even took the time to discuss abortion:

> Since everything is interrelated, concern for the protection of nature is also incompatible with the justification of abortion. How can we genuinely teach the importance of concern for other vulnerable beings, however troublesome or inconvenient they may be, if we fail to protect a human embryo, even when its presence is uncomfortable and creates difficulties?

And Francis removed any doubt concerning his thoughts about abortion during a 2018 general audience to tens of thousands of people in St. Peter's Square. Speaking off the cuff, the pope compared abortion to hiring a hitman and asked "how can an act that suppresses an innocent and helpless life that is germinating be therapeutic, civilized or even simply human?"[46]

Nor is abortion the only traditionally pro-life issue that Pope Francis has embraced as part of his CLE. In describing the practices of euthanasia and assisted suicide as "always wrong," the pope calls out a "technical and individualistic" culture that hides "behind alleged compassion to justify killing a patient."[47] In *Amoris laetitia*, Francis even condemns gestational surrogacy and "the world politics of reproductive health" as the result of "commercialization," "industrialization," and "consumerism."[48]

So while Pope Francis has given special consideration to what some may consider "liberal" (to use the problematic binary) life issues like protecting God's creation and welcoming undocumented immigrants and refugees, he has also spoken up strongly and clearly for the more traditional pro-life issues. In short, he is quite solidly within the CLE tradition of Bernardin, John Paul II, and Benedict XVI. But at the same time his pontificate represents the leading edge of this tradition, and he uses new lenses and metaphors to speak to a new generation. To a new moment in the Church and the world. In what follows I highlight what are, in my view, his two most significant contributions to the CLE. First, a negative: resisting the throwaway culture. Second, a positive: promoting a culture of encounter.

Throwaway Culture

Pope Francis uses "throwaway culture" to name the opposite of what the CLE seeks to affirm. This culture fosters "a mentality in which everything has a price, everything can be bought, everything is negotiable. This way of thinking has room only for a select few, while it discards all those who are unproductive."[49] It reduces everything—including people—into mere things whose worth consists only in being bought, sold, or used, and which are then discarded when their market value has been exhausted.

Human beings have inherent, irreducible value, but when a throwaway culture finds them inconvenient it deems them "inefficient" or "burdensome" and they are ignored, rejected, or even disposed of. The pope responds to such a culture by defending the universal dignity of every person without exception. By upholding the "internal consistency" of such dignity across a host of different issues, Francis undermines the throwaway culture.[50] In reducing the person to a mere product in a marketplace—one that can be used and then thrown away—our culture makes what philosophers call a category mistake. Persons are ends in themselves, with inherent and irreducible value, and must never be put into the category of things that can be merely discarded as so much trash.

The most serious and obvious example of reducing a person's inherent value to that of a mere thing is their being violently discarded and killed. Christians especially are called to resist this violence because Jesus commanded them to do so. Throughout his life he took pains to call out deadly violence and instructed his followers to "love one another as I have loved you" (John 15:12). Pope Francis resists a throwaway culture that employs violent and (often) state-sponsored practices like war, genocide, terrorism, and the death penalty. But he also argues that this same violent culture includes practices like abortion (which discards a child as inconvenient[51]) and euthanasia (which treats the elderly like "baggage" to be discarded[52]). Francis also has concern for what violence does to the perpetrator. In his address to Congress, for instance, he said that when we are repeatedly violent we become a "prisoner" who is "trapped" by our own violent habits. We ourselves become murderers and tyrants, Francis warns, when we imitate their violent practices.[53]

But the CLE is concerned not only with explicit violence such as killing, but also violence within the structure of our societies. In *Amoris laetitia* Francis echoes John Paul II in saying that the dignity of the person "has an inherent social dimension."[54] That is, respecting life cannot be about simply resisting the aggressive violence of throwaway culture, but also the violence within its social structures. Francis insists that the commandment "Thou shalt not kill" applies clearly to our culture's "economy of exclusion." In the pope's view, "Such an economy kills."[55]

The exclusion with which Francis is concerned need not be conscious exploitation and oppression. It can be unconscious practices that lead to certain people becoming "outcasts" or "leftovers." The pope uses particularly harsh language in condemning theories of economic growth that ignore or discard human beings if they are deemed a net drag on such growth. The homeless person who dies of exposure; the child without adequate health care who dies of an easily-treatable disease; island-dwelling peoples threatened by climate change. What Francis calls "a globalization of indifference" considers such people as mere afterthoughts. The dignity of these vulnerable people is inconvenient for those who benefit from a global consumerist culture, so we ignore the poor and marginalized, gradually becoming "deadened" to their cries. The love of money (something Francis calls "the dung of the devil") supplants the primacy of the human person, and the logic of consumerism exercises dominion over us and our culture.[56] Those thrown away in the process do not matter.

A primary value in throwaway culture is maintaining a consumerist lifestyle, but to cease caring about who is being discarded, most of us must find a way to no longer acknowledge their inherent dignity. Instead of language that affirms and highlights the value of every human being, throwaway culture requires language that deadens our capacity for moral concern toward those who most need it. Rehumanize International, a CLE activist group, has researched how this works (both historically and today) with different populations including racial minorities, the elderly and disabled, prenatal children, immigrants and refugees, enemy combatants, and incarcerated inmates.[57] Patterns develop whereby these populations have been or are named as non-persons, sub-humans, defective humans, parasites, and objects, things, or products. The following chapters note how many vulnerable populations are first named like this, then discarded.

Although technology has helped connect those who wish to be connected, it has also helped facilitate the detachment by which the throwaway culture can flourish. For instance, I can now press two buttons on my smartphone and hours later a product will arrive at my door. I have no idea who procured the materials out of which the product has been made. I have no idea who assembled the product. I have no idea who shipped the product, nor do I know who delivered it. I don't know how much profit the corporation that sold me the product is making or what they are doing with the money I give them. I don't know if the people involved in bringing the product to me were paid a wage fair in their social circumstances. I don't know the effect that this product's manufacture has had on their local economies. I have little to no idea about the ecological impact associated with making this product. In short, consumerist culture has detached us so totally from encounter and connection that—barring some unusual circumstance—we aren't inclined to think about how we are contributing to a culture in which people are used and thrown away. The social structures of consumerism are designed to keep us laser-focused on maintaining a certain lifestyle to the exclusion of nearly everything else.

Critiquing throwaway culture, Francis insists, also means critiquing our culture's focus on autonomy, privacy, and moral relativism. In the face of a throwaway culture's violence and injustice, it is simply not appropriate that we retreat into our private spaces and "live and let live." When autonomy becomes our primary value, Pope Francis says that we succumb to "blind forces" of "self-interest" and "violence."[58] In the spaces abandoned by our appeals to autonomy, privacy, and moral relativism, throwaway culture uses and discards the most vulnerable with impunity.

Culture of Encounter

Although Pope Francis wishes that we resist throwaway culture, he is well aware that merely offering the negative message "don't do this" isn't enough. Admonitions may convict us of our complicit role in violence and injustice, and perhaps push us to seek alternatives to our current practices, but we also need a new imagination or framework for doing things differently. Francis's positive message, the antidote to throwaway culture, is what he calls a "culture of encounter."

Well before Francis, the CLE focused on the most vulnerable by reflecting the "sheep and goats" parable in Matthew chapter 25. Jesus insists that we have a fundamental duty to encounter him in the least among us. Every supporter of the CLE is called to give particular care to those without power on the margins—to those who find it difficult or impossible to speak up on their own behalf. We owe special concern for the least among us, Francis says, "no matter how troublesome or inconvenient they may be."[59]

Such concern, however, transcends enacting laws or donating money. While these are good and often morally essential things to do, Pope Francis summons us to go beyond them, get our hands dirty, and move ourselves out of our safe spaces to the peripheries where we can encounter the excluded and marginalized. Contemporary consumerist culture pushes us to have our experiences mediated "by screens and systems which can be turned on and off on command," but the culture of encounter to which Francis calls us insists on a "face-to-face encounter with others, with their physical presence which challenges us, with their pain and their pleas, with their joy which infects us in our close and continuous interaction."[60] In this regard the pope—like Christ himself—seems to focus particularly on children, a focus at the core of the CLE. Today's most vulnerable children, the pope says, are found hiding underground to escape bombardment, on the pavements of a large city, at the bottom of a boat overladen with immigrants. Let us allow ourselves to be challenged by the children who are not allowed to be born, by those who cry because no one satiates their hunger, by those who do have not toys in their hands, but rather weapons.[61]

He is referring unmistakably to children who are victims of war, abortion, and poverty.

Such encounters are necessary not only for Christians, who are called to find Jesus in these relationships and be evangelized by them, but for anyone who wants to avoid the trap of deciding in advance what people need before getting to know and love them. The wealthy and privileged often determine the problems and solutions without having a single conversation with those who need the help. Not only does this disrespect the very people we are called to prioritize and honor, its ignorant posture often gets the proposed solutions tragically wrong.[62]

Pope Francis also insists that we work to build a culture of encounter even if there are "no tangible and immediate benefits." Genuine encounter requires a posture of hospitality—and such encounters will be understood as good and fitting even if there seems to be no utilitarian reason for engaging. It is an inherently good thing that people, previously strangers, encounter each other in the setting of hospitality. Francis maintains the necessity of this even if there is some danger associated with opening one's person or space to another. He insisted, for instance, that Catholic parishes house 500,000 refugees displaced by conflicts with ISIS.[63] And who can argue with him? While it is possible that doing so involves some danger, it is shameful that countries which waged the wars that allowed ISIS to come about have not shown hospitality to the people those wars have displaced.

Significantly, taking the side of the vulnerable as Pope Francis suggests is not mere pacifism. Surely, if an unjust aggressor threatens the marginalized, deadly violence may be necessary to protect them. Though he does not think that individual nations should decide when such violence may be required (especially given the long history of cloaking wars of conquest under the mantle of protecting the vulnerable) he did give what some have called a "cautious yellow light" to air strikes against ISIS.[64] Such violence, surely, should be a last resort, and must achieve a good greater than the harm that is caused—but Pope Francis does envision a CLE that leaves room for rare cases in which deadly violence is necessary to defend the vulnerable. Such cases will be rare precisely because we are called to encounter each other in the spirit of Christ's mercy. This, he says, is God's central message: that we are to show to others the mercy shown to us.

It may be easy to judge and dismiss those we are called to encounter and support, and who therefore are difficult to love. But this is often the reason they find themselves on the margins of our culture. Francis simply (but insistently) focuses us on God's command to show mercy. Of course, this means exhausting every other possibility before using deadly violence, but such love goes well beyond this. It means cultivating a general attitude of mercy—developing habits that resist the temptation to judge, even (and perhaps especially) when someone is easy to judge. Cultivating a habit of mercy is necessary if we are to have regular, genuine, judgment-free encounters with those on the margins.

This is especially important in public discourse within today's culture. A culture of encounter, characterized by mercy for those we are tempted to judge, means being in intellectual solidarity with those who hold different opinions than we do. It means listening first, presuming good will, and tolerating views that we find uncomfortable. Francis provided an example of this in his opening of the controversial Synod on the Family. Having heard through the grapevine that some might be afraid to speak up against the pope's point of view, he urged his fellow bishops to offer their disagreements with him and others in honest and direct ways but always with "humility" and an "open heart."[65] This stands in marked contrast to much public discourse concerning the issues that this book will discuss. Far too often, students and others demand "safe spaces" and that those with different points of view be marginalized. But a commitment to encounter those on the margins in the spirit of mercy means resisting these understandable impulses and, like Pope Francis, welcoming and engaging those with different points of view.

Pope Francis's culture of encounter also recognizes the mutuality of all creation. In *Laudato si'* Francis highlights the fact that non-human creation belongs not to us but to God. Creation has an intrinsic value independent of human beings. In this remarkable passage, the pope connects the sufferings of human beings to the sufferings of God's other creatures:

> Mary, the Mother who cared for Jesus, now cares with maternal affection and pain for this wounded world. Just as her pierced heart mourned the death of Jesus, so now she grieves for the sufferings of the crucified poor and for the creatures of this world laid waste by human power.[66]

Francis takes non-human suffering so seriously that he believes even Jesus' Blessed Mother makes it a priority. And who—if not deadened to their cries and detached from their dignity—cannot be moved by the sufferings of elephants poached for their ivory or pigs made to live most of their lives in gestation crates? These are vulnerable, voiceless creatures, pushed to the margins, whose dignity is radically inconvenient for human beings who have power over them. They are subject to terrible violence, the result of a consumerist culture that cannot think of them except as things to be bought and sold. Especially those in urban or suburban cultures, who are almost totally removed from the tangible reality of God's creation, struggle to establish a genuine culture of encounter between human and vulnerable non-human animals. But if we take the mutuality of all creation seriously, we need to face the hard truths about our relationships with other animals.

Finally, a culture of encounter asks Christians in particular to resist the temptation to be ruled by right/left arguments over the policies of nation-states. An undue focus on such arguments impedes authentic participation in the culture of encounter to which Pope Francis calls us. As we saw in the introduction, participating in this binary political culture requires us to define ourselves by our opposition to the political "other." Furthermore, as Pope Francis says in *Evangelii gaudium*:

> In her dialogue with the State and with society, the Church does not have solutions for every particular issue. Together with the various sectors of society, she supports those programs which best respond to the dignity of each person and the common good. In doing this, she proposes in a clear way the fundamental values of human life and convictions which can then find expression in political activity.[67]

And writing in *Laudato si*, the Pope insists that articulating a resistance to throwaway culture goes deeper than policy or politics:

> [The] "use and throw away" logic generates so much waste, because of the disordered desire to consume more than what is really necessary. We should not think that political efforts or the force of law will be sufficient to prevent actions which affect the environment because, when the culture itself is corrupt and objective truth and universally valid principles are no longer upheld, then laws can only be seen as arbitrary impositions or obstacles to be avoided.[68]

Technical policy proposals are important, but they are not the focus of this book—which, again, seeks to discuss foundational questions about values and convictions. For those who disagree (at least for the moment) on politics and policy, a focus on value and convictions can provide common ground and the basis for fruitful encounters that may, down the road, lead to a different outcome.

CLE Principles and Conclusion

Cardinal Bernardin knew that the CLE might appear deceptively simple, but in practice is challenging and complex. He also knew that there was room for growth in the set of ideas he was proposing:

> The concept itself is a *challenging* one. It requires us to broaden, substantially and creatively, our ways of thinking, our attitudes, our pastoral response. . . . Although some of those who oppose the concept seem not to have understood it, I sometimes suspect that many who oppose it recognize its challenge. Quite frankly, I sometimes wonder whether those who embrace it quickly and whole-heartedly truly understand its implicit challenge.[69]

The CLE is problematic because it hasn't been articulated with a systematic moral vision. Without such a vision, those who practice the Consistent Life Ethic certainly could be accused of playing "Calvinball"—a game in which players make up the rules to serve their own interests. But considering the tradition unfolding from Bernardin, to John Paul II, to Benedict XVI, and now to Francis, a series of powerful, grounding CLE principles can be articulated and applied across a wide range of issues:

1. It is always **wrong to radically reduce someone's inherent dignity for some other end**, especially by aiming at their deaths.

2. Using **violence ought to be resisted at every turn**, not only because of its effect on the victim, but also because of its effect on the agent of violence. It is permissible to use deadly force to protect one's vulnerable neighbor, but mercy requires that such violence be strictly regulated and absolutely the last option used.

3. In every circumstance **give priority to protecting and supporting the lives of the most vulnerable, especially those who cannot speak up in their own defense.** In some circumstances, such as gross neglect of our duty to aid, we may be morally responsible for the deaths of those we could have saved.

4. **Resist appeals to individual autonomy and privacy that detach us from our duty to aid** and slouch toward a relativistic consumerist culture that rewards the powerful and discards the vulnerable. These vulnerable include not just those who are alive today—those marginalized due to their age, race, gender, level of ability, and more—but also generations to come.

5. **Resist language, practices, and social structures that detach us from the full reality and dignity of the marginalized**—especially dignity hidden by the broader consumerist culture.

6. Focus on creating a culture of encounter, especially with those we have most difficulty showing mercy and love. **Go to the peripheries, even when there is risk, showing hospitality and care for the stranger**—especially (but not only) if we are responsible for their need in the first place.

7. Acknowledge **mutuality, not only between human persons currently living, but also between current and future generations, and between human persons and the rest of non-human creation.** This includes a concern for those suffering, marginalized creatures who, though subjected to terrible violence, cannot speak up in their own defense.

So much for abstractions. The rest of the book will focus on how these CLE principles speak to some of the most difficult and polarizing practical issues of our day, especially because the exhausted culture war vision from the 1970s is clearly on its way out. As the following chapters go through the issues, at some points some readers may find my arguments to be hopelessly conservative, while at other points others may conclude I'm a wacky far-left liberal. This is to be expected. The CLE troubles our liberal/conservative binary, and to the extent that a reader has been formed by this political culture, the arguments that follow may be challenging.

Given this challenge, it would help to keep in mind what Archbishop Gomez said at a recent conference on Catholic social teaching and political polarization: "There are no single-issue saints."[70] If we hold a particular moral principle and believe it is true, then we must apply that principle consistently across a range of issues. During my undergraduate studies in philosophy one of my mentors explained that having a moral principle is like getting on a bus, not like getting in a taxi. In a taxi you can tell the driver where you want to go, but on a bus you have to follow the route wherever it leads. We can't tell our moral principles where we want them to go. If we do, we surely leave ourselves open to the throwaway culture's pernicious tendency to discard those whose dignity is invisible or whom we find the most inconvenient. We risk applying our concern to one person or group when it suits our interests and ignoring another person or group when it does not. But when we follow our moral principles wherever they lead (even, perhaps, to places we don't want to go) we resist the ways in which bias and self-interest can hurt our ability to protect and support those on the margins of our culture.

Chapter Two

Sex Practices and Cultures

Admirers of Pope Francis may find it somewhere between odd and scandalous that the first set of issues we will discuss concerns sex practices and cultures. Hasn't Francis taken us beyond his predecessors' unfortunate obsession with sex? Isn't Francis the pope who asks, "Who am I to judge?" and who focuses on social justice? So why begin here? Isn't this taking the Church backward?

Part of the disconnect here is the way much of the media have covered the last three popes. Francis's predecessors held classic CLE positions, writing about and advocating for issues that range across the US political binary imagination. Unfortunately, most media paid more attention to what the popes had to say about sex than what they had to say about, say, the rights of immigrants or ecological protection. But in its coverage of Francis, the media has directed far more attention to his statements about protection of the environment and the rights of immigrants than to his statements concerning sex. But he has said many things on this topic, especially in his 264-page apostolic exhortation on marriage and family, *Amoris laetitia*. It discusses everything from the hookup culture to the relationship of sex to procreation. It uses explicit throwaway terminology when speaking about contemporary sexual culture: "In our own day, sexuality risks being poisoned by the mentality of 'use and discard.' The body of the other is often viewed as an object to be used as long as it offers satisfaction and rejected once it is no longer appealing."[71] In other contexts (about which we will see more below) Pope Francis has focused on pornography, human sex trafficking, and the relationship of contraception to sexually-transmitted infections (STIs).

Furthermore, sex is one of the most polarizing issues in our culture-war-infected politics and has gained even more prominence in our post-#MeToo moment. The CLE of course strongly rejects obsession over sex to the exclusion of other issues. Disagreements over sex are also the starting point for disagreements about other topics considered in this book, so for that reason alone it is important to begin here, at the root of so many conflicts. And, as is the case with these other topics, sexual issues cannot be abandoned to a private zone of autonomy, no matter how strongly our culture resists. How we think and act regarding sex affects vulnerable populations, many of whom our current sexual culture uses and discards like trash. Sexuality constitutes the deepest parts of our human identity, and the vulnerabilities that accompany sexual intimacy (profound bodily and emotional intimacy, risk of contracting STIs, pregnancy, parenthood, etc.) demand a special concern for these relationships. Furthermore, the violence in our sexual practices today—particularly when alcohol and/or issues of power imbalance are involved—is something that CLE must engage. We will discuss in more detail below, but our post-#MeToo moment demands that we abandon our hyper-autonomous "leave people alone to do what they want" approach to these questions. Instead, our priority must be for those vulnerable populations at risk in a culture that imagines them as things to be used and thrown away.

This chapter will begin by examining sexual practices, paying close attention to how violence, consumerism, and an undue focus on autonomy detach us from the inherent dignity of the human person. Too often, however, Christians' critique of sex is negative. The chapter will also present a positive, alternative sexual culture—one focused on encounter and hospitality—that offers a more life-giving option. This book will not shrink from direct challenges to the CLE perspective, and this chapter will conclude by responding to charges that a sexual culture of encounter and hospitality (1) is unrealistic, (2) would lead to more STIs and overpopulation, and (3) is a vestige of a patriarchal understanding of sex and is therefore bad for women.

A Violent Sexual Culture

Recall that Francis is particularly concerned with violence which "treats others as mere objects," given that those who use such violence fail to acknowledge that by their very nature human beings have dignity and so must not be reduced to mere objects. The so-called "hookup culture" (the dominant attitude toward sex in contemporary music, movies and social media) is premised on violence that objectifies the human person. A quick glance at the website "Texts from Last Night" (a cultural phenomenon with nearly four million Twitter followers at the time of this writing) reveals this culture. Here is the first text I encountered as I did my research for this chapter:

"Chick in class has 69 tattooed on the back of
her neck. Target acquired."

What better example of the attitude that characterizes hookup culture? In only fourteen words, this text refers to a woman in degrading language, uses a violent image to describe a plan to hook up with her, and invites us to think about the social influences that led this woman to get such a tattoo. In less than ten minutes you can find dozens of similar examples on the site. In the few I cite below, particularly note attitudes that degrade and dehumanize a sexual "partner" (for most, that word implies an emotional connection that the relationship does not include) and detach the aggressor from the dignity of the person being used. Also notice how much the hookup culture involves alcohol, porn, and preying on vulnerable people who want substantial relationships:

"I don't give a damn about what he wants to
do with his life. Personalities are for pussies."

"On the way home she put on a necklace with
her name on it and wrote my name in sharpie
across my chest so that in the morning we
could avoid the awkward Idk who the fuck
you are conversation. Best. Girl. Ever."

"I can't stream porn because Xbox is taking all
the Internet. I thought having a male room-
mate would make life easier."

> "hey give me heads up if you're feeling vulner-
> able tomorrow night"

> "the number of desperate girls at the gym
> right now is unfair. it would be cruel not to let
> one blow me."

> "Ya know, since we do have alot [sic] of sex
> with each other i figure i should wish you a
> happy valentines day"

Undoubtedly these texts display a bit of dramatic performance, but they do provide a window into hookup culture. Of course, in the past hookups did happen, but they tended to be hidden from public view. Our contemporary sexual culture publicly and proudly celebrates them as a positive good.

Though in a previous generation we might have reduced this to a product of men, perhaps no one exemplifies hookup culture better than (the early) Ke$ha. Our cultural shift to celebrating hookup culture is demonstrated by the way many women and girls, rather than critique such attitudes and practices from a feminist perspective, embrace the hookup culture as their own. Ke$ha's chart-topping 2011 song "Blah, Blah, Blah" exemplifies this shift. In the music video, which included her duct-taping a man's face and ripping off his pants, she sang these lyrics:

> I don't care where you live at
> Now turn around boy, let me hit that

Don't be a little bitch with your chit chat
Just show me where your dick's at

Stop talk talk talking that blah, blah, blah
Think you'll be hitting this? nah, nah, nah
In the back of my car, car, car
If you keep talking that blah, blah, blah, blah, blah

So cut to the chase kid
'Cause I know you don't care what my middle name is
I wanna be naked, and you're wasted

The song employs offensive references typically used to denigrate women and girls—but now used to denigrate men and boys. Ke$ha describes a man who wants to talk before (or instead of) having sex as "being a little bitch"—just as of one of the texters-from-last-night described men who have personalities as "pussies."

This culture has been expanded and intensified through technology, particularly with apps like Tinder (which invented the swipe right, swipe left way of sorting potential matches) and Bumble (which permits only women to make the first communication). In the *New York Times*, Lauren Peterson writes of her 2017 college experience with these apps:

> Dating apps allow you to set obvious parameters: age range, distance parameters, and so on. But there are also unspoken rules: a deadline for the relationship (in our case graduation);

what feelings shouldn't be expressed, from affection ("Thinking of you!") to criticism ("It bothers me when you do x"); and boundaries on what shouldn't be shared about your personal life (family details, past loves). And you can regulate how much you want to integrate the person into other spheres of your life.[72]

Lauren describes how she became emotionally attached to one of the matches she was seeing, told him of her real feelings and, in classic hookup culture fashion, was promptly cast off. Later in her essay, Lauren admits that she had "broken the rules" of the culture in which she was participating. After the relationship fizzled due to the "power imbalance" she opened Bumble again and saw, almost comically, that 1,946 men had swiped right on her profile during the six weeks she was seeing Michael. Lauren concludes by admitting, "It's easy to dismiss dating apps as insincere, objectifying and sketchy," but she nevertheless holds onto hope that they can connect her to people for whom she is "willing to bend the rules."

The role of alcohol in hookup culture cannot be overstated. Writing in *Jezebel*, for instance, Sarah Hepola wonders

what my sex life would even look like if alcohol hadn't been there. Alcohol gave me comfort in my own body, and it allowed me to turn my erotic curiosity and hunger for experience into an action plan. I was tired of being the stuttering girl sucking in her stomach after the lights went out. I wanted to be the woman who roamed wild and free. Alcohol also helped me cut the girlish strings on my heart, an action my college years demanded. Three months into my freshman year, I split a six pack with a dashing sophomore, and we wound up partially clothed on his bed, my bare legs wrapped around his waist, my hands around his neck. I pulled back slightly and asked him the question, the naive question of a girl who does not yet understand her fate: "What does this mean?" He looked past me, into his studio apartment, and then back into my eyes. "It means that I'm a 19-year-old boy, and we're having fun."[73]

Sarah writes that she didn't need alcohol to be physical with her trusted high school boyfriend, but in college she had to have it to feel safe. "This is the question I asked myself at 18," she said. "If sex means nothing to the guy, and I'm going to be tossed aside anyway, then why don't I drink myself to the point where it no longer hurts?"

Let's pause here to highlight key aspects of the hookup culture to which we will be returning several times in this chapter. First, at a basic level, it is often viewed as a game in which the strong and aggressive "player" "wins" by using another person as a means of getting the sexual action he or she sets out to get. Second, it involves detaching from the reality and dignity of another person so as to use them as a mere object, with no moral or emotional strings attached.

Third, though this generally involves men preying upon and using vulnerable women (who, more often than men, are looking for relationship intimacy), more and more women are also buying into the predatory violence of hookup culture. Fourth, hookup participants often use alcohol to detach themselves from the reality of the situation—not only by overpowering the natural inhibitions that prevent making poor sexual choices, but also by making it easier to ignore a partner's humanity. Fifth, the desire for a genuine encounter or relationship with another person—because it contradicts the culture of no-strings, detached use of another—is dismissed as (often feminine) weakness.

Pope Francis laments that sexual culture has become part of a broader throwaway culture. In *Amoris laetitia* he notes that if we detach ourselves from the value of everything, then everything becomes disposable—even the people in our most intimate relationships.[74] And he has good reason to lament such detachment, especially given the serious consequences of the hookup culture's violence.

Consequences of the Hookup Culture

More often than is acknowledged, an alcohol-facilitated hookup should be considered sexual violence. Sometimes the violence is obvious, as when one partner tries to resist but is physically overpowered, or when a partner is given a date-rape drug. More often the violence involves a predator's calculated attempts to buy a "target" enough drinks so that person will be easier to "acquire." And even more often it simply involves sex with someone who has been drinking to the point where it is impossible to make a genuine choice to have sex. Especially given this last consideration, a conclusion is difficult but obvious: much of the sex taking place in the hookup culture is, in fact, sexual violence. To be clear: a violent rape is by orders of magnitude worse than a buzzed hook-up. But we cannot draw a big bright line between hookup culture and rape culture.

Though violence can be purposefully ignored or if acknowledged can be dismissed as "being a little bitch," such acts have serious consequences. Being treated violently as a sexual object can destroy a person's self-esteem and even cause serious depression or other mental illness—especially when a partner has been manipulated into thinking that the one with whom they are being intimate cares about them as a person. Sometimes the one being used stops seeking self-worth outside the hookup culture and seeks only to become the most desirable sexual object possible—even if this involves developing an eating disorder, becoming obsessed with the gym, destroying one's skin (and dramatically increasing the risk of cancer) in the sun or in a tanning bed, or getting hookup-welcoming tattoos.

Violent acts also affect the perpetrator. Over time, using another can grow more and more violent. Once another's body becomes a mere object of conquest and pleasure after having "a couple drinks," how much worse can it be to use a person's body when drunk? And if it is OK to use a person's body when drunk, what is wrong with using that person's body after buying drinks to get them drunk? And then what's wrong with simply using that person's body, period, full stop? All violent acts, including acts of sexual violence, gradually destroy the agent's sensitivity to the dignity of the human person—making it easier and easier to commit more (and more serious) violent acts in the future. (The final chapter on state-sponsored violence will explore this in more depth.)

But the ideas and attitudes that lead to this point are slippery but clear. Once using another's body for conquest and sexual gratification becomes socially accepted—and especially when it is promoted and valorized in the name of sexual freedom and liberation—distinguishing why example A is bad, but example B is acceptable, and example C might even be good becomes difficult. Such blurred moral lines, coupled with deference to sex as belonging to a private zone of autonomy, makes it easier for victims of sexual violence to become invisible and for morality to "stay out of people's bedrooms."

Even if one is fortunate enough to escape such violence, the hookup culture has a more insidious and serious effect: sexually transmitted infections. Despite the wide availability and social celebration of contraception, so-called "safe sex" (strongly supported by multiple centers of power in US culture) has caused an explosion in STI rates. In the face of this, the CDC recently sounded the alarm: new cases of STIs have reached record highs.[75] In New York City, more than one in four individuals has an STI—and across the United States one in four teenage girls has an STI. Given these statistics, the fact that "only" 50,000 new cases of HIV infections are diagnosed each year, remarkably, is considered a victory.

Some think the hookup culture applies only to single people, but it has also infected countless marriages. The culture strongly resists committing to just one person—thus, unsurprisingly, the *New York Times* reports continued increases in rates of spousal infidelity.[76] Researchers also see that cheating has increased significantly in relatively new marriages. "In younger couples, the increasing availability of pornography on the Internet, which has been shown to affect sexual attitudes and perceptions of 'normal' behavior, may be playing a role in rising infidelity." And sociological studies show that when married men use pornography, the chance of divorce doubles. When used by women, the chance of divorce triples.[77]

Because the hookup culture has created goals, habits, and expectations for sexual behavior that are incompatible with marriage, the capacity for intimacy necessary to make a permanent commitment often is destroyed. Even those who seek genuine commitment often fail because the surrounding culture has drilled dysfunctional attitudes about sex into them decades before they met their spouse. Moreover, the sobering statistics of spousal rape make it clear that marriages have not been able to avoid the violence of the hookup culture.[78]

Happily, after decades of a "stay out of people's bedrooms" culture of sexual autonomy and moral relativism, in October 2017 the #MeToo movement finally began to expose and confront the dominance of violence in our sexual culture and the huge number of that culture's victims. The #MeToo movement has revealed the terrible stories connected to the transactional nature of sex that hookup culture normalizes and celebrates. Gone are the "bad ol' days" of looking the other way when men use their power (physical and otherwise) to coerce women into having sex. Our culture is now all-in with deep concern about what goes on in other people's bedrooms, especially the bedrooms of powerful men. Protecting vulnerable populations from violence, it is now clear, requires such concern. We still lack the cultural tools to generate a positive replacement model (see more on this below), but post-#MeToo it is clear that what we got now ain't working.

The principles laid out in the previous chapter make it clear why the CLE must take the issue of sexual attitudes and practices seriously. To claim dismissively that the proper response to hookup culture is to stay out of people's bedrooms, privileging the autonomy and privacy of individuals to live as they see fit and avoiding "pelvic issues," is to be complicit in the terrible consequences of hookup culture. Those who adhere to the CLE, therefore, not only must refuse to participate in and support such a culture, but out of concern for the vulnerable populations wounded by this culture must actively, forcefully, and publicly challenge it and seek to replace it. Our post-#MeToo moment demands nothing less.

A Consumerist Sexual Culture

Driven primarily by the goal of maximizing profits, businesses (especially large corporations) spend huge sums of money to hire the best experts on human behavior to advise them on marketing in the best venues via the best media to give them the best chance of convincing consumers to buy their products. Doing so has some merit. Businesses and corporations often satisfy an important need or create a new product or service, such that their customers can flourish in genuinely positive ways. Problems arise, however, when businesses make a profit by luring customers into an addictive and vicious cycle of consumption-dissatisfaction-consumption-dissatisfaction.

Businesses, it should go without saying, use our sexual culture to make a profit. Dozens of times a day, television commercials and programs, internet ads and clips, and movies and music videos bombard us with hyper-sexualized images. Those that make the most money promote a particular vision and understanding of sexuality—one which plays on the particularly powerful neurochemical intensity (especially for young people) of sexual desire. Although we are inundated with millions of images, especially in the age of the smartphone, a sexualized image is still particularly effective at capturing our attention. From a very early age we are immersed in imagery designed to shape our notions of sexuality. We absorb them into our understanding and expectations so that subconsciously they become the norm.

Human nature does not change, but sexual standards do. A brief comparison of women's poses in Renaissance paintings and Marilyn Monroe's in the 1970s or the pornographic images so readily available today shows the arbitrariness of what is considered desirable. But it can nevertheless hurt people on a massive scale. To meet the current arbitrary standard it is necessary, particularly for women, to adopt an unhealthy lifestyle. More than ten million American women are suffering from an eating disorder, even those who are middle aged or older.[79] Such disorders have become problematic not just for women—men or boys now comprise 15 to 20 percent of the cases. Many spend excessive time at the gym and many more feel great guilt about—and even hatred of—their own bodies. Diabolically, some corporations profit by generating dissatisfaction with our sexuality (and especially with our bodies) in order to sell us their products. We are inundated with ads for certain foods or drinks, supplements, diet pills, gastric surgeries, clothing, make up, dermatological drugs and treatments, hair replacement, hair removal, hair coloring, drugs that aid in sexual preparedness or performance, altering skin color, exercise equipment, gym memberships, personal training, or even plastic surgery. Time and time again we are urged to buy a product or procedure to fulfill our desire for sexual and romantic relationships.

Of course, the images projected by models or Hollywood stars are airbrushed and digitally manipulated; no one could achieve such personal transformation without unhealthy practices (or, at the very least, a trainer, dietician, cook, and plastic surgeon). Brilliant marketing strategies entice us to keep trying to satisfy our hunger and thirst for sexual attractiveness by buying more products. The holy grail for those who promote profit-generating consumerist habits is the ability to create a deep and powerful desire that can never be satisfied. In theory, since the goal is impossible to achieve, desire for it could produce a lifetime of product purchases.

Porn: King of Consumerist Sexual Culture

Many men, and an increasing number of women, will recognize an essential part of this story that we have not yet addressed. The effect of consumerism on our sexual culture cannot be understood without examining the role of pornography. Some of what follows below may be difficult to read, but pornography has such a profound power over our sexual imagination and practice that we can no longer not talk about it, even in polite company.

Today's ubiquitous laptops, tablets, and smartphones make, at the touch of a button, an astonishing amount and variety of porn available anywhere, on demand. A survey of people aged eighteen to twenty-six revealed that roughly two-thirds of young men and one-half of young women find viewing pornography to be acceptable, and nearly nine out of ten young men and one in three young women reported consuming pornography.[80] Even considering that respondents may not report such things honestly, nearly half of all the men surveyed reported consuming it at least once a week. Not surprisingly, the study concludes that the more younger adults accept and consume pornography, the more likely they are to engage in casual sexual behavior. Those who use porn daily have, on average, five times the number of lifetime sexual partners as do those who never use. Furthermore, again recalling the connection between alcohol and hookup culture, the study finds a significant correlation between consistent use of pornography and binge drinking.

Nor is this phenomenon limited to young people. It is difficult to estimate the profit purveyors of porn make, especially given the international nature of the business, but it is likely in the dozens of billions of dollars.[81] The industry dominates the internet; more than 12 percent of websites offer pornographic products. One in four search engine requests are for porn. Nearly half of Christians describe porn as being a problem in the home, and, increasingly, women too, not just men, are suffering from porn addiction. Children's exposure to porn is particularly disturbing. A child first experiences online hardcore porn, on average, at age eleven, a fact that disturbs even established porn actors[82] and is associated with high and increasing numbers of minors who sexually assault other minors.[83] And even more ghastly: more than 100,000 websites provide child porn, sharing thirty to fifty million files daily. And these numbers continue to climb.

A exposé by *The Atlantic* on "The Hidden Economics of Porn" has blown the lid off how a couple of big corporations have made monstrous profits by manipulating consumers' sexual desires.[84] Just like Amazon and Google, they use a consumer's search and purchase history to create an algorithm that will generate further suggestions carefully crafted to keep the user wanting more. These companies know that masturbating to a computer screen will ultimately be an unsatisfying experience, one which—if they play their cards right—will result in the consumer coming back.

But without being offered the thrill of a genuine encounter with an actual person, consumers become desensitized or bored and require new ways to be excited.

This means piquing their interest by slowly but steadily pushing the sexual envelope toward the forbidden. Some readers may be surprised that in many states scenes depicting sex between family members have become the most-searched-for clips.[85] In their book *The Porning of America*, Carmine Sarracino and Kevin M. Scott note that one of the most popular porn websites, "Scream and Cream," presents all forms of "violent extreme forced sex fantasies," the sounds of rape having the highest audio quality. More and more, porn depends on real degradation.[86] Corporations entice potential viewers with an actress's "first anal" experience, her pain clearly part of what the customer is paying for. Over the past several years hardcore porn has gravitated toward humiliation and degradation that cannot in any sense be defined as "acting" or "performance." For instance, on a website called "Pinkeye," a man not only ejaculates on a woman's face, but also holds her eyelid open so that her eyeball will become irritated and inflamed.[87] Nor is this uncommon: a recent study found that 88 percent of the 250 most popular porn movies show aggression toward women.[88]

In a remarkable cultural development, more and more celebrities are publicly and strategically telling their porn-addiction stories, describing how it has damaged their lives. British comedian and actor Russell Brand, in a stunning YouTube video that has well over three million views,[89] says "I was exposed to such a lot of it from such a young age, it's affected my ability to relate to women." Brand, after linking the breakup of his marriage to porn, offers a lament that reflects Catholic teaching on sex: "Our attitudes toward sex have become warped and perverted and have deviated from its true function as an expression of love and a means for procreating." American comedian and actor Chris Rock told a similar story during his 2018 Netflix special.[90] "I was addicted to porn," Rock said. "You get desensitized. When you start watching porn, any porn will do. Then, later on, you're all fucked up and you need a perfect porn cocktail to get you off." Rock also linked his porn addition to cheating on his wife and the breakup of his marriage. This list of celebrities (including Cameron Diaz[91]) speaking out about their porn addiction continues to grow.

The porn industry exemplifies how big business attempts to create dissatisfaction and detachment among their customers to make them "come back for more" of a product. And boy, have they been successful. Sarracino and Scott point out how porn "has so thoroughly been absorbed into every aspect of our everyday lives—language, fashion, advertisements, movies, the Internet, music, magazines, television, video games—that it has almost ceased to exist as something separate from the mainstream culture, something 'out there.'"[92] David Simon, co-creator of *The Wire*, recently argued that even if we aren't consuming porn directly, we can't help but consume its logic. It is now "a multibillion-dollar industry and it affects the way we sell everything from beer to cars to blue jeans." Simon said, "The vernacular of pornography is now embedded in our culture."[93] Importantly, Sarracino and Scott note, porn has shaped the sexual encounter that hookup culture presumes. The hookup "perfectly mirrors the sex that is typical in a porn movie." Almost always "impersonal, and undertaken without commitment," it is nothing more than mutual satisfaction of lust. In the image of an ideal hookup, the bodies and clothing of women (and, increasingly, of men) mirror those of porn stars.

Sarracino and Scott see some value in pornography, but do not support the direction it is taking. Our "sexual freedom was indeed hard-won" against "religious fanatics," they claim, and so they are convinced that we should not go "backwards." But autonomous sexual freedom and privacy has led to the devastatingly dysfunctional sexual culture that the CLE is challenging. The culture has failed to address the underlying systems of physical and structural violence that lead not only to the way porn and other media distort sexuality, but also the way actual hookup culture does as well.

And it isn't only religious conservatives waking up to this fact: Pope Francis's concern about the effect of porn on children[94] reflects an explosion of multi-partisan worry surrounding these issues. A piece in the *New York Times* gives even "liberal parents" tongue-in-cheek permission to "freak out about porn."[95] *The Washington Post* claims that the social science is now irrefutable: porn is "a public health crisis."[96] *The Huffington Post* connects the dots between porn and the sex trafficking industries,[97] a link that has also caught Pope Francis's attention.[98] *The Atlantic* draws attention to the fact that most of those who use porn regularly nevertheless believe it to be "morally wrong."[99]

Calls are growing on Capitol Hill for legislative action, and even ultra-liberal countries like Iceland and Britain have sought to ban online pornography.[100] Private companies like Starbucks and Tumblr have also recently banned porn. These moves may mark the beginnings of a cultural shift, which is all to the good, but porn problems are symptoms of more fundamental issues. *GQ* claims that porn is "rewiring men's brains"[101] and *New York Magazine* points out that porn "deadens men to real women."[102] Though high use of porn correlates with having more sex partners, it also correlates with having less sex overall.[103] More and more, people are coming to prefer porn over "the real thing."

A Flooded Market—and the End of Sex?

It should also be said that, especially in the context of a pornified hookup culture, sex itself becomes just another product to be negotiated and consumed. The culture sees nothing inherently sacred in sex. Nothing that would exclude it from any of the other goods markets distribute. Via a particular culture shift—one that the provocative French novelist Michel Houellebecq argues has been underway for some time—the sexual revolution, widely understood to be a liberation movement, is in fact the intrusion of capitalist values into the previously sacrosanct realm of intimate life.[104] The market has done to sex what it often does to consumer goods: it has made the products cheaper and much more plentiful, especially if you are a man.[105]

Increasingly, in the sexual marketplace men find the rules of exchange confusing—wrongly believing they are owed sex as a result of the transactions they thought were taking place. Many people in many quarters have made admirable attempts to resist occasions of sexual violence by ratcheting up the value of autonomy and consent. States like New York and California have written into the law that, unless consent to sex is explicit and alcohol free, it is sexual violence. But as Jon Zimmerman argues in *The Washington Post*, this movement has run up against the cultural presumption that there is nothing wrong with casual sex—and this creates a profound internal tension.[106] For how can one really know what someone else wants if they only know them casually, if they have just met? Sure, two perfectly sober people can stop kissing, robotically follow a legally-mandated script, and make a "bedroom contract between sexual vendors," but that removes from the experience much of the magic and allure that lead most to want sex in the first place.

Considering what we have seen thus far, it should be no surprise that people are having less sex today than they did a generation ago. The Centers for Disease Control and Prevention's Youth Risk Behavior Survey reports that from 1991 to 2017, high school students who'd had intercourse dropped from 54 to 40 percent.[107] It is striking that today's young people are on track to have fewer sex partners than the previous two generations did at the same age. And the trend does not describe only young people: On average, US adults had sex nine fewer times in 2014 than they did in the late 1990s.[108] By now we can posit lots of causes for such trends: the ubiquity of porn, the high risk of contracting an STI, the risk of sexual violence, increasing focus on consent-focused legalisms, and (frankly) the pervasiveness of really bad sex, disconnected from a genuine encounter with a person.

If these trends continue, we may glimpse the problems to be faced if we take a close look at Japan, which has been dealing with these trends far longer than the United States has. This startling statistic was first reported in 2015: 47 percent of young Japanese women aged sixteen to twenty-four "despise" sexual contact. (For young men of the same age, the number is 25 percent.) The statistic was so shocking that many doubted its veracity—but Politifact rates it "True" without qualification.[109] Remarkably, the number of girls between sixteen and nineteen who despise sexual contact jumps to a whopping 66 percent. And nearly one-third of all Japanese people enter their thirties without sexual experiences of any kind.[110]

The Japanese government predicts that by 2065 the country's current population of 127 million will decline by nearly forty million. Facing a depopulation rate unprecedented in modern times, by necessity Japan has become a world leader in using robots to do the jobs human beings no longer can do—including caregiving for a disproportionate elderly population. To put it in perspective, the Japanese buy more adult diapers than baby diapers.[111] Life-like sex dolls perform the functions human beings no longer do. Even though these dolls are in the early stages of technological development, a significant number of Japanese men prefer them to real life women. One man said, "My wife was furious when I first brought Mayu [his sex doll] home. These days she puts up with it, reluctantly."[112] And this

trend is beginning to appear in North America as well—
the first sex doll "brothel" opened in Toronto in 2018.[113]

According to the Foundation for Responsible
Robotics, Android love dolls, which cost between $5,000
to $15,000, can perform fifty automated sexual positions
and can be customized down to nipple shape and pubic
hair color.[114] Personality traits can also be programmed into
these robots. One model, the "Roxxxy TrueCompanion,"
has several different personality settings, including "Wild
Wendy" or "S&M Susan" if you're in the mood for either
of those. There are also settings designed to simulate rape.
If you touch "Frigid Farrah" sexually, for instance, she is
programed not to be "appreciative of your advance."[115]
Objects made to look like human beings and designed to
be subject to sexual violence can be ordered and delivered
to one's home.

The rapid rise in the sophistication of artificial intelligence, coupled with better robotics technology in general,
will make the sex robots of the future even more lifelike. If
most or even all of these cultural and technological trends
continue, is it overly dramatic to wonder whether human
beings will no longer have sex with one another? Even with
the technology in its infancy, already 27 percent of young
people say they would take up a relationship with a sex
robot.[116] Especially given the turn to artificial reproductive
technology (discussed in detail in the next chapter), fair-
mindedness, I think, requires us at least to consider the
possibility. And even considering the possibility suggests
that something is clearly, deeply, and urgently wrong with
our sexual culture.

An Alternative Sexual Culture: Encounter and Hospitality

Many of my undergraduate students can articulate quite clearly how it feels to be caught in a hookup culture. A good number claim they are miserable. Clearly, unrestrained choice to use another sexually makes people anything but free, happy, and flourishing, but they often can't see any other viable option. Though in fact they don't want to play, they often find that their least bad choice is to participate in the game. They find themselves coerced by cultural structures.

CLE supporters must work hard, then, not merely to critique the current sexual culture, but to develop an alternative—and go out to the peripheries as a means of effecting cultural change. The first step is to be direct and honest in discussions about sex. Honesty means facing the problem underlying most of the issues considered in this chapter: a misunderstanding and mistreatment of the human person. Instead of seeing a sexual partner's irreducible dignity, our culture turns them into an object of our will to be used and discarded. Often under the influence of alcohol, our sex partner's dignity (and our own) is stripped away, reducing them to a thing to be used. In place of this culture, thrust upon us by previous generations' desire for autonomy and by corporate greed, the CLE offers a different understanding of sexuality. It requires us to respect the irreducible dignity of the human person by engaging in a genuine encounter with a person who is an end in themselves, never a mere means to some other end.

But honesty requires us to go further and—rejecting moral relativism—ask this question: "What is sex for?" One does not need to be part of the Christian or Jewish traditions (both of which respect God's command to "be fruitful and multiply") to understand that, while sex properly understood is about a genuine encounter with another person, the biological act is clearly also geared toward the creation of offspring. This biological force is so strong that attempts to circumvent it often are ineffective. In typical use, a condom fails 13 percent of the time. In typical use the contraceptive pill fails at a rate of 7 percent. The biological connection between sex and procreation is so strong that pregnancy can even occur after sterilization.[117]

A new sexual culture, one that takes the biological nature of sex seriously and is guided by CLE values, will have the following characteristics:

- It will be skeptical of calls to avoid hard questions by appeals to individual autonomy and privacy. Especially where issues of justice and nonviolence are at stake, it will instead go out to the peripheries and work to change the culture.

- It will refuse to reduce others' dignity by using them as sexual objects, particularly if they are vulnerable. Doing so is an act of violence that not only injures one's partner in profound and lasting ways, but also harms the perpetrator.

- It will insist that the profound biological, psychological, and spiritual stakes in sexual relationships require a genuine encounter and a mutual personal relationship that has a proportionate level of depth and seriousness.

- It will resist the ideas and practices by which our culture makes it acceptable to use one another sexually. This will include resisting not only the hookup culture that alcohol and corporate porn facilitate, but also a contraceptive mentality which gives participants the false impression that they can use each other "safely."

- It will give appropriate respect to the fact that sex, both biologically and theologically, is strongly connected to procreation. Honoring this fact means transforming our sexual culture through a posture of hospitality and welcoming the stranger.

Given these principles, what is the proper place for sexual relationships? One might think that a call to limit sex to a permanently committed marriage reflects a "conservative" view, but progressive Christian ethicist David Gushee (a one-time advisor to Barack Obama's presidential campaign and promoter of LGBT rights within Evangelical and other Christian communities) says, "We need to begin within our own communities in calling one another back to the norm of sexual abstinence outside marriage and fidelity within marriage, regardless of how very difficult it seems to practice this norm today."[118]

Gushee does not call us back to a time when the culture was dangerously close to being anti-sex. (Indeed, to "go back" now would mean to celebrate the 1960s and '70s sexual revolution, when the seeds of the hookup culture were planted. For college students today, this is the sexual ethic of their grandparents!) Instead, especially given current trends, Gushee's is a progressive call to *more and better sex*—sex characterized by genuine encounter, mutual relationship, hospitality, and nonviolence. It is a call to be honest about the fact that two people who have sex have chosen, as John Paul II put it in his "theology of the body," to give their partner a mutual and total gift of self. As should be clear, by having sex we offer our physical and (if it has not been dulled by the pornified hookup culture[119]) emotional self to our partner in a most vulnerable way. Understanding sex as a gift of self to another—not merely using another for conquest and pleasure—honors this fact.

A 2016 article on this new sexual culture featured in (of all places) *Cosmopolitan* magazine includes interviews with several young women about living out the alternative, progressive sexual culture that the CLE calls for.[120] Tellingly, one interviewee lamented that young men who realized her views on sex made many frustrating assumptions about her, presuming that she fit "the virgin archetype," or was "conservative," not "fun," or not "a sexual being." A CLE-inspired alternative to the current sexual culture is anything but anti-sex. In fact, for those caught in the pathetically bad sex of the hookup culture, it provides a beacon of hope that good sex is possible. It may even provide a beacon of hope for those who worry that the current culture is careening toward the end of sex altogether.

Furthermore, the biological and theological connection between sex and creating new life also exemplifies the true power and depth of what is at stake. Deciding to have sex with one's partner (even with contraception, given its relatively high failure rate) can be a choice to allow that person to become the mother or father of your child, and to offer yourself as the mother or father of their child. The alternative sexual culture supported by the CLE respects the flourishing of genuine, loving encounters between couples, and in the spirit of hospitality welcomes new life that may spring from the relationship. This alternative culture calls couples to have sex when they have committed to giving themselves to each other totally, in the spirit of a unifying encounter and an open hospitality to new life.

This is the unambiguous sexual ethic Pope Francis proposes. In *Amoris laetitia* he insists sex "by its very nature" is ordered to procreation. A child is not an external add-on but springs forth from the center of the "mutual giving" of the couple's love; the child does not appear at the end of a process, but "is present from the beginning of love as an essential feature." True love is open and cannot be closed in on itself; no sexual act between spouses should "refuse this meaning." Marriage, the pope says, is a friendship marked by passion, but a passion always directed toward a unifying encounter. The all-encompassing character of such union requires it to be "exclusive, faithful and open to new life." In the pope's words, it "shares everything."[121]

Objections

> Objection #1: *Isn't this proposal unrealistic? In most corners of today's culture, if one were to offer it in casual conversation, without the context of the rest of the chapter, it would almost certainly be met with skepticism, if not outright laughter. Many would claim that it is, at best, an idealized vision of sex, and if the CLE is going to have any impact on how people actually live their lives it needs to be more grounded in the reality of what actual people can do. Even married couples, for instance, can't possibly engage in sex always as a mutual and total self-gift. Life gets in the way: responsibility for children, sickness, stress at work, exhaustion—all these things can make sex something less than ideal. Furthermore, isn't it hopelessly naïve to think that people in the grip of the hookup culture could do something like what the CLE proposes? Shouldn't we be more realistic and lower our expectations—perhaps especially for what young people can achieve?*

These are understandable and important questions, but they have good answers. First, before all else, the CLE must be realistic in its approach. Dogmatic views disconnected from the reality of everyday people and experiences will never become a viable alternative culture. But if we pay attention to history, we know that cultural attitudes toward sex can shift dramatically. The ancient Greeks thought that sex between a man and a boy was not only acceptable but a positive personal and social good. During the late Middle Ages, the concept of love included a respect for women and a spirituality totally foreign to today's hookup culture. Equally foreign are the nineteenth century Victorian public sexual ideals of modesty and chastity. And the fundamental changes brought by the sexual revolution during the second half of the twentieth century are well known.

Many of my students believe their generation has sex much more frequently than their parents did at their age, but we saw above that they are wrong. The backlash against the hookup culture beginning to form among young people complicates their views of sex. Hookup culture still predominates (72 percent of college students claimed to have had at least one one-night stand), but a quarter said that they were saving themselves for the right person. This is up 19 percent since 2002.[122] And a backlash from young people could easily become even more dramatic, especially after #MeToo. How long before the clear connection between hookup culture and sexual violence is challenged more broadly? How high do STI rates need to rise? What level of saturation of porn must be reached? How unhappy do people have to become with their (lack of) relationships and increasing isolation? Ke$ha's arrival on the music scene received attention mostly because as a young woman she was saying what men and boys have been saying for decades; but is what she was saying all that interesting? People who made money off her music marketed it as pushing boundaries, but it was the same old and tired routine of the last fifty years, and this chapter has documented its disastrous results.

An authentically feminist approach—one that challenges rather than accepts male models of sex—will call this lifestyle into question. It will strive to undermine the values and forces that drive the hookup culture. Young people are already starting to question the sexual ideas and values of their grandparents' generation. It will be interesting to see if large numbers follow through and begin to change the culture significantly. At any rate, given what history shows and what we know is already happening, a CLE-inspired cultural shift in our sexual practice cannot be deemed "unrealistic." In fact, history suggests that young people eventually will reject the sexual assumptions and values of their parents and grandparents. A sexual culture grounded in the values of encounter, mutuality, and hospitality is waiting to replace hookup culture.

What about people who do wait for marriage? Is the ideal of sex as total and mutual self-gift realistic? A sexual ethic founded in the writings and values of celibate male clerics risks not acknowledging the experience of married couples (and especially women—see below). Certainly, it is unrealistic to expect that every instance of married sex be total self-gift. However, we should keep before us the incidences of sexual violence even within a marriage. Falling short of the ideal because one is tired from work or because the baby is crying is one thing but using a spouse's body is another. We need to acknowledge that many relationships will fall short of the ideal but reducing another's body into a means to achieve one's own sexual end—that is, completely rejecting the ideal—is never acceptable.

> Objection #2: *Won't this lead to overpopulation and more STIs? One can agree that hookup culture is facilitated by a contraceptive mentality,* [123] *but still argue that it is necessary to address overpopulation, the ecological devastation that it causes, and high STI rates. Better to have safe sex with contraception than try to encourage a practice that will have such devastating consequences.*

The CLE, because it emerges from a culture of hospitality and welcome (especially for vulnerable populations whose dignity is deemed inconvenient), doubts the claim that there are too many people. A brief look at history and current population statistics and trends offers good reasons for such doubt. Academics and public intellectuals have always predicted overpopulation catastrophes, but all those predictions have been mistaken. Today, the countries with substantial reproductive growth are in the developing world, using energy and emitting carbon at rates that are tiny when compared to what people in developed countries use. Meanwhile, countries in reproductive decline actually produce the highest carbon emissions (thanks to unprecedented consumerism). This book will have more to say about this in future chapters, but those concerned about ecological degradation and developing sustainable energy should not focus on population rates (especially among people of color in developing countries). Privileged Westerners should turn a critical eye toward their own consumerist practices. The problems some arrogantly construe as "overpopulation" do not come from sexual and reproductive practices, but from political and economic injustice—which can often be traced back to the violence of Western colonialism. The developed West must not repeat this mistake with a new colonialism, this time an attempt to convince poor people of color in the developing world that they must adopt the values of a violent, consumerist, throwaway sexual culture.

Furthermore, history demonstrates that artificial population control doesn't work. In the fourth and fifth century, as the empire was beginning to collapse, Rome desperately sought to repopulate itself but failed. China's one-child policy caused a disproportionate number of female children (both prenatal and neonatal) to be killed, with the result that tens of millions of men will not find partners. Some economists also believe that the low birthrate means China will not generate enough new workers to support its mercurial economic growth.[124] Like ancient Rome, present-day China is now trying urgently but without much success to repopulate itself.[125]

Making contraception and abortion normative at the service of a consumerist culture has also caused populations in the developed West to decline dramatically, with similarly problematic results. This is particularly true for countries with large social welfare systems that protect the poor—given that they need an ever-increasing population of workers to pay taxes that support expensive government programs. Many Western governments have foreseen these problems and incentivize their citizens to have more children through tax breaks and other economic rewards. Russia has designated a holiday to create time off work for baby-making sex.[126] Even when considered as a whole (and, as mentioned above, distinguishing between cultures that consume massive resources and those that do not), the world does not have an overpopulation problem. Contrary to the received wisdom in many circles, all over the world population growth is slowing; the United Nations predicts that in two generations the world's total population will actually begin to decline.[127]

Also contrary to the received wisdom, contraceptives do not solve the STI problem. For some time, Pope Benedict and others in the Catholic Church have been pointing this out, but the developed West has been greeting these claims mostly with disbelief and derision. That is until Edward Green, a secular social scientist at Harvard, pointed out that contemporary social science supports Benedict's view.[128] Paradoxically, using contraception can increase STI rates within a given population. This is, in part, because people generally have riskier sex when they feel safe. In addition, however, some cultures believe that people in a relationship who use contraception (especially condoms) show a lack of trust in one's partner—despite the fact that infidelity (spurred, ironically, by the idea of "safe" contraceptive sex) often remains a problem in the relationship. Furthermore, using the birth control pill or other hormonal contraception, while creating a sense of security that leads to riskier sexual choices, provides no protection against STIs at all.[129] Interestingly, according to the *Journal of International Development*, the rate of STI infection in Uganda went down dramatically because "the lack of condom promotion" contributed to success in "behavior change strategies."[130] These considerations explain why the United States (despite wide availability and celebration of contraception—coupled with overwhelming educational and media campaigns encouraging so-called "safe sex") continues to see ever-increasing rates of new sexually transmitted infections.[131]

Melinda Gates, a leader in exporting Western neocolonial assumptions and practices via the Bill and Melinda Gates Foundation, claims to be "hopeful" that Pope Francis will change his views on contraception.[132] But when asked about fighting HIV in Africa, the Pope refused to say that contraception was the answer. Instead he argued that we should focus our concern on broader problems of sexual culture.[133] And in *Amoris laetitia*, the pope also noted that a decline in population due to culture and reproductive health policies "will lead to economic impoverishment and a loss of hope in the future."[134] In terms of ecology, Pope Francis said in *Laudato si'* that to "blame population growth instead of extreme and selective consumerism" is evidence that we are "refusing to face the issues" of what really drives environmental degradation.[135]

> Objection #3: *Doesn't this understanding of sex hurt women? Christians should be honest about the fact that our tradition has not done a good job of listening to women's voices and perspectives. Almost all institutions over the last two millennia have done a poor to horrific job in this regard, but this still leaves the Church with a serious limitation. In fact, we should reserve special criticism for Christianity insofar as it continues to rely on*

an outdated understanding of sexuality while failing to take women's experience seriously. Before the birth control pill was available and normative, women had little control over their sexual and reproductive lives. Women could not compete with men equally, especially for employment, because they bore the burden of childbearing. Contraception has empowered women to make autonomous and private sexual choices—beginning a family only if and when they want to. Indeed, the birth control pill sparked the revolution that made women's liberation possible.[136] It is easy for men (especially celibate men like Catholic priests) who do not have to bear the burden of childbearing to speak of "hospitality to new life" as essential to sexual relationships. While the CLE may make some important criticisms of the hookup culture and pornography (especially as they promote sexual violence, which disproportionately hurts women), it goes too far if it calls into question the normativity of contraception and tries to connect sexuality to being open to new life.

The CLE warns that cultivating and guarding autonomous and private moral space does not lead to true freedom and flourishing. This is especially true in a broader sense of all our sexual choices, and CLE feminists have argued that giving women more sexual choice, without examining the social and cultural forces that shape and coerce those choices, has badly damaged women and the struggle for an authentically feminist liberation. There is no doubt that the pill (along with abortion) has allowed women to space and avoid bearing children, but at a cost that CLE feminists want to talk about more openly.

For starters, a near-exclusive focus on autonomy and privacy does not question the male, consumerist forces and ideas that have shaped what is thought to be flourishing sex and family life. It is expected, for instance, that a certain socially-determined "stability" be established before getting married and having children. Welcoming new life might be good, but first you have to support yourself without relying on a community of family and friends. This perspective presupposes a consumerism-driven standard of living—a standard which, as we have seen, is governed by cycles of dissatisfaction. You need to make it to the next level: get the bigger promotion, buy the bigger house, live in the better neighborhood, pay off your student debt, etc. As a result, many people put off marriage and children until much later in life, often their late thirties and early forties. This even though child-bearing is much riskier for women in their late thirties and forties—and family-building is much more difficult in one's forties and fifties. Tellingly, those who marry at thirty-eight are three times more likely to get divorced than those who get married at twenty-eight.[137]

These same forces also push us to define ourselves by our jobs. In a male-dominated consumerist culture, asking "What do you do?" really means, "How do you earn money?" The power behind this social expectation is so strong that many will move far away from families and other support networks to get exactly the job they want. It is problematic that some feminists criticize consumerism for placing financial autonomy before all else, but do not consider how the same forces motivate contraception and sexual choice. The framework and goals set up by men to benefit men may make contraception seem necessary to compete equally with men. But instead of accepting those forces and participating in them, CLE feminists push for authentic systemic change—change that will lead to better sex, better relationships, better families, and better communities.

Many also claim that the pill is important for women's health and liberates them to participate autonomously and privately in our sexual culture. But we have already shown how male and consumerist forces have shaped sexual attitudes and practices in ways that hurt women.[138] Indeed, the pill not only exposes women to a male-dominated understanding of sexuality, but despite exceptional situations where it does relieve serious health problems, contemporary science demonstrates that in most circumstances the pill can damage women's health in profound ways. In light of such problems, the social expectation that the pill be used throughout their child-bearing years (fueled by the more general patriarchal assumptions that women bear responsibility for contraception and that the male, unpregnant body is normative) is not feminist. Pill-protected sex, of course, does not protect against STIs and can even increase a woman's chances of contracting HIV.[139] Furthermore, the pill is a group 1 carcinogen[140] and the pharmaceutical industry has paid hundreds of millions of dollars in liability to women whom contraceptives have harmed.[141] Using the pill also brings with it an increase in the risk of breast cancer.[142] The pill's correlation with significantly higher rates of depression and suicide, particularly with regard to adolescent girls, has also come under investigation.[143] (Some argue that women should use intra-uterine devices or other long-acting contraception, but these devices have even worse side effects.[144])

Despite widespread use of the pill, about half of pregnancies are unintended.[145] But because women have been "liberated" to "choose" to have "safe" sex (and also abortion, especially when contraception fails), it is women themselves who are left to deal with the consequences of unintended pregnancies. Because the responsibility for reproductive choice falls solely on women—who are now supposed to have autonomous control over their sexual and reproductive decisions—in the context of our hookup culture a predatory man who uses a woman (in a relationship or not) has little incentive or expectation to take responsibility for his actions if she becomes pregnant—and not a few times (as we will see later in this book) he may pressure his partner to have an abortion.

As Helen Alvaré has frequently pointed out, the social expectation that accompanies the pill's availability, coupled with the hookup culture, hurts women, especially when they pursue actual relationships:

> For decades, and to the present day, a robust literature—economic, sociological, and psychiatric—indicates that the complete separation of the idea of sex from the idea of procreation

does not in fact favor women's preferences about sex, dating, or marriage. . . . Economists have pointed out how this leads to a market in which sex becomes the price women pay for even casual relationships with men; women are drawn into this market against their preferences, feeling they have no choice. . . . Women's reproductive lives are more, not less, outside their control in a sex and mating market dominated by the notion that it is not sex but "unprotected sex" that makes babies.[146]

Shifting responsibility to the woman, as some economists predicted decades ago, has led to the feminization of poverty,[147] something to which the CLE must give serious attention because of its special concern for vulnerable impoverished populations. Alvaré also points out the growing race and class divide in this regard:

[T]he poor and racial minorities give birth outside of marriage far more often than their more privileged sisters. In 2007 (the most recent year for which we have data), the birth rates among single women varied drastically according to race and ethnicity. The figures were: 72 per 1000 African American women of childbearing age, 106 per 1000 Hispanic women, and 32 per 1000 non-Hispanic white women. A mere 7% of college-educated women gave birth outside of marriage as compared with 50% of women who did not go to college.[148]

In the fight for justice for vulnerable women, those who uphold the CLE cannot be satisfied with the rhetoric of autonomy and privacy. Unable to escape a patriarchal, consumerist sexual culture, these women are sacrificed at the altar of sexual autonomy, allowing the privileged to detach themselves from the irreducible demands of dignity for all.[149] In proposing a different way to think about our sexual culture, we should go out to the peripheries with hope, and perhaps even a bit of confidence. We can take heart, for instance, from the example of Anna Keating, who works as coordinator of Catholic life at hyper-secular Colorado College. It might be the last place you'd expect a favorable reaction to skepticism concerning the contraceptive mentality, but she's had great success in opening up young women (of all faiths and of no faith) to consider a genuine alternative to their sexual culture—particularly when it comes to the patriarchal assumption that women's equality depends on pumping their bodies full of hormones that demonstrably damage their health and their broader well-being.[150]

Conclusion

This chapter could not consider every issue relevant to the vast, complex topic of sex and sex cultures (the next chapter, for instance, will consider reproductive technologies in more detail), but it has sought to take an honest look at the explicit and structural violence in our sexual culture. It has argued that the CLE must challenge such a culture—proposing an alternative that offers an enthusiastic "yes" to good sex by promoting genuine encounter, mutuality, and hospitality; and a firm "no" to bad sex dominated by a consumerist-driven focus on autonomy, privacy, detachment, conquest, and using others' bodies.

Of course, many, many more questions remain. For instance, some use of the pill is clearly consistent with the CLE—especially to ensure a woman's health, as in the case of dangerous endometrial growth and the risk of ovarian cancer, or when an irregular period causes terrible cramps and dangerous bleeding. Exceptions for other complex reasons—such as in the case of controlling STI transmission via prostitution (something that Pope Benedict appeared to consider a legitimate step in controlling STIs[151]) or protecting someone who is the victim of repeated sexual violence—require more careful and detailed consideration than this chapter can accommodate. Whether sexual relationships between lesbian or gay persons can meet the requirements of the CLE is also a complex issue that could not be adequately addressed in a chapter that already is the longest in this book. I encourage readers to ask these questions within the CLE framework and expand the discussion beyond the scope of this book.

Let me conclude by invoking Pope Francis's call to mercy. People trapped in a destructive and consumerist sexual culture have been wounded and are hurting. This is what violence does. People with such wounds need a field hospital that offers love and healing—not disdainful words that add to their pain. Like Jesus speaking to the crowd surrounding the woman caught in adultery, a CLE-inspired sexual ethic will put sexual sinfulness in the context of the sinfulness that all human beings share. Each of us surely is responsible in some way for the consumerism that has produced our current sexual culture, and therefore shares some degree of moral blame. Yes, it is important to show that our current sexual practices are detached, violent, and ugly. But it is even more important to imitate Jesus' mercy and love with a positive message calling our culture to alternative sexual practices that are unifying, welcoming, and beautiful.

And lest the reader worry I'm finishing with flowery abstractions thrown in at the conclusion of the chapter, let us return to the story of Ke$ha. She now goes by plain Kesha, and her dropping the dollar sign from her name is symbolic of her more general rejection of a consumerist sexual culture that used her in nearly every way a person can be used. In 2014 she checked into rehab and began the process of turning her life around. In a moving letter to "her 18-year-old self" she wrote:

> The bad news is, you nearly killed yourself on the road to success, fueled by fear of failure, crippling anxiety and insecurity. You will become severely bulimic and anorexic and the worse your disease gets, the more praise you will get from some people in your industry. And this will really, really mess with your head. But when you're trying to live up to an unrealistic expectation, it's never going to be good enough. No matter what you do. . . . You're still in a society that worships photo-shopped super models. We all still feel the pressure to look like

them because that's a symptom of a society that emphasizes all the wrong things and this will be an everyday struggle -- and you must be strong 'cause over time you will gain confidence and you will learn that words and art do matter.[152]

Apparently, the love and support of her fans kept Kesha afloat long enough to begin to resist. "You will meet kids who tell you that they struggle with many of the same things you've struggled with, or more," she wrote. "And that will change you." Hello, culture of encounter.

The poster-child for the consumerist hookup culture ended up being coerced down an all too predictable path of self-destruction. But due to the love and mercy others showed her she is now one of the most important resisters of the very culture she once personified. And now, as this chapter was being written, the new Kesha released her first song in four years, one that marks her struggle out of the horrific life she once led.

She titled the song "Praying."

Chapter Three

Reproductive Biotechnology

Introduction

The CLE is committed to consistent reasoning and making connections between issues, so several chapters in this book will approach the same topic in different contexts. One chapter will discuss homelessness with respect to pregnant women and another with respect to military veterans. One chapter will examine how racial discrimination impacts abortion practices, while another chapter will connect it with incarceration. The previous chapter addressed the birth control pill in the context of sex practices and cultures. This chapter will focus on how it relates to consumerism and technology in reproductive practices. We will look at such practices in light of the CLE's concern about a person's dignity being so reduced as to become a mere tool of another's will, especially those who are vulnerable and at risk of being used and discarded. As in the previous chapter, we will also consider the challenges leveled against the CLE position.

From the beginning, however, it should be noted that biotechnology is moving quickly into mainstream cultural practices. Ethics, however, which tends to adapt itself slowly, lags behind. It is likely that some of the technological capabilities and practices written about here will be outdated soon after this book comes out. But the ethical principles and reasoning will not go out of date, and thus can be used to evaluate new reproductive biotechnologies as they emerge.

Opposing the CLE's Principle of Hospitality

The contraceptive pill is ubiquitous. One in five American women use it. And nine in ten use it not because of a medical diagnosis, but to prevent a new life from being formed as a consequence of having sex. This is one way in which technology can promote an inhospitable sexual culture. Using the pill is, however, a very particular rejection of hospitality—a refusal to welcome a new life coming into existence via the process that naturally produces life. A different rejection of hospitality involves refusing to welcome an already-existing human being. Some argue that the birth control pill can be an "abortifacient"; that is, the drug not only can prevent ovulation, but also can prevent an early member of *Homo sapiens* from implanting into the uterus. And though drug companies once marketed the birth control pill as having an abortifacient effect, most scientists and ethicists (including several who identify as pro-life) now believe it does not.

One can also separate sex from hospitality toward human life by taking a drug called Plan B, sometimes referred to as the "morning after pill." As both names imply, it is designed to be used when birth control has failed or when a couple has had sex without birth control but wants to avoid pregnancy. It is also an important part of a standard procedure, even in Catholic hospitals, to care for women who are victims of sexual violence. There is more controversy about whether Plan B is an abortifacient—especially because it is indicated for use up to seventy-two hours after unprotected sex, and some studies have shown Plan B to be effective up through 120 hours.[153] Eminent pro-life ethicists, however, argue that the chance of Plan B having an abortifacient effect is vanishingly small.[154]

Ella is a drug specifically designed to be used within five days of having sex.[155] In this case there is less controversy about its abortifacient properties given that Ella's own website says it "may also work by preventing attachment to the uterus." The FDA agrees, saying that Ella "may also work by preventing attachment (implantation) to the uterus."[156] In recent years there has been significant controversy about whether the US government should force institutions like hospitals and universities to cover Ella as part of their employee insurance packages—especially if such institutions are run by religious orders or others with strong moral concern for what they understand to be the violent death of a vulnerable member of the human family.[157]

Finally, there is RU-486, sometimes called "the abortion pill." Though it differs in several ways from Plan B or Ella, it is often confused with them. Taken after an early member of *Homo sapiens* has connected to her mother's uterus, it is prescribed to women up to ten weeks into pregnancy. RU-486 actually includes two drugs, one that cuts off the pregnancy hormone to the prenatal human child and another that expels the child from the mother's body.

This kind of biotechnology, obviously, clearly demonstrates a lack of hospitality to early human life.

Technologies That Create Life without Sex

Based on what we saw in the previous chapter, it is clear that the CLE would be skeptical of a biotechnological culture that attempts to separate sex from hospitality to new life. We will examine this in more detail later in this chapter. However, other biotechnologies engage in a similar kind of separation—but one that makes the creation and (selective) welcoming of new life possible outside of sex. Mary Louise Brown's 1978 birth demonstrated the possibility of generating fellow members of our species via in vitro fertilization (IVF). Infertile couples, fertile couples who want to have quality control over the reproductive process, or individuals who would like to raise a child "of their own" (as opposed to adoption or fostering a child), can use sperm and ova to create a child in a laboratory dish.

Many hundreds of thousands of babies have been born this way, and it is becoming even more common as many women and men who delay having children until later in life lose the ability to conceive a baby sexually. As contraception made it possible to think of sex apart from procreation, IVF allows us to think of procreation apart from sex. This has led to speculation that the "end of sex" discussed in the previous chapter may be made possible by IVF becoming the default method for human reproduction.[158] Even pieces in mainstream outlets like National Public Radio have wondered whether advances in IVF technology, particularly when used to choose certain genetic traits, "will make sex obsolete."[159] A related problem comes from our diminished biological and social capacity to procreate via sex. Sperm counts are half of what they were only forty years ago.[160] The US fertility rate just hit a historic low,[161] and some European countries are now paying their citizens to have children.[162] Combine these concerns with the trendlines mentioned in the previous chapter concerning porn and sex robots, and it becomes clear that sex between two people being the normative way human beings reproduce is facing challenges never seen in human history. Tech giant Apple is betting on IVF: they do not provide childcare for their employees—but do provide free egg-freezing so ova can be used later for IVF.[163]

To the understandable delight of an increasingly number of infertile people, the power of IVF has become extraordinary. For instance, Rajo Devi Lohan was able to conceive via IVF and bear a child when she was seventy years old (though she died soon after doing so).[164] Because it becomes likely that older parents will not live long enough to raise IVF-created children, many fertility clinics do not permit women over a certain age to use the procedure. But given Western culture's focus on reproductive autonomy, these restrictions cannot be sustained for long. When they first started doing IVF, fertility physicians in the United Kingdom were asked to consider social factors like age, but in 2005 it became illegal to refuse a fertility customer on this basis.[165]

IVF success also diminishes the later in life one uses it. Women under thirty-five have a success rate of 35 to 40 percent, but for those over forty the rate plummets to less than 10 percent. It is much more expensive than conceiving a child by natural means (often over $40,000 per live birth[166]). Thus, IVF becomes an option only for those with significant resources, and it becomes understandable why many couples in the United States try to maximize their resources by creating many more embryos than they hope to use. If they fail the first or second time, there are "extra" embryos. But these "extra" embryos create a huge ethical problem, given that most are discarded as medical waste or used for research.[167]

In addition to these moral complications, a child born via IVF is significantly more likely to have heart defects, cleft lip or palate, disconnection between the esophagus and stomach, blockage or other problems with the anus, club feet, spina bifida, and chromosomal abnormalities like Down syndrome. The later a mother uses IVF in her life, the greater the increase in these already substantial possibilities. We will examine this topic in greater detail when we discuss abortion and euthanasia in the case of disability, but it seems that our communities—or even the parents themselves—do not place the same value on disabled children as on those who meet their expectations for health and achievement. Consider, for instance, that between 70 and 90 percent of prenatal children thought to have Down syndrome are killed via abortion. Such abortions are so frequent that, even though many more babies are being conceived with Down syndrome, the overall rate of older human beings with this disability in the United States is declining.[168]

Often the reason for an abortion after IVF has nothing to do with a birth defect. Especially given that IVF users are significantly more likely to have twins or triplets, consider this remarkable story presented in the *New York Times*:

> As Jenny lay on the obstetrician's examination table, she was grateful that the ultrasound tech had turned off the overhead screen. She didn't want to see the two shadows floating inside her. Since making her decision, she had tried hard not to think about them, though she could often think of little else. She was 45 and pregnant after six years of fertility bills, ovulation injections, donor eggs and disappointment — and yet here she was, 14 weeks into her pregnancy, choosing to extinguish one of two healthy fetuses, almost as if having half an abortion. As the doctor inserted the needle into Jenny's abdomen, aiming at one of the fetuses, Jenny tried not to flinch, caught between intense relief and intense guilt.

"Things would have been different if we were 15 years younger or if we hadn't had children already or if we were more financially secure," she said later. "If I had conceived these twins naturally, I wouldn't have reduced this pregnancy, because you feel like if there's a natural order, then you don't want to disturb it. But we created this child in such an artificial manner — in a test tube, choosing an egg donor, having the embryo placed in me

— and somehow, making a decision about how many to carry seemed to be just another choice. The pregnancy was all so consumerish to begin with, and this became yet another thing we could control."[169]

The Effect of Consumerism

Consumerism, as we saw in the previous chapter (and will see throughout the book), enables throwaway culture. The West's reproductive biotechnological culture is no exception. It permeates and drives the processes that disconnect sex from hospitality and openness to new life, as well as the processes that disconnect attempts to have children from sex. Consumerism shapes potential parents to believe they must achieve a certain lifestyle and level of autonomy before having children—and, indeed, that they must be able to give their children the same lifestyle and level of autonomy.

The consumerism driving reproductive biotechnology can also impact others connected to the IVF process. Some are connected directly, as when a surrogate mother rents out her womb to another individual or couple who wants a child. As with other kinds of renting, the market determines price. One American company, Circle Surrogacy, charges clients an estimated $90,000 to $130,000 to hire a surrogate mother (not including the cost of donor eggs)[170]—less than $40,000 of which goes to the woman. Still, $40,000 is a substantial sum, leading some ethicists to criticize surrogacy as de facto exploitation of poor women by biotech corporations.

The worry increases when a corporation outsources gestational labor to poor women in developing countries. Driven by a desire to grab market share by lowering the cost, some companies seek poor women who will gestate a child for far less money. India was an early leader in the "surrogate mother industry" that served wealthy women from developed countries. The cost has been driven down to about $14,000, while Indian women generally receive less than $5,000 for their gestational labor.[171] Thailand has had a similar experience with commercial surrogacy. Consumerism there reached its peak when a Japanese billionaire purchased sixteen surrogate children.[172] In both countries, exploitation became so rampant that the Indian and Thai governments banned commercial surrogacy altogether.[173]

In the United States and other countries in the developed West surrogacy has brought complex legal problems. For instance, in certain US states and in the United Kingdom the surrogate mother is the legal parent until the child is handed over to those who paid for her gestational services. This has caused emotional confrontations, as in the following case:

Margaret (not her real name), a 42-year-old single mother who has two other children, said:

"They may not be my eggs but I grew these babies inside me. I nourished them to birth and went through a life-threatening emergency caesarean to have them.

"I would be devastated if they are taken away from me now. The law regards me as their mother and I regard them as my children."

She said: "I decided to become a surrogate mother because I wanted to help a childless couple.

"But it was also important to me that there should be a friendship between me and the parents and that this contact continued after the birth.

"When it became clear to me that this couple, who are both professionals, saw this as just a business arrangement, and me as some sort of incubator, I changed my mind and decided to keep the children.

"I then bonded with the babies and now I love them dearly. It doesn't matter that they are a different race to me. I feel like their mother."[174]

Sometimes the parties disagree about whether a pregnancy should continue at all. For instance, a Canadian couple had paid a woman to carry their child to term, but then learned that the child likely had Down syndrome and asked the surrogate to have an abortion. The mother refused, putting the case in a "legal limbo."[175] There was a contract between the three parents, but courts sometimes dissolve such contracts in favor of family law, which often forces biological parents (the donors of the egg and sperm) to support their children. In the United States this is complicated by the fact that the parents can sometimes sue the surrogate mother for breach of contract. Yet the law says that a surrogate has the right to make reproductive decisions in a "non-coercive environment." In the case above, once the parents who paid for the surrogacy backed off and made it clear they would not accept the child, the surrogate mother ended up having an abortion anyway because she felt that raising this new child would put a burden on her already-existing family.

Though the US American legal tradition is uneasy with treating children and reproductive capacities as things to buy and sell, the twin totalizing forces of autonomy and consumerism are pushing society in a permissive, hands-off direction. Other countries, however, are taking a more skeptical approach. Sweden recently banned all surrogacy in their country—whether commercial or altruistic. Writing in *The Guardian*, Swedish journalist and anti-child trafficking activist Kajsa Ekis Ekman argued that Swedish rejection of "an industry that buys and sells human life"— in which "babies are tailor-made to fit the desires of the world's rich"—is "a true step forward for the women's movement."[176] Indeed, she notes that in February of 2016 "feminist and human-rights activists from all over the world met in Paris to sign the charter against surrogacy, and the European Parliament has also called on states to ban it."

Left wing French feminist intellectuals and politicians have called for a global ban on the practice, describing it as a form of neocolonialism. Ekman goes so far as to say we have "started outsourcing reproduction to poorer nations, just as we outsourced industrial production previously."

But what about cases in which eggs needed for IVF are procured from an outside source? This is a commercial process in the United States as well, subject to the same market forces as other products that are bought and sold. College-educated women—on whom the IVF market has a special focus—may be familiar with advertisements asking them to "donate" their eggs. And given the consumerist market forces in play, they don't want eggs from just *any* young woman, of course. Consider this story from the *Yale Daily News*:

> A healthy, attractive Yale female who has proven her academic achievement with an SAT score of 1500 or above can earn a cool $25,000, provided that she is also a nonsmoker. All she has to do to collect the money, according to a recent classified ad in the Yale Daily News, is donate her eggs to a loving couple.

> Similar ads, usually placed by egg donation facilitation agencies, run in college newspapers across the country. Tiny Treasures LLC, a Somerville, Mass. brokerage agency that is responsible for recent ads in the News, offers specialty advertising services

that place ads in college publications. In a process akin to that of college admissions, Tiny Treasures requires all prospective donors to mail copies of their SAT scores and college transcripts with their applications, both of which have direct bearing on the amount of compensation received. The agency suggests first-time donors receive between $2,000 and $5,000, but students who qualify as "Extraordinary Donors"— those with SAT scores above 1250, ACT scores above 28, college grade point averages above 3.5 or those who have attended Ivy League universities — receive between $5,000 and $7,000 for their services.

Compensation for egg donors varies, with donors negotiating their own fees, although the agency offers suggested rates. A classified ad in the Columbia Spectator from "a stable NYC Ivy League couple" seeks an Ivy League student, between 5-foot-7 and 5-foot-10 tall, of German, Irish, English or Eastern European descent. Compensation was listed as $25,000.[177]

Nor is this process limited to the Ivy League. A study of 100 advertisements in sixty-three colleges across the United States found that twenty-one specified a minimum SAT score. Half offered more than $5,000 and among this group 27 percent specified an "appearance requirement." The bigger the money, the choosier the client. Above the

$10,000 level, most ads "contained appearance or ethnicity requirements."[178] One advertisement in the *Stanford Daily* offered a whopping $100,000 for a suitable woman's eggs.[179]

But what to do if the price is too high or if (as in Canada, Australia, and the United Kingdom) selling eggs commercially is illegal? One company offers a solution: go on an egg-buying vacation.[180] They offer seven- to ten-day stays in places like Cancun, Ukraine, Panama, and South Africa where there are "high quality clinics" that offer "a broad range of ethnic donors, equivalent services and success rates, and at a drastically reduced cost." How can they get the costs, as they claim, 80 percent cheaper than in the United States? The answer is simple:

> Wages and the cost of living in other countries can be much less, so prices for services and payments to egg donors reflect this difference. In addition, the same brand name fertility medications are priced for the market they are selling in, so fertility medications for the donors are up to 50% less expensive.

And many of these women are desperate. For example, thousands of emigrants from the Soviet Union live in Cyprus, where "Russian-language newspapers often place advertisements seeking 'young healthy girls for egg donation.'" Women from Russia and Ukraine sometimes fly in just to donate eggs, "desperately needing the money for rent and utility bills." Some women even depend on this "as their main source of income, going through the process of being injected with hormones at least five times a year." In light of this the UK government recently completed a formal crackdown on reproductive technology companies explicitly organized to exploit poor and desperate women for their eggs.[181]

Given the companies' desire to make as much money as possible, many donors are not told about the complications and risks involved in the procedure. The documentary film *Eggsploitation*, for instance, tells the stories of many women (both in the United States and abroad) who had major health problems as a result of their donations. The powerful drugs that donors must take carry risks—"ovarian hyper-stimulation syndrome," as well as "pulmonary infarctions, fluid imbalances, stroke, clotting, perforation of the bowel or bladder, bleeding, production of adhesions which cause future infertility, and death. Long-term risks include breast, ovarian and endometrial cancers and future infertility." Abstract description of the problems is bad enough, but seeing the faces connected with the stories is heartbreaking.[182]

Because the supply of sperm is far more available, it doesn't command as much money as egg donation. Nevertheless, sperm donors face similar problems and exploitation. Sperm banks can and do market their products based on men's physical appearance and SAT scores, but even more disturbing is the sheer number of biological children that a single donor can create. The *New York Times* recently reported that one donor was the confirmed biological father of more than 150 children—and counting.[183] Some of these cases involve relatively small communities where there is a legitimate worry about possible sexual relations between half-brothers or -sisters. A Maryland woman who was artificially inseminated recently went on a crusade to find the more than thirty-five other children of her donor who, like her son, had a genetic disease that without treatment was fatal.[184]

Beyond Infertility

If reproductive biotechnology were used only to respond to infertility as a medical problem, it might be considered a procedure that needs to be reformed and properly regulated. But when reproductive autonomy rules the day, moral or legal judgments in this area are suspect. The only rules appear to be those of a consumerist marketplace. Presumably, to be open-minded and non-judgmental about reproductive autonomy and privacy means that the purchase of a child (or children) via IVF need not be limited to one or two parents. Biotechnology has already created situations in which a child might have five people referred to as parents: (1) the egg donor, (2) the sperm donor, (3) the surrogate mother, (4) parent/progenitor A, and (5) parent/progenitor B.[185] Depending on how you define the term, today's IVF children could have even more parents, as gametes can now be engineered to contain the genetic information of multiple people.[186] At a certain point, the term "parent" (or even "progenitor") loses its meaning, so a new vocabulary will need to be developed to describe the relationship status of those involved in the buying process.

For some years now, it has been possible to examine embryos created by IVF before implantation into a woman's uterus. And the examinations are becoming more precise. Preimplantation genetic diagnosis (PGD) could be done out of concern for health or medical issues—such as when embryos with a relatively high chance of inheriting a genetic disease are discarded. But as problematic as such a practice is, especially considering the CLE's concern about throwaway culture, what is done now is even worse. People can use PGD technology to select desired traits. IVF parents can now be offered choices based on sex, likely eye or hair color, height, and even complexion and body build.[187] And in the case of one undesired embryo, a parent driven by raw reproductive consumerism created an online advertisement stating her willingness to trade the female embryo she had created for a male one.[188] Before long PGD and embryo (de)selection will be bypassed altogether and gene-editing will be used to create a child with the desired biological traits. Embryos will be created through IVF and then, after some are chosen (and the "excess" ones are thrown away), they will be edited to eliminate what those with power have decided are genetic diseases.[189]

William Saletan points out that such reproductive practices are now so widespread it is difficult to imagine how our culture could ever go back. The presumption of reproductive autonomy is so strong that even sex-selection has become routine in IVF procedures, especially for a second child:

> Worldwide, the number of embryos and fetuses discarded for being the wrong sex is in the millions. In this country, the number of clients paying for sex-selective PGD is in the thou-

sands and growing. Nearly half of U.S. clinics that offer PGD have used it for nonmedical sex selection, and 40 percent of Americans approve of this practice.[190]

For instance, as I was writing this chapter, I came across an advertisement on the website of a company called The Fertility Institutes:

> If you want to be certain your next child will be the gender you're hoping for, be aware that no other method comes close to the reliability of PGD. While traditional sperm-screening techniques have a success rates of 60-70%, only PGD offers virtually 100% accuracy. Get free DVD and more info now! Free financing available![191]

We may be headed down a slope beyond even these practices. If we accept reproductive autonomy, then can we really prevent potential parents from choosing diseases for their children? Consider that some deaf parents have already claimed that outlawing PGD in order to select deaf children for themselves would essentially be admitting that deaf people's lives are not as good as other lives.[192] Some deaf parents, along with many others in our culture at large, claim that a life without hearing can actually be a richer one that they can choose to share with their children.

You may feel disturbed at this trend. Even if we could avoid the slippery slope via regulation by law (and it is difficult to imagine this happening without challenging our culture's near fanatical focus on reproductive freedom and choice), Saletan points out that doing something only on the national level probably will not work. Yes, some European countries have made some practices illegal—but the United States has not followed suit and US-based companies now offer their European customers attractive travel packages. Surely, then, the answer is to change the laws in the United States. But even if that huge (and, frankly, unlikely) feat is accomplished, business will go elsewhere. The Fertility Institutes has already opened a branch office in Mexico specifically to avoid this kind of regulation.

The CLE Critique

How might a CLE advocate respond to the reproductive culture and its technological practices? The previous chapter examined some aspects of how biotechnology affects women, but the problems here are even deeper. A consumerist culture asks women to delay having children until they have amassed enough wealth to reach our expected independent standard of living. In part because family and the broader community offer little support to be both mothers and professionals, women (rather than men) are expected to avoid pregnancy by taking a drug with serious side effects. Furthermore, considering the market for IVF, a consumerist culture identifies women even more strongly with their reproductive capacities—often exploiting them (especially the financially vulnerable) by using their eggs and their uteruses in order to make reproduction without sex possible. This process also reinforces unhealthy attitudes toward female beauty and body image because the market pays more to egg donors with traits that match a socially-constructed notion of female beauty.

In addition to these important concerns about women, the CLE must also highlight how IVF and other reproductive biotechnologies instrumentalize children. Like many other practices critiqued throughout this book, IVF reduces the dignity of a vulnerable population, making them mere tools of our will. And children's dignity is reduced dramatically: they are brought into (and taken out) of existence when and how powerful adults wish. At times this reduction of dignity is direct and obvious, as when PGD is used to determine which human embryos are unacceptable and so can be discarded, even simply because they are female. RU-486 and Ella (and perhaps even the morning after or birth control pills) are used to decide whether to discard human beings at the very beginning of their lives. Human embryos are destroyed in the process of using their stem cells to do research. In each of these cases, totally helpless and vulnerable members of the human family are abandoned or killed in ways that the CLE simply cannot tolerate.[193] Pope Francis has been explicit about this—no research can justify the destruction of human embryos.[194] This default to reproductive autonomy must be resisted by a preferential option for the vulnerable who cannot speak for themselves—particularly when a culture of consumerism radically reduces their dignity and turns them into mere marketplace products. In *Amoris laetitia*, Pope Francis decries how in the ancient Near East children were viewed as "without particular rights and even as family property"[195]—the same view that the throwaway culture has of very young children today. Francis contrasts this view with the one Jesus lived out, one that commands us to let "the little children come" to him—even privileging vulnerable children over powerful adults.

The CLE also highlights the impact of reproductive biotechnology (especially when paired with surgical abortion) on the lives of another vulnerable population: disabled children and adults. Using prenatal reproductive biotechnology to discard and kill the unwanted sends a clear message to older people with disabilities: it would have been better had you never existed. These practices also indirectly affect the resources available to persons with disabilities. In a culture driven by autonomy and privacy, a mother who did not use PGD or abortion to eliminate the "problem" now must sleep in the bed she made. Because she chose not to discard or kill her disabled child, it is up to her to "take responsibility" for her choice.

The CLE also calls attention to how this technology affects the vulnerable poor—especially in the context of a market. The poor already have the deck stacked against them because, as chapter 5 discusses in detail, they lack access to education, healthy living options, and supportive family structures equal to what people of means have. And this new biotechnological path not only exploits the vulnerable poor for use of their gametes and uteruses but will also widen the gap of inequality between them and the privileged by selecting IVF-generated children for traits that will provide even more competitive advantages in the marketplace.

Our current use of reproductive biotechnology does violence to vulnerable populations—women, children, people with disabilities, the poor—in ways that those who follow the CLE must resist. These populations have irreducible value and must be supported and defended against a biotechnological assault on their dignity. But how? The problem is rooted in the mistake that put us on the wrong track in the first place: disconnecting reproduction from sexuality.

Instead of thinking about children coming into the world via "reproduction" (a word that has clear consumerist overtones and implies a "product" that is made) we should think about it in terms of "procreation." We should understand ourselves as cooperating with God's creative power and accepting children (if and when they arrive) as a gift, not something for which we have a right. Pope Francis notes, again in *Amoris laetitia*, "A child deserves to be born of [the sexual love of a man and woman], and not by any other means." People are not owed children as the kind of things to be purchased in a market. Sexual love and the transmission of life are "ordered toward one another." God made man and woman to "share in the work of his creation" and entrusted "to them the responsibility for the future of mankind, through the transmission of human life."[196]

A culture that understands sex as a pornified hookup with someone from Tinder after texting for a couple days, and reproduction as something done via IVF in our late thirties, after we've had our fun and reached a certain standard of living, is in serious trouble. It has a profoundly mistaken view of children as products we make and choose for ourselves—and rejects Francis's understanding of how children are to come into our lives: namely, as a "grateful and enchanted welcome of a gift."[197] This approach acknowledges children's unconditional dignity independent of the will and desire of those who choose them. Many of the throwaway culture's violent practices stem from this fundamental mistake. And if we do not change course, many more will follow.

Objections

> Objection #1: *This view is anti-science and anti-technology. Indeed, it is anti-progress. The Church needs to get out of the Dark Ages and let science and technology continue to make progress.*

Let us examine this charge more carefully—after all, this objection could mean several different things. It could mean that someone who holds with the CLE position considers *all* scientific and technological developments to be problematic. But such a claim is patently false, especially given that organizations which support the CLE—like the Catholic Church—run hospitals and universities all over the world and pour billions and billions of dollars into scientific and technological research. As a matter of fact, in the late Middle Ages the Catholic Church invented the modern hospital and research university. In modern times, the Vatican works to support and even organize research initiatives to explore how to use non-embryonic stem cells to cure illnesses.[198] Note that in late 2011 the Vatican made a formal agreement to support the adult stem cell research work of NeoStem, a New York-based biopharmaceutical company.[199] Far from being anti-science and anti-technology, the CLE supports using science and technology to aid vulnerable populations.

And surely no one wants to support science and technology with no moral limitations. We are all "anti-science" regarding some science—like what the Nazis practiced. David Gushee reminds us to not limit our concern about science to this historical era:

> It wasn't just Nazis who were interested in such [deeply immoral] projects, at least the milder forms of them. The early twentieth century advent of serious advances in birth control, for example, as well as in sterilization techniques, tempted many do-gooders around the world to seek to suppress the birth rates of the bad in favor of the good. If American readers of this book are feeling pretty good about our country right now, this might be a good time to say that the United States was the very first nation to undertake compulsory sterilization for eugenic purposes.[200]

It is not "anti-science" to believe that morality should discipline and limit how science and technology develop in a culture.

But perhaps there is a more sophisticated "anti-science" objection. Isn't the CLE anti-science specifically regarding *reproductive* technology? Such an objection flows nicely from the well-worn claim that religious people and institutions are obsessed with sexual practices—and their medieval, anti-science approach demands that we do everything "naturally," without the aid of science and technology. The truly vulnerable who are abandoned, so the argument goes, are those who wish to participate with God in the beautiful creation of a child, but are forced to abandon their hope because of narrow-minded, backward, anti-science, and anti-technology attitudes.

But even this more sophisticated version does not ring true. Recall, first, that the CLE questions any practice that involves bringing a child into the world primarily to satisfy the individual will. It challenges us on why we would seek our own biologically-related child, for instance, rather than becoming a parent for the vulnerable children waiting to be adopted or fostered. As mentioned above, the CLE understands parenthood as a gift that may or may not be given to us, not as something one is owed as a means of fulfilling a desire to have biologically-related offspring.

Moreover, the CLE's concerns are consistent with using science and technology to help a couple *cooperate* with God in procreating. In this sense, CLE organizations like the Catholic Church are remarkably *pro*-sex and will support reproductive biotechnology insofar as it affirms sex, particularly when it is procreative. For instance, in its most recent bioethics document the Vatican upholds biotechnologies that address infertility by repairing damaged or diseased procreative organs or mechanisms. Drugs that help women ovulate more regularly or produce more eggs, or that help men achieve erections or higher sperm counts, for instance, are legitimate.[201] The fact that the Church "supports Viagra but not the pill" is sometimes cited as an example of Catholic inconsistency and even misogyny, but in this context it is clear where such distinctions come from. Viagra, a kind of biotechnology that facilitates the connection between sex and procreation, is different from biotechnologies used to undermine that connection. So, bottom line: one need not be anti-science or anti-technology to accept the CLE's position on reproductive biotechnology. Without doubt, science and technology are doing wondrous and completely moral things to help couples connect sex and the gift of procreation.

> Objection #2: *This view fails to respect privacy, choice, and personal freedom. The judgements about appropriate use of biotechnology are based on personal values. Some are the "crunchy" or "all natural" type who strive to be "in tune" with "fertility rhythms" of our ecological world—but not everyone is like that. One might be interested in resisting the cultural practices of self-centered consumerism—but not interested at all in a "natural" perspective. A pluralistic culture needs to make room for those who see things differently. Plus, don't we want to avoid imposing religious values upon those who do not share them? After all, is it really any of our business how others bring children into this world? Who are we to claim that one person's private behavior is morally problematic?*

These questions resonate strongly in the hyper-autonomous culture of the United States. Especially regarding the weighty issues surrounding reproduction, we hesitate to impose our understanding of the good onto those who think differently. In this context, being labeled "anti-choice" is almost as negative as being labeled anti-science. But just as almost everyone is anti-science in some circumstances, at times almost everyone is anti-choice as well. Many believe, for instance, that vulnerable populations (like prenatal or neonatal children who are racial minorities, are female, and/or have mental disabilities) need to be protected from the reproductive choices of powerful people who would simply eliminate them—perhaps through abortion or infanticide—because of their race, gender, or disability.

Those who uphold the CLE cannot let appeals to privacy and freedom divert public attention from the violence that certain biotechnologies visit upon vulnerable populations. For instance: following the IVF process, the youngest members of the human family ("excess" human embryos) are destroyed or discarded. Women and girls are exploited for their reproductive capacities, reinforcing the harmful view that females have value because of their appearance and their ability to bear children. The expectation that children be raised without physical or mental flaws (especially when a consumerist culture determines what counts as a flaw) undermines the dignity of vulnerable populations—both prenatal and postnatal. These examples alone demonstrate why the CLE resists a hyper-autonomous reproductive culture's urge to value choice above defense of the most vulnerable. The CLE says it time and time again:

unrestrained choice and autonomy put vulnerable populations at unacceptable risk.

But there is another vulnerable population yet to be considered: *future* children. The CLE resists the choices of the powerful who dominate and even kill the vulnerable to accomplish the ends they desire. The CLE insists that decisions about procreation be made based on the good of a vulnerable future child. Is it justice for children—does it give them what they are owed—to bring them into existence via a process that involves five (or more) parents? Or with only one parent? Or a parent who is likely to die within a few years of the child's birth? Or parents not committed to raising a child throughout childhood? Or parents who bring a child into the world but do not commit to raising that child together? For decades, US family law has preferred stable, committed two-parent families, given that social science demonstrates that this is generally in the best interests of children's flourishing.[202] Too often our culture has begun to focus on reproductive autonomy and freedom without examining how these choices affect vulnerable future children.

> Objection #3: *Human embryos are not really a vulnerable population. One could argue, in the best interests of our future children, that we should regulate reproductive biotechnologies such as IVF so they can be used only by married couples who are permanently committed to each other and to raising children together. But who really thinks that the embryo is a person like us? Sure,*

the embryo is "alive," but it is nothing more than a tiny clump of cells without a human form or shape. Furthermore, it is not even clear that an embryo is an individual: a single embryo can split or segment and become two embryos. Plus, two embryos can combine to form a single embryo. And though it is difficult to determine the exact rate at which it happens, many millions of human embryos appear to die spontaneously as a result of natural miscarriages. Those who uphold the CLE do not seem to behave as if we have another human holocaust in our midst; does anyone really think that the embryo has interests comparable to older human beings that look and act more like us? Perhaps human embryos deserve moderate moral respect given that they can eventually become human persons, but no one really thinks they count as a vulnerable population and that their interests, for instance, should outweigh the interests of married couples who wish to have children via IVF.

This objection deserves careful consideration—and, in truth, the complex issues it raises will need elaboration in the next chapter. At that point we will explore the relationship between a "human being" and a "person," but for now we should note that contemporary biology clearly describes the human embryo as an organism belonging to the genus and species *Homo sapiens*. A sample of 5,502 biologists from 1,058 academic institutions assessed statements representing the biological view that "a human's life begins at fertilization." Ninety-five percent agreed.[203]

After fertilization, the egg and sperm cease to be gametes (which belonged to other organisms) and begin to exist in a new state, as a human organism with its own principle and pattern of growth and development, its own genetic code, and an XX or XY chromosomal pattern. It is true that human embryos appear to die at what seems like a high rate, but the science is not clear about how high that rate actually is and whether the beings that die are fully-formed embryos or malformed entities that never completed the process of fertilization. But even admitting for the sake of argument that half of fully-formed embryos may die before they have a chance to develop, it is not clear what follows from this. At many times in human history the infant mortality rate for human beings was also around 50 percent. This, of course, implied nothing about the moral value of such infants.

Responding to challenges based on individuality and twinning/combination is more difficult. But consider that "a female human becoming pregnant and bearing a child" is another example of one human being becoming two human beings, and we wouldn't claim that the woman was not an individual person before pregnancy because of this. It is not clear, therefore, that we ought to deny that an embryo is an individual person because that one living being may later become two organisms. However, it does at least seem remarkably odd to imagine—as happens with human embryo combination—that one individual human person can combine with another individual human person to become a single human person. At the very least, we must say that human life at this stage of development works in a very different way than does human life at other stages. It might come as a surprise that the Catholic Church has reacted to this complex situation by refusing to make the positive claim that a human embryo, in fact and beyond doubt, *is* a human person. Instead, erring on the side of caution when the facts do not present a clear answer, the Church chooses her words very carefully: the embryo is to be treated *as* a person.[204] From this perspective, within a CLE framework, human embryos are considered part of a completely vulnerable population at risk of being discarded and destroyed because they are disabled or the wrong gender or thought to be useful for research. Such a population deserves special consideration given how those who, within a context of total reproductive autonomy, will use their power to radically reduce the embryos' dignity by treating them as a mere means to a reproductive end.

Conclusion

As mentioned in the previous chapter, those of us who support the CLE must hold our judgmental fire. Today, our social and reproductive choices are made in powerful social and political contexts that can coerce behavior. Most people of child-bearing age have grown up in a context that affirms using these technologies, making it difficult to imagine living any other way. We can and should be firm in standing against their use—while at the same time showing genuine mercy to those coerced by our consumerist throwaway culture, especially if they are dealing with the devastating disappointment of infertility.

Even a hostile throwaway culture sometimes produces stories that offer hope. Consider, for instance, the experience of Janeen and Sean, a couple dealing with the pain of infertility after IVF failed.[205] Their feelings of inadequacy and disappointment were relieved when they adopted Deklyn, a son they welcomed with joy. And sociological evidence confirms Janeen's and Sean's experience. Researchers at the Gothenburg University in Sweden have found that couples who adopted after failed IVF reported a higher quality of life than couples who were successful in their IVF attempt.[206] Their advice? As soon as they realize that they are facing the challenge of infertility, couples should strongly consider adoption.

And as a father who struggled for years with infertility and has three adopted children, I could not agree more. But adoption is not for everyone and many church communities put such a high value on children that they may unintentionally push couples toward some of the artificial methods discussed in this chapter. Instead of judging others, we should instead be thinking about ways infertile couples can live out a culture of encounter and hospitality—including by welcoming neighbors and other community members into open homes that resist the closed off, disconnected US consumerist culture. This will take time, however, given that it is normative (for lay people) to be in the Church as a family with children. Especially if we truly understand that children are a gift we are not owed, then we must begin to establish language, practices, and social structures for people to encounter and welcome them into their lives in ways which take into account the fullness of that reality.

Chapter Four

Abortion

Introduction

In his recent book for Oxford University Press, the historian Daniel K. Williams points out that before *Roe v. Wade* significant parts of the US pro-life movement originated within the anti-war movement.[207] It is no accident, however, that most people connect the term "pro-life" with opposition to abortion. This is logical because the prenatal child (or fetus—more on terminology follows below) belongs to a uniquely vulnerable, exploited, and discarded population subject to terrible violence. Abortion's a moral and legal complexity, however, comes from the fact that the mother of a prenatal child herself often belongs to a vulnerable, exploited, and discarded population—and the unique relationships in pregnancy can cause traditional moral reasoning to fall short sometimes.

The CLE is well-positioned to dive into this complexity. Binary and simplistic "us vs. them" arguments that pit vulnerable populations against each other dominate abortion discourse in the United States, but the CLE rejects such thinking. As this chapter will demonstrate, construing the argument in terms of "pro-life vs. pro-choice" conceals more than it reveals. When applied equally and consistently to both of these vulnerable populations, CLE principles can establish a distinctive approach to abortion that provides a way to transcend the limits of the seemingly-interminable abortion culture war.[208]

In their approach to the CLE, Cardinal Bernardin, Pope John Paul II, and Pope Benedict XVI all recognized the priority of abortion. Given the confusion about Pope Francis's views, recall what was presented in chapter 1: although Pope Francis did argue that we should address more issues than abortion alone (very much a CLE approach), he did condemn the practice in the strongest possible terms—going so far as to say that the prenatal child, the least among us, bears the face of Christ. In a recent trip to Ireland (in the wake of that country's referendum to revoke the constitutional rights of prenatal children) the pope criticized a "materialist throwaway culture" for denying such children "the very right to life."

This chapter will return to what Francis has said about specific issues related to abortion. We will begin, however, by examining US abortion culture—focusing on people's beliefs about abortion and on our abortion practices. Then we will critique this culture using CLE principles. Finally, the chapter will address two crucial objections: the claim that a prenatal child, while a human being, is not a person; and that even if the prenatal child is considered a person, it is possible to maintain a pro-choice position.

US Abortion Culture

In trying to determine what our culture thinks about abortion, we might consult polls concerning who identifies as pro-life and who identifies as pro-choice. Or perhaps we might identify those who support *Roe v. Wade* and those who do not. But such metrics not only perpetuate the artificial "us vs. them" culture war, but also don't reveal much about what people think about actual instances of abortion. To this point, a PRI poll found that seven-in-ten Americans say the term "pro-choice" describes them somewhat or very well, yet nearly two-thirds say the term "pro-life" describes them somewhat or very well.[209] Identifying as pro-life or pro-choice often reveals less about what one thinks about abortion and more about one's broader tribal and political loves and hates. Polls about *Roe v. Wade* reveal something similar. They show that a high percentage of Americans don't know much about what *Roe* says or does. A Pew Forum study done on the fortieth anniversary of *Roe*, for instance, revealed that 38 percent of Americans think *Roe* is a decision about something other than abortion. For those younger than thirty, that number rose to 56 percent.[210] Furthermore, of those who know that *Roe* was about abortion, many don't know even the basic details of the decision. Many wrongly believe, for instance, that overturning *Roe* would make abortion flatly illegal, when in fact it would merely return the issue to state legislatures for them to decide.

A more authentic picture requires looking at poll questions on specific kinds of abortions. Gallup has long found that twelve weeks, or the end of the first trimester, is a key marker for US Americans' views on abortion. In 2018, for instance, Gallup found that before week twelve of pregnancy, 60 percent want abortion "mostly legal." After week twelve, however, they found support for mostly legal abortion "plummets" to 23 percent. Terms like "pro-choice" or "pro-life" do not capture US Americans' complex views on abortion. Again, the labels conceal more than they reveal.

At the moment, abortion restrictions after week twenty are a key point of US debate—especially because some biologists believe that at this stage abortion causes a prenatal child to feel pain.[211] (Pain medication is given to babies in the NICU born just days after this threshold.) Not surprisingly, given the numbers above, a 2018 Marist poll found that more than 60 percent believe abortion should be illegal after twenty weeks.[212] Interestingly, and perhaps counter-intuitively for those formed within US abortion discourse, a higher percentage of women support such a ban than do men.[213] (In other circumstances women are also less accepting of abortion than men are. The Gallup poll referenced above asked about the specific case of aborting before week twelve a fetus thought to have Down syndrome: only 44 percent of women thought that such abortions should be legal, but 56 percent of men did.) Though 60 percent of US Americans say they approve of legal abortion in the first trimester, when asked whether they want abortion legal in the first trimester "for any reason," support drops to 45 percent. These statistics underscore the importance of asking about specific instances of abortion; when we do, it becomes clear just how inadequate the binary between "life" and "choice" is.

Its inadequacy is clear when views of millennials are examined. Though they tend to identify as strongly pro-choice, millennials consistently support bans on abortion after twenty weeks at higher rates than older generations.[214]

Furthermore, according to the General Social Survey, during the 1970s and 1980s young adults were more likely than people from older generations to think abortion should be legal in most or all circumstances. About twenty years ago, however, the GSS surveys started showing a shift: increasingly those most likely to oppose legal abortion in most or all circumstances were young adults. But even though millennials have become more anti-abortion, only 36 percent are willing to identify as pro-life.[215] Again, the life/choice binary cannot capture the complexity of what people think about abortion.

Abortion Practices

Since 1973, when *Roe v. Wade* invalidated almost all state laws restricting abortion, over fifty-three million prenatal children have been killed via abortion in the United States—nine times the number of Jews killed in the Nazi Holocaust. By the time they are forty-five years old, more than 30 percent of US American women have had at least one abortion.[216] The numbers are dramatically higher among African Americans—indeed, in New York City African American babies are more likely to be aborted than brought to a live birth.[217]

These numbers may seem astounding, but the context in which these abortions take place needs to be examined. Fewer than one in twenty abortions are done in the circumstances where the mother's life or health is in danger or because of sexual violence. However, structures of poverty—something about which the CLE is most concerned—appear to be significant forces in driving the choice of abortion. Those who are "poor" (below federal poverty level) account for nearly half of all abortions in the United States, while those who are "low income" (within 100-200 percent of the federal poverty level) account for about another 25 percent. Having a baby, especially when one already has a child, can be devastating for the economically vulnerable. In such a situation pregnancy can even push someone toward homelessness: the age at which a person is most likely to be homeless is one year old.[218]

Of the hundreds of thousands of women in the United States who have an abortion every year, 25 percent are middle or upper class. That suggests our abortion rate cannot be reduced to issues of structural poverty alone. Rather than an exceptional, heartbreaking choice chosen only in dire circumstances, often abortion is a back-up when birth control fails or when pregnancy does not go according to the consumerist plan. Recall that the previous chapter presented a particularly disturbing example from the *New York Times* about a couple who, after getting pregnant through in vitro fertilization, "reduced" twins to a singleton pregnancy through abortion:

> "Things would have been different if we were 15 years younger or if we hadn't had children already or if we were more financially secure," she said later. "If I had conceived these twins naturally, I wouldn't have reduced this pregnancy, because you feel like if there's a natural order, then you don't want to disturb it."[219]

Those who offer the procedure, like Mount Sinai Medical Center in New York City, report that such "pregnancy reduction" is on the rise.

Like many IVF users, the couple in the article above were in their forties, and pregnancy at that age raises the risk of disability. This is another major reason for abortion: the prenatal child is diagnosed as not meeting the desires of one or both parents. The abortion rate of babies with Down syndrome in the United States is very high—somewhere between 70 and 90 percent.[220] Denmark and Iceland have pledged to use abortion to become "Down syndrome free."[221] In nations like these the social expectation to have an abortion is so strong, pushed in particular by physicians and other health care providers, that a mother must have great inner strength to resist it. The case of Courtney Baker, whose physician pressured her to kill her daughter Emersyn even after Courtney had refused and given her daughter a name, is, unfortunately, not all that unusual.[222]

Lower Abortion Rates

Later we will focus on the wrongful discrimination underlying many abortions, particularly as an outgrowth of the throwaway culture's consumerism in IVF practices. But there is some good news as well: abortion numbers in the United States are down significantly—in fact, at their lowest point since *Roe v. Wade*.[223] And though the number of prenatal children killed each year remains mind-numbingly high, the fact that hundreds of thousands of children are not killed each year is a triumph that should be celebrated, no matter one's position on abortion.

It is not clear why the rate has gone down. *Vox.com*, for instance, assumes that it must be a consequence of using contraception.[224] But traditional contraception has saturated the culture for decades, and there has been no significant uptick in usage rates that would explain such a massive abortion decline. Counterintuitively, abortion strongly correlates with the *use* of contraception: more than half of women who have an abortion report using contraception in the month they got pregnant.[225] Furthermore, states that receive robust Title X funding for family planning and have comparatively few abortion restrictions have higher abortion rates than states that do not have strong funding for family planning programs and have more abortion restrictions.[226]

Those who are honest with the data and yet want to argue that contraception is responsible for lower abortion rates look for factors other than use of the condom and pill (both of which increase the likelihood of hookup sex while having relatively high failure rates due to user error). The factor they cite is increased use of more effective long-acting contraception like the IUD. The *Vox* article makes this claim, but doesn't give actual numbers of young adults using long-acting contraception during the period when abortion rates fell—and with good reason: those numbers, according to the CDC, "remain low."[227] And given the facts presented in previous chapters (particularly that long-acting contraception devices produce a higher-than-usual dose of hormones and present other health risks) they cannot be the solution. Especially if women's health is the price for social equality with men.

Intellectually honest people must also reckon with the fact that contraception, because it separates sex from procreation in our cultural imagination, creates a perceived need for abortion. Contraception has made it possible to have the mistaken belief that consent to sex isn't consent to supporting a child (unless it is men being required to pay child support—more on this below). Before widespread contraception, the facts of reproductive biology itself were enough to make that case. But today, as I've argued elsewhere, our contraceptive mentality dupes us into ignoring the obvious biology of sex and procreation.[228] Pro-lifers, by seeking abortion restrictions that protect vulnerable prenatal children with the law, are often strangely accused of wanting to "punish people for having sex." Rather than seeing pregnancy as an obvious part of what sex is designed to do, a contraceptive mentality promotes a culture that disconnects sex and procreation. In a contraceptive mentality, consent to sex cannot be consent to support a child, and when contraception fails abortion must be there as a failsafe to maintain that disconnect.

In a culture that disconnects sex from procreation, a child showing up in a woman's body isn't understood as a clear biological aspect of what it means to have sex, but as an intrusion or parasitical invasion. Pro-lifers are described as cruel "forced birthers" who want to compel women to gestate children for whom they are not responsible. In an unusually honest article, abortion-rights activist Ann Furedi makes this case. She cites the failure of traditional contraception and the fact many women reject long-acting contraception in arguing that Melinda Gates and others are wrong not to include abortion in the Family Planning 2020 summit because "abortion is necessary as a supplement to contraception."[229]

Others attribute the decline in abortion rates to a nationwide explosion of laws restricting and discouraging abortion. From twenty-week bans, to waiting periods, to nixing abortion funding, over the last two decades many US states have enacted hundreds and hundreds of these laws. Indeed, the steepest drop in abortion rates took place following the 1992 Supreme Court decision *Planned Parenthood v. Casey,* which permitted many more abortion restrictions than did *Roe v. Wade,* which it replaced. The *Vox* article misleadingly claims that no correlation can be found between states where abortion rates fell and those that had passed new laws restricting abortion between 2011 and 2014, a time when rates of abortion declined dramatically. But there is no reason that the impact of such laws would be felt only a year or two after being enacted. This is especially true given that it takes laws several years to build up enough cultural steam to change deeply-ingrained cultural attitudes and practices.[230]

One factor has been given only scant attention—increased social support for women and parents. In my book *Beyond the Abortion Wars,* I highlight programs created since 1992:

- Family and Medical Leave Act (1993)

- Mickey Leland Childhood Hunger Relief Act (1993)

- Mental Health Parity Act (1996)

- Newborns' and Mothers' Health Protection Act (1996)

- SCHIP – The State Child Health Insurance Program (1997)

- Unemployment Compensation Act (2010)

- Healthy, Hunger-Free Kids Act (2010)

I also argue that the most important factor in reducing abortion rates may be the 2010 Affordable Care Act. This law not only expands Medicaid health benefits to poor women (and men), but even provides substantial government assistance in buying health insurance to those with incomes up to four times the federal poverty level. Furthermore, the Affordable Care Act also includes provisions for the Pregnant Women Support Act, legislation that pro-lifers have pushed for many years.[231] Among other things, this part of the Affordable Care Act:

- increases the tax credit for adoption and makes it permanent;

- eliminates pregnancy as a preexisting condition;

- requires SCHIP to cover pregnant women and their prenatal children;

- requires that prenatal care be covered by all insurance carriers;

- makes grant money available to states for home visits by nurses, pregnancy counseling, ultrasound equipment, campus childcare, and the like.

Common sense suggests that with more social support vulnerable women have resources they previously lacked—and thus are less likely to choose abortion. But, unfortunately, this issue has not been studied in detail. European countries, for instance, generally provide more social support for parents and have lower abortion rates than does the United States. Spain, for instance, saw a reduction in abortions as a result of offering a "universal child benefit."[232] In Hungary, the abortion rate fell by 33 percent from 2010 through 2018 after it started providing "maternity support, paid childcare leave, family tax benefits and housing allowance, tax allowances that encourage young couples to marry, vacation benefits, no-charge holiday camps for children, subsidized textbooks, and decreased utility costs."[233] It is highly likely that increased support for women and parents from 1992 through the present—especially the Affordable Care Act—is contributing to the steep decline in US abortion rates.

Consumerism and Autonomy

The twin forces of consumerism and autonomy—though they loom large in every chapter—are especially important in examining abortion. Some consider the autonomous right to abortion to be important because they see it as necessary for women—who can get pregnant—to function in today's work force, or at least function in it the same way men do. The consumeristic standard of living supposedly necessary to be "successful" is driven in large part by the costs of homeownership, which (except for the rich) presumes two full-time workers. And often two full-time workers also require expensive childcare. The demanding work schedule necessary to maintain such a lifestyle seems incompatible with raising children (or even being pregnant). Because of short-term profit maximization, most companies and other institutions often do not provide their employees (and especially women) the opportunity, even on a part-time basis, to be both parents and workers. As we will see below, some use the very possibility of child-rearing as a reason to discriminate against female employees.

Given these social demands, abortion is big business—and like almost all enterprises subject to market forces, it is driven largely by money. According to their own figures,[234] by providing over 330,000 abortions each year, Planned Parenthood generates $400,000,000—far and away the most of any abortion provider. Given such profitability, it is no surprise that for every adoption referral it does, Planned Parenthood procures 333 abortions. It is simply not in Planned Parenthood's financial interest to encourage women to choose anything but abortion.

Whistleblowers, including a former clinic manager, have confirmed that Planned Parenthood is driven by profit. Perhaps best known is Abby Johnson, a former clinic manager in College Station, Texas, and now a pro-life activist. Johnson claims that she would direct her staff to "turn every phone call, every client into a revenue generating client, no matter how you have to do it." She also has firsthand knowledge of Planned Parenthood's immoral practices.[235] These include failure to:

- properly account for and maintain separation between government funds prohibited from use for elective abortions and those funds derived from other sources that are not subject to such limitations.[236]

- notify parents when a vulnerable girl is seeking an abortion, including instances when the minor girl is the victim of an act of statutory rape under applicable state law.

- provide a woman undergoing an abortion with accurate and relevant information regarding the stage of her pregnancy, including the opportunity to view ultrasound imagery that may affect her decision to undergo an abortion.

- detect and act upon instances where a girl or woman is brought to the clinic under some degree of coercion, up to and including instances where she is subjected to human trafficking.

Johnson is currently leading a charge to sue Planned Parenthood, alleging that they "knowingly committed Medicaid fraud from 2007 to 2009 by improperly seeking reimbursements from the Texas Women's Health Program for products and services not reimbursable by that program" and "filed at least 87,075 false, fraudulent, or ineligible claims with the Texas Women's Health Program. As a result, Planned Parenthood wrongfully received and retained reimbursements totaling more than $5.7 million."[237]

The abortion giant has even put profits ahead of the basic rights and dignity of its employees. Many local Planned Parenthood chapters, for instance, have fought their employees' attempts to unionize, only agreeing after intense public pressure. Excellent reporting from a friendly media outlet, *Rewire*, has exposed Planned Parenthood's history of intimidating labor unions.[238] That history was on full display recently in Colorado when officials suggested that Planned Parenthood employees could face backlash if they went ahead with their plans to unionize.[239] The *New York Times* also did a recent exposé on how Planned Parenthood mistreats its pregnant employees, uncovering "discrimination that violated federal or state laws — managers considering pregnancy in hiring decisions, for example, or denying rest breaks recommended by a doctor."[240]

A recent and horrifying example of the abortion industry's greed came to light in the case of a Philadelphia abortion clinic run by Dr. Kermit Gosnell. A grand jury report indicted Gosnell and other clinic workers on charges that his "Woman's Medical Society" was driven not by a concern for women's health, but by profit. The report noted:

> [T]he only question that really mattered was whether you had the cash. Too young? No problem. Didn't want to wait [for the twenty-four-hour waiting period mandated by law]? Gosnell provided same day service. The real

key to the business model, though, was this: Gosnell catered to the women who couldn't get abortions elsewhere – because they were too pregnant. Most doctors won't perform late second-trimester abortions, from approximately the 20th week of pregnancy, because of the risks involved. And late-term abortions after the 24th week of pregnancy are flatly illegal. But for Dr. Gosnell, they were an opportunity. The bigger the baby, the more he charged.[241]

Gosnell's patients would come in during the day, pay, and then be given labor-inducing drugs. He would then show up later that night to see if any were ready to deliver. Some would have already fully delivered by the time he got there, and he would simply kill these infants. He was also a deadly threat to mothers; the indictment cites dozens of examples of women he had butchered and even killed as a result of his practices. On one occasion, after keeping a patient's mother waiting for hours, Gosnell sent the girl home without telling either of them that fetal parts remained inside her. Over the next several days, as infection set in, Gosnell insisted that the girl was fine, but her mother later rushed her daughter to the ER, unconscious and near death.

Dr. Gosnell has been convicted and has been rightly locked away for the rest of his life, but providers like him get away with such mistreatment of women—sometimes for decades at a time—in part because of a culture of autonomy and non-interference concerning abortion practices. Ostensibly liberal abortion-rights activists ask, "Who is the government to come between a woman and her doctor?" Despite their power over life and death (for both mother and prenatal child), abortion providers are given autonomy to do nearly whatever they like. As the pro-choice columnist Linda Greenhouse has pointed out, *Roe v. Wade* was not primarily about women's rights, but about protecting physicians from legal liability and giving them autonomy to practice medicine in this area as they wished.[242] Even someone like Gosnell at first was caught and investigated not because of his illegal abortion practices, but because of his illegal drug prescription practices.

But the autonomy that *Roe* invokes for doctors would come to be attributed to the women seeking an abortion. Any reason at all will do. For instance, a federal court recently cited women's autonomy in striking down an Indiana law banning abortions aimed at prenatal children with Down syndrome.[243] The Democratic Party platform, hyper-concerned to protect and expand the autonomy of abortion choices, now includes the following:[244]

- a call to repeal all "federal and state laws and policies that impede a woman's access to abortion"—support for abortion rights in this platform is deemed "unequivocal";

- a call for repeal of the Hyde and Helms amendments, which prevent taxpayer funds from being used to pay for abortions;

- an assertion that "reproductive health"—which includes access to "safe and legal abortion"—is "core to women's, men's, and young people's health and wellbeing."

Of course, such autonomy goes only one way. The platform also removed a commitment, which had been included in the 2012 platform, to religious liberty in the context of abortion. The push now being made in some abortion rights circles is what I sometimes call the "abortion is awesome" gambit. From this perspective, abortion should not be discussed as "safe, legal, and rare"—in part because seeking that abortion be "rare" stigmatizes a medical procedure (increasingly being called "abortion care"[245]) that is "core" to our "health and well-being." Abortion, for any reason at any point in pregnancy and paid for with tax dollars, should be available to anyone who wants it with no restrictions whatsoever.

As demonstrated earlier in this chapter, however, US Americans reject such extremism, preferring that abortion be restricted after the twelfth week of pregnancy and in many other contexts as well. Furthermore, many health care providers are now refusing to participate in US abortion culture—so much so that there is a shortage of physicians willing to do elective abortions. (California and New York have responded to the problem by making it legal for non-physicians to do these kinds of surgeries—a dubious proposition if the goal is women's health.) Even though abortion rights groups are scrambling to train new providers of abortion in medical school, they are now encountering another problem: a lack of buyers and managers of abortion clinics.[246] Despite permissive laws and a general libertarian sense of "live and let live," US Americans have profound moral problems with our abortion practices.

A CLE Critique

It is difficult to imagine a more vulnerable human being than a prenatal child. She cannot speak up in her own defense. She depends totally on others. Some who would diminish her dignity say that her total dependence is a reason to continue to treat her with radical inequality—making her even more vulnerable. Because of her fundamental vulnerability Pope Francis has said that she bears "the face of Christ" as the least among us. As a result, the CLE argues that she deserves not only equal treatment; she deserves special consideration and protection. Her protection and support are an essential part of a preference for the most vulnerable.

Our culture finds a prenatal child's dignity deeply inconvenient. We saw in previous chapters that abortion is crucial as a backstop to contraception so hookup culture can function. But as powerful as this motive is, another is even more serious. The *Planned Parenthood v. Casey* decision mentioned above defended the killing of prenatal children as necessary for "women to participate equally in the economic and social life of the Nation." We've knit abortion—the killing of prenatal children—deeply and tightly into our cultural fabric. And true to form for the throwaway culture, we even change the way we speak about this population so as to erase their dignity. When a prenatal child is wanted, we speak about "baby bumps," "baby showers," "babies kicking," and "healthy babies." When unwanted we switch to language by which a prenatal child can be more easily discarded as a mere object—words or phrases like "fetus," "product of conception," "parasite," "terminating pregnancy," and "abortion care."

But Pope Francis resists this rhetorical sleight of hand that turns prenatal children into things: "So great is the value of a human life, and so inalienable the right to life . . . that no alleged right to one's own body can justify a decision to terminate that life, which is an end in itself and which can never be considered the 'property' of another human being."[247] For Francis, abortion is the product of throwaway culture that encourages "a cold calculation of what we have and what we can use. Then even life is reduced to a one-time-use consumer good."[248]

Pro-life feminists, who consistently find the CLE attractive and powerful, are more than interested in refusing to capitulate to a poisonous, patriarchal political culture that pits vulnerable women against their vulnerable prenatal children. Acting on behalf of the vulnerable means acknowledging that there are at least two vulnerable people involved, and always having a focus on mothers as well. It is barbarous to pit women against their own children—and insist they imitate the unpregnant bodies of men—so they can have economic and social equality. It is especially barbarous when we don't support women in their choice to keep a child. Pregnancy discrimination against women has been found to be "rampant inside America's biggest companies."[249] Childcare is beyond the means of many families, especially vulnerable single women. And (at the time this book goes to press) the United States is the only country in the developed world that does not offer some level of mandatory paid family leave for women.

All this has consequences. For instance, some of the most important reasons women report having fewer children than they would like include:[250]

- "Child care is too expensive" – 64 percent

- "Worried about the economy" – 49 percent

- "Can't afford more children" – 44 percent

- "Not enough paid family leave" – 39 percent

- "No paid family leave" – 38 percent

The United States has made important strides in supporting women, but the facts are clear: "[T]he gap between the number of children that women say they want to have (2.7) and the number of children they will probably actually have (1.8) has risen to the highest level in 40 years."[251]

This leads many pro-lifers to call abortion the "unchoice."[252] A consumerist throwaway culture requires abortion and coerces women into it as the price of admission. Pro-life feminists have long argued that the widespread expectation women will have abortions—rather than be offered social support to raise their child—benefits men. Some European countries are even exploring the possibility of sanctioning male coercion of abortion. Nearly

40 percent of Danish people, for instance, believe that "a man should be free to choose a 'judicial abortion' if the woman chooses to have the child against his will." After all, "[M]any men have been angry about paying the price for 18 years [of child support] for a one-night mistake."[253] The youth wing of Sweden's Liberal Party has proposed that "men should be given an equal say in whether or not they wish to become a parent, and be granted the option to cut any lawful responsibilities."[254] Within the developed West's consumerist throwaway culture, this makes sense. Why should a woman's right to choose offset a man's right to participate in hookup culture? Shouldn't he have the right to choose as well? How can consent to a one-night stand possibly be consent to welcome and support a new human being for eighteen years?

This explicit coercion isn't limited to Europe, obviously. In *Beyond the Abortion Wars* I note that multiple studies have found a strong correlation between abortion and "intimate partner violence," especially when a woman has had multiple abortions.[255] I highlight the story of NBA guard J.J. Redick and the "abortion contract" he and his former girlfriend agreed to. According to the *Huffington Post,* the contract stipulated that if his ex was pregnant, she must end the pregnancy and provide proof of the abortion. The two would then be mandated to maintain a social relationship for another year. If Redick bowed out of the relationship before that time, the contract indicated that he would pay her $25,000.[256]

Sometimes explicit coercion comes from the male partner as well as his family. A young woman named

Maegan Chen claimed she was dating Star Wars actor Mark Hamill's son Nathan when, despite being on the pill, she became pregnant with his child.[257] His first reaction, as is typical, was to insist that she get an abortion. It was "the only way he would be there for me." Maegan had already had one abortion and, despite telling him she didn't want to go through that again, he continued the pressure until she agreed to take RU-486 at seven weeks. But when the abortion didn't work Maegan insisted that, considering "everything she had done to this baby," she now intended to "love her forever." Once Nathan's family got involved, the pressure on Maegan got worse. One e-mail read, "If you'd had the procedure, then [Nathan] would have felt closer to you for that, for knowing you cared about him and his feelings. Your time in London would have been fabulous. You would still have a relationship with him now. You still could, if and only if, you have the procedure." Another e-mail read, "Mark and I told you that if you choose to do the procedure we would be more than willing to pay for it. Do not use that as an excuse. It is not an excuse. We could and would pay the clinic if and when it is done but at this point we are not going to contact you again."

Most find such stories shocking and disgusting. What better examples to support the pro-life feminist argument that abortion legitimizes the irresponsibility of men and pressures/coerces the choices of women? Because of pressure and coercion, every major pro-life organization in the United States wants mercy and not judgment for women who are abortion's second victims.[258] During the Church's 2015 "year of mercy," Pope Francis expressed particular concern for women who have had abortions. The pope, though standing for the prenatal child in the strongest possible terms, stands as well for women:

> The tragedy of abortion is experienced by some with a superficial awareness, as if not realizing the extreme harm that such an act entails. Many others, on the other hand, although experiencing this moment as a defeat, believe that they have no other option. I think in particular of all the women who have resorted to abortion. I am well aware of the pressure that has led them to this decision. I know that it is an existential and moral ordeal. I have met so many women who bear in their heart the scar of this agonizing and painful decision.[259]

Again, abortion has (at least) two victims. As the pro-life activist group New Wave Feminists argues: "When our liberation costs innocent lives, it is merely oppression redistributed."[260]

The CLE gives close attention to another population disproportionately hurt by abortion—the economically vulnerable. In the United States, three in every four abortions are performed on poor and low-income women. Given the economic pressures mentioned above, it is not difficult to see why. If a woman cannot afford to take time off work or pay for childcare—especially if she has other mouths to feed—abortion can seem like the only way out. And the broader culture, perniciously, suggests that economic problems can be eased by making abortion as accessible as possible rather than by helping the economically vulnerable have any other choice. Some in the public debate even claim that denying women abortions increases their likelihood of poverty. Politically-oriented studies released near the anniversary of *Roe v. Wade* drive home this point.[261]

Of course, for the economically vulnerable population abortion is an unchoice. No level of poverty ever justifies intentionally killing the innocent, but the CLE has to acknowledge the close relationship between poverty and abortion—to save the lives of at-risk prenatal children born into poverty and to recognize the face of Christ in their impoverished mothers. An essential part of the CLE's approach to abortion involves listening to the voices of the poor. Economically vulnerable people don't see abortion as a liberating experience or something that they "choose." On the contrary, many hate that they are pushed into killing their own children to keep themselves above water economically, and resent privileged abortion-rights activists talking about it in such glowing terms and pushing it on them.[262] The economically vulnerable are nearly three times as likely as the well-off to believe abortion ought to be illegal in all cases.[263] Furthermore, despite having more abortions overall, poor women confronted with an unintended pregnancy are less likely to choose abortion than are rich women—despite the serious economic consequences for doing so.[264] Level of education tracks very well with income, and reliable data show that the more education a person has, the more morally permissive his or her view of abortion—and vice versa.[265] College-educated women are much more likely to think that an unplanned pregnancy can "ruin your life," whereas high-school-educated women are more likely to respond to abortion with moral outrage.[266]

This is also true for vulnerable racial minorities. The Bronx, where I teach at Fordham University, is dominated by such communities—and nearly 40 percent of Bronx pregnancies end in abortion.[267] Jason Riley, an African American columnist for the *Wall Street Journal*, wrote an important article highlighting the pervasiveness of abortion in many African American communities.[268] Between 2012 and 2016, he notes, black mothers in New York City terminated 136,426 pregnancies and gave birth to 118,127 babies. In 2014, 36 percent of all abortions in the United States were performed on black women, who make up only 13 percent of the female population. These statistics help explain why certain clinic owners target communities with large percentages of racial minorities when deciding where to build their facilities. As an example from Cleveland shows, they also promote abortion through billboard campaigns—with slogans alike "Abortion is Necessary" and "Abortion is Good Medicine."[269] There is strong evidence that such racial targeting is not peculiar to Cleveland.[270]

Despite having much higher rates of abortion than do whites, people of color are more skeptical of abortion. Fifty-one percent of whites claim to want abortion legal in "most" or "all" cases, but only 49 percent of blacks and 43 percent of Hispanics do. These differences are even more pronounced among Democrats.[271] Eighty-one percent of white Democrats support broad abortion rights, but only

66 percent of black Democrats hold that view.[272] Blacks and Hispanics also want more diversity of opinion on abortion within the Democratic party. Thirty-five percent of white Democrats support Democratic candidates who think abortion should be generally legal; but for black Democrats that number plummets to 7 percent. Remarkably, 40 percent of Hispanic Democrats believe only Democratic candidates who think abortion should be *illegal* should be supported.[273]

Given the diversity of views on abortion among people of color (again, especially among Democrats) there is good reason why privileged white abortion activists should hesitate about going all-in with phrases like #shoutyourabortion and "abortion is good health care." Instead of pushing unlimited abortion on people who don't want it, our attention should be drawn to inadequate social services for vulnerable populations who choose to keep their children. It should also focus on our maternal mortality rate. Despite the United States' massive wealth, that rate is the worst in the developed world.[274] African American women are most at risk: nearly four times as likely to die during pregnancy than white women are. There are many reasons for this—from higher rates of obesity and hypertension to lack of access to prenatal care, quality health care institutions, providers, and insurance.

But a crucial factor—and perhaps the most important one—has been largely overlooked, perhaps because it is just too terrible to face directly. Abortion correlates with *deadly* intimate partner violence, as shown by a study in the *Journal of Midwifery & Women's Health*. It found that, over eight years, 43 percent of maternal deaths in Washington, DC, were homicides.[275] As reported in *Women's Health* magazine, a ten-year study of traumatic injuries among women of childbearing age was presented at the 2017 annual meeting of the American College of Obstetrics and Gynecology. It found that pregnant women are more likely to suffer violent trauma—and are twice as likely to die after trauma—than nonpregnant women. And these frightening numbers may be even higher given irregular reporting requirements and the fact that 77 percent of maternal deaths take place before twenty weeks gestation, when a fetal death certificate is not required.

A Culture of Extreme Violence

We should expect to find a connection between such violence and the abortion culture—which, as pro-life feminists have been pointing out for decades, operates with the patriarchal impulse to solve problems with deadly violence. And the violence of the physical act of abortion is so brutal, in fact, that our culture refuses to face it directly. (Protesters who hold up signs that display the remains of a prenatal child dismembered in an abortion are roundly mocked and pushed to the margins of culture because they show the horror.). We can't even face it *indirectly*. We instead refer to abortion with euphemisms that help us refuse to face the reality of the violence done to the prenatal child. We do not "dismember a living child": rather, we provide women "abortion care" by which the "products of conception" are "removed." But in other contexts, language concerning a prenatal child subjected to violence takes on another tone. The infamous Scott Peterson, for instance, was sentenced to death for killing his pregnant wife, Laci, because the state of California charged him with double murder.[276] And when Remee Lee's boyfriend tricking her into killing their "fetus" by taking RU-486, the state of Florida responded by passing the Offenses Against Unborn Children Act.[277]

The CLE insists that the violence of abortion be faced directly. It calls us to stop using double-speak and Orwellian euphemisms that hide the fate of vulnerable populations. In *Beyond the Abortion Wars*, I cite an abortion provider's congressional testimony concerning a procedure called "Suction Dilation and Evacuation" that he has performed over 100 times. It is difficult to read, but facing the abortion culture honestly means not shying away from its medical and clinical reality:

> With suction complete, look for your Sopher clamp. This instrument is about thirteen inches long and made of stainless steel. At the business end are located jaws about 2 ½ inches long and about ¾ of an inch wide with rows of sharp ridges or teeth. This instrument is for grasping and crushing tissue. When it gets hold of something, it does not let go. A second trimester D&E abortion is a blind procedure. The baby can be in any orientation or position inside the uterus. Picture yourself reaching in with the Sopher clamp and grasping anything you can. At twenty-four weeks gestation, the uterus is thin and soft so be careful not to perforate

or puncture the walls. Once you have grasped something inside, squeeze on the clamp to set the jaws and pull hard – really hard. You feel something let go and out pops a fully formed leg about six inches long. Reach in again and grasp whatever you can. Set the jaw and pull really hard once again and out pops an arm about the same length. Reach in again and again with that clamp and tear out the spine, intestines, heart and lungs.[278]

He continues to describe the challenges he sometimes faced in retrieving the child's head. This description clearly illustrates the gruesome reality of the procedure. Despite such details, even though a clear majority of US Americans reject second trimester abortions, US politics and Supreme Court decisions currently make it nearly impossible to pass a bill restricting abortion before twenty weeks, much less twelve. As this book goes to press our current law even forbids requiring that aborted children have the dignity of a proper burial.[279] Not only does the way in which their lives are thrown away erase their dignity, but the way their remains are discarded makes them invisible as well.

The CLE also concerns itself with the effect of abortion on the agent of violence. What must performing or assisting in such violent procedures do to a person? Fewer and fewer health care providers do abortions, and fewer and fewer are being trained. More and more are leaving the industry altogether. Consider Gail, who describes her life before working in a Planned Parenthood abortion clinic:

I used to be really happy, loved life, saw beauty everywhere before I started working there. Then, I started working at Planned Parenthood, and I was always sad, always tired, and really depressed. . . . How I felt coming home each day from the abortion center was like a soldier who had come back from war. The emptiness. That's how I felt. Empty. I don't believe we were created to see so much death.[280]

A recurring theme throughout this book is the psychological trauma of participating in violence. Whether visited upon prenatal children, criminals, soldiers, people requesting euthanasia, or even non-human animals, participation in such killing scars the human soul. The purveyors too are victims of violence.

One might struggle to have sympathy for health care providers who by participating in abortion have abandoned their duty to heal and not harm. But the CLE insists that our primary response be mercy. This species of love—which can serve as a conduit of grace into the life of someone cut off from mercy—has had a tremendous impact on clinic workers. To address their pain, Abby Johnson has started an organization provocatively named "And Then There Were None."[281] Members reach out to abortion clinic workers with the goal of helping people like Gail find a way to leave the industry. Because of her insider experience, Johnson can speak to workers with informed authority—and a lot of mercy and love. (Indeed, one of their mottos is "Love One Out!") Despite skepticism from some more traditional pro-life figures, Johnson has had great success. Many clinic workers, disturbed by their violent practices, want to find the way out that Johnson's organization provides. As I write this chapter, their fliers say they have helped over 430 abortion workers leave their clinics, including seven physicians. Such people have gone from being dealers of violence and death—slowly killing themselves in the process—to being powerful champions for children and women at risk of abortion. The testimonials of many of these champions appear on the And Then There Were None website. The mercy and love of Abby and her growing community is already strikingly powerful—and will grow more so in the future.

Pope Francis has described abortion as a "white glove" crime akin to Nazi killings.[282] He was referring to our current practice of prenatal testing and with the diagnosis of a possible disability killing the prenatal child. Is the Nazi comparison too dramatic? We saw above that in the United States, 70 percent of prenatal children diagnosed with possible Down syndrome (and there is a false positive rate of over 5 percent[283]) are killed via abortion. In France the figure is 80 percent and in Denmark and Iceland, almost 100 percent. Even though people with Down syndrome rate their lives as happier than those deemed "normal,"[284] the Netherlands is actually holding public debates about their disproportionate demand upon community resources.[285] Manufacturers of prenatal testing technologies sell their products to insurance companies by citing the cost-effectiveness of finding Down syndrome earlier in pregnancy—the implication being that an abortion will probably save money. Some health systems and insurance companies go so far as to deny basic health care to prenatal children with a serious health diagnosis if the parents decide not to abort.[286] Such pressures coerce parents into considering abortion when they otherwise would not. And, beyond structural coercion, some philosophers even argue that parents who receive a prenatal diagnosis of Down syndrome have a "moral duty" to kill the child and that those who defend their lives are practicing "Down Jihadism."[287]

The CLE looks to defend and honor vulnerable populations at risk for terrible violence. For instance, in the United Kingdom some disabled communities are pushing to apply abortion laws equally to abled and disabled prenatal children.[288] The CLE also attempts to mitigate the strain that raising disabled children can put on families—and acknowledge that, sometimes, a decision to abort really is a misguided attempt to save a child pain and suffering. But especially when a prenatal child receives a supposed terminal diagnosis (again, there are significant levels of false positives), the CLE points out other options that honor the dignity of this person who has the face of Christ. For example, perinatal hospice, which is dramatically underused, not only allows the medical team to verify the prenatal diagnosis, but guarantees a pain-free, honorable, nonviolent death for children who will not survive after birth.[289] Given the impact of prenatal violence on mental health, women who choose this option appear to have better psychological outcomes than those who choose abortion.[290] It is difficult to imagine a practice that resists throwaway culture more directly than perinatal hospice.

Those who follow the CLE do everything they can to resist the horrific abortion culture—and do so in a way that avoids the false choice between personal and social supports (which address "demand") and justice under law for prenatal children (which focuses on "supply"). The CLE also refuses the false choice between protecting and supporting prenatal children and protecting and supporting their mothers. And, though prenatal children and mothers at risk for abortion are already a vulnerable population, the CLE demands a special focus on those within that group who are even more vulnerable: the poor, racial minorities, and the disabled. As much as possible, it tries to have a real-life, genuine encounter with these vulnerable populations, going to the peripheries to listen and gather wisdom from their life experiences.

But there are objections to the CLE on abortion. I imagine many reading this chapter want to jump to specifics of public policy—and, indeed, it is something I think about quite a bit. This is the source, I suspect, of many important and thoughtful objections. Can a religious point of view become law? Don't laws against abortion lead to unsafe illegal abortions? How is it possible to codify exceptions for women who are victims of sexual violence, whose lives are threatened by a pregnancy? These are important objections, and in other places I've tried to address them.[291] But this book, again, seeks to avoid the pointed discussions of policy and politics that currently assail and divide our culture. Instead, I wish to focus on underlying values. US Americans need a different moral and political imagination before we can have a genuine debate over abortion policy.

Objections

> Objection #1: *A prenatal child is not really a member of a vulnerable population. It may be true that the prenatal child—at any stage of development—is a member of the species* Homo sapiens *and part of the human family. But one could still question why being a member of* Homo sapiens *matters at all. This is actually "speciesism"—akin to racism or sexism—which wrongly discriminates against non-human species and gives humans a pride of place we don't deserve. After all, why should a fetus count as a person when it seems to have few morally valuable traits? Perhaps after week twenty or so the fetus can feel pain, and even earlier than that has a beating heart and brainwaves, but many thousands of species have these traits and we don't typically think of them as having the right to life as a person.*

There does seem something deeply wrong, even from a Christian religious perspective, about declaring all *Homo sapiens* to be persons with rights and all non-*Homo sapiens* to be non-persons with no such right. If we met, for instance, a Hobbit like Bilbo Baggins or a Kryptonian like Superman, or some similar alien creature who was like us in all morally-relevant ways, it wouldn't do to say that this was a non-human who could be enslaved or killed without violating their personal dignity. Angels, of course, are also non-human persons. So if the CLE is to respond to this objection fairly it must do better than simply citing the science on who or what counts as a member of the species *Homo sapiens.*

In chapter one of my book *Peter Singer and Christian Ethics*, I explore in philosophical detail whether a prenatal child's potential conveys personhood. Please go there if you would like the full argument.[292] (I make a shorter and more accessible version of the same argument in chapter two of *Beyond the Abortion Wars*, and what follows is an even more condensed version of that argument.) Many argue against a prenatal child's personhood because certain traits and abilities have not yet developed: to feel pain, move around, engage in relationships, act rationally, become aware of one's self, develop a moral sense, and so on. Once human beings develop these traits, some believe, their moral status increases. Prenatal children who can feel pain are worth more than those who cannot; human beings who can engage in relationships are worth more than those who cannot; those who are rational and self-aware are worth more than those who are not. And so on.

But almost no one is willing to follow this view to its logical conclusion by applying it to other living beings. If a prenatal child becomes a person with a right to life when she can feel pain, does that mean that *any* being that feels pain is a person with a right to life? Dogs? Pigs? Chickens? Rats and mice? To avoid this conclusion perhaps a more sophisticated trait can be chosen, such as rational thought, self-awareness, or capability of making free and moral choices. It is true that a prenatal child does not have these traits, but neither does a newborn. Children cannot be guilty until they are capable of rationality, morality, and free choice—capacities that don't develop until many years after birth. A child demonstrates self-awareness when she can recognize herself in a mirror, but this doesn't happen until several months after birth. Furthermore, because elephants, dolphins, and the great apes all pass the mirror test, from this perspective they too would qualify as persons.

The problem with a "Trait X" approach is that it leads to claims that almost no one wishes to accept. Picking a "lower-end" trait leads to granting personhood with a right to life to animals like mice and rats; picking a "higher-end" leads to denying personhood to newborn infants. Happily, there is an alternative approach. And it builds on an important difference between the prenatal human child and the other kinds of beings like those mentioned in the comparisons above: the potential of each being. Obviously prenatal children have the potential—thought of in terms of probability—of gaining Trait X. Does that potential alone make them persons? Not at all. Following this principle wherever it leads, what should we think about a fertility lab tech who rinses spare sperm and egg cells down a drain? It looks as if he destroyed something with the potential to be a person. Did he do something terribly wrong? Furthermore, cloning technology has revealed that each of our human body cells has the potential to be turned into an embryo. If I scratch the outside of my hand and kill some skin cells, am I killing a bunch of persons? After all, they had *the potential* to become persons, didn't they?

The problem here, rather than actual disagreement, comes from confusion over the meaning of the word "potential." The Greek philosopher Aristotle used language that distinguished between two different senses of this concept; English lacks that subtlety. The first understanding concerns what we mean by "probability" or "chance." From this perspective, a being has potential to become X if that being has *a percentage chance greater than zero* of becoming X. But the second understanding refers to potential of a different kind—that which *already exists* inside a being as the kind of thing that it already is.

Two examples may help illustrate the difference. If you are very morbid, perhaps in an attempt to get you to get off the couch and become more active, someone might say "you need to remember that you are a potential corpse and will die someday. Get out there and live." But perhaps you have had a teacher or coach, also in an attempt to get you off the couch and live life, who said, "You have so much potential! Don't waste it!" Both statements use the word "potential," but they mean very different things. In the first example, yes, *your body* has a certain percentage chance (basically 100 percent!) of becoming a corpse, but it isn't true that *you* become a corpse. In fact, in saying that you have died, the point is that you are *not* the corpse. On the other hand, when your teacher says that you need to work hard to "reach your potential" she is speaking of the potential that already exists inside of you. It is part of who you are as a human person. It is potential based on the nature of the kind of thing that you already are.

Or a carpenter might say "A tree is a potential desk," whereas a biologist might say, "A sprouting acorn is a potential oak tree." Again, the word is used in two different ways. A tree has a certain percentage chance of being used to make furniture, and in that sense is a potential desk. But it makes no sense to treat a tree as if it is a desk. In fact, for a tree to become a desk it must be cut into pieces, shaped, fastened together, and so forth. It ceases being a tree and *becomes a new kind of thing*. I like to name this process a "nature-changing event." But what about the sprouting acorn's potential to become an oak tree? Does it need to become a new kind of thing to reach its potential? Not at all. It needs energy and the right environment to become the kind of thing it already is. No "nature-changing event" is necessary. In a real sense a sprouting acorn is *already an oak tree*. Indeed, if a certain kind of oak tree had special legal protection, killing such a tree even at this early stage would be illegal.

Supporters of the CLE see that potential in the first sense of "mere probability" or "percentage chance" is not morally significant. Skin cells, or sperm and egg separated from one another, have the potential, but to become persons they would have to undergo a nature-changing event. Skin, sperm, and egg cells would have to cease to be cells that are part of another organism and *become a brand-new organism*—a new member of the species *Homo sapiens*. This is not true of the prenatal child or newborn infant. These are already human organisms—and thus already have potential inside because of the kind of things they already are. Because of their nature. No "nature-changing event" is necessary. They require only energy and the right environment to express their potential to become *the kind of thing they already are*. It is clear how we acknowledge such potential when a prenatal child or newborn is said to have a "disease" or "injury." Something accidental to her nature is frustrating her ability to express her potential within. Healing the disease or injury is not a nature-changing event. The potential always inside her came to be fully expressed. When healed, a diseased or injured person can fully express who she already was.

Because the prenatal child has a personal nature (as do angels, Superman, Bilbo, and so forth)—the same nature as anyone reading this book—she absolutely does belong to a vulnerable population, a population with the dignity that, according to the CLE, makes it always wrong to kill her.

> Objection #2: *A prenatal child's total dependence on the mother's body justifies certain kinds of abortion. Indeed, it appears that much of US law is based on this assumption. Most Constitutional scholars believe that US states cannot restrict abortion before viability—that is, before the prenatal child can live outside the mother's body. A totally dependent prenatal child has less moral value than someone who is autonomous and independent. Furthermore, the prenatal child's total dependence on the mother means that the mother's duty to stay physically connected changes once the child can live outside of her body.*

The CLE will of course utterly reject any idea that vulnerability born of dependence on another is a reason to think of a vulnerable individual as somehow less than those who are more autonomous. Certainly, we owe someone who is so utterly dependent even more moral concern than those who are not as dependent. Second, it just isn't clear that a newborn infant is any less dependent than a prenatal child. Both are 100 percent dependent on others for their survival and flourishing. Are we prepared to say that the newborn human being is also less valuable because of his total dependence? Finally, viability is a strange moral marker for moral status and value given that it is often a function of different local and cultural levels of medical technology. From this perspective, a twenty-three-week-old prenatal child would count as a person in New York City, but the same twenty-three-week-old prenatal child, due to limitations of technology, would not count in the mountains of Afghanistan. The same prenatal child in Kansas City fifty years ago would not count as a child, and for the same reason, but she would count as a person in Kansas City today. Ten years from now we are likely to have an artificial placenta, and this will push viability back very early in pregnancy;[293] but how could this technological development possibly change the moral status of a creature? The moral kind of thing one is? One's moral value as a person does not come from accidental traits like one's physical, social, or temporal location, but rather the irreducible dignity that comes from being the kind of creature one is.

Objection #3: *A mother doesn't have a duty to support a child with her body. Often, when supporters of abortion rights say they are pro-*

choice, they are not denying the personhood of the prenatal child, but rather standing up for the autonomous right of a mother to do as she wishes with her body. What makes abortion complex is that there are two bodies intimately connected with each other. The CLE insists that directly killing innocent persons, because it radically reduces their dignity to a mere means to some other end, is always wrong. But not every failure to aid is wrong—even if one foresees but does not intend that death will be the result. For instance, one may hear of a post-hurricane disaster overseas and a call for personal aid to help dying victims, but a failure to aid people who will die without it may not always be wrong. Something like this may be true of an abortion of pregnancy. After all, the word "abort" just means to stop. It is better to think about abortion as the stopping of aid to a child rather than aiming at their death.

In *Beyond the Abortion Wars*, I highlight the famous 1971 article written by pro-choice philosopher Judith Jarvis Thomson, destined to be read for decades to come by hundreds of thousands of undergraduate students. In the article, Thomson (for the sake of argument only) concedes that prenatal children count as persons but tries to show that one could still be pro-choice based on a woman's autonomous right to her body. Here is her famous analogy:

You wake up in the morning and find your-self back to back in bed with an unconscious violinist. A famous unconscious violinist. He has been found to have a fatal kidney ailment, and the Society of Music Lovers has canvassed all the available medical records and found that you alone have the right blood type to help. They have therefore kidnapped you, and last night the violinist's circulatory system was plugged into yours, so that your kidneys can be used to extract poisons from his blood as well as your own. The director of the hospital now tells you, "Look, we're sorry the Society of Music Lovers did this to you—we would never have permitted it if we had known. But still, they did it, and the violinist is now plugged into you. To unplug you would be to kill him. But never mind, it's only for nine months. By then he will have recovered from his ailment, and can safely be unplugged from you." Is it morally incumbent on you to accede to this situation? No doubt it would be very nice of you if you did, a great kindness. But do you have to accede to it? What if it were not nine months, but nine years? Or longer still? What if the director of the hospital says, "Tough luck. I agree. [B]ut now you've got to stay in bed, with the violinist plugged into you, for the rest of your life. Because remember this. All persons have a right to life, and violinists are persons. Granted you have a right to decide what happens in and to your body, but a person's right to life outweighs your right to decide what happens in and to your body. So you cannot ever be unplugged from him."[294]

Would you be guilty of killing an innocent person, and thus erasing his dignity, if you decided to disconnect yourself from the violinist? Thomson argues that most of us would not feel guilty, despite knowing that the violinist will die without our aid, and despite the fact he is a person with a right to life.

She then notes that the woman who has an unintended pregnancy is analogous to being attached to the violinist. Both the violinist and the prenatal child are persons with a right to life but removing one's self from such a person is morally acceptable. Thomson says that it is of course within your right (and a pregnant woman's right) to choose to be a "good Samaritan" by staying connected and giving aid, but you do not have a *moral duty* to do this.

Thomson is correct in one respect: removing yourself from the violinist is not the same as directly killing the violinist. Doing so doesn't make the violinist's death the "object"—as it is called in Catholic moral theology—of your act. If someone else came along and against all odds saved the violinist, you would not be upset—because you were not choosing the violinist's death; you were refusing to use your body to keep the violinist alive. And in fact, Catholic moral theology permits certain kinds of "indirect" abortions of pregnancy—such as when a cancerous uterus is removed with the child inside or when a fallopian tube must be removed in cases where, regrettably, the child starts growing rather than in the uterus. In both cases death is foreseen, but not intended. And a proportionately serious reason justifies the action: trying to save the life of the mother.

But Thomson's argument clearly gets much wrong as well. Getting pregnant is almost never analogous to randomly getting attached to a violinist. As previous chapters have discussed in detail, our culture still connects a choice to have sex and responsibility for children who result from that decision. Men who are pressed to pay child support, even after a random hookup, cannot complain in court that consent to sex does not entail consent to supporting their child. If after giving birth a mother discards her newborn child, she cannot complain to social services that she had no duty to support this child simply because she had sex. No, for those children acknowledged to be persons with full dignity, our culture insists that consent to sex includes consent to support them—sometimes in very, very dramatic and burdensome ways. Thomson's analogy fails to capture the CLE insight that we have a special responsibility for the needs we ourselves create—and that, in having sex, we bear a special responsibility for the need of any child that may result. And if Thomson and others like her are serious about conceding that the prenatal child counts as a person, then when it comes to parental duties of support that child in the womb should count the same as a newborn infant or older child.

But now a crucial question presents itself. What about pregnancies that result from sexual violence? Such cases constitute a very small (even tiny) percentage of abortions in the United States overall, but nevertheless should be treated with utmost seriousness. In such cases, of course, the woman has not chosen to have sex and thus the analogy to the violinist makes a good deal more sense. In both cases the use of violence might support the argument that there is not the same kind of special duty to support a child. Indeed, this claim underlies views of many (including 60 percent of pro-lifers) that abortion should be allowed in the case of sexual violence—especially if the resulting death is merely foreseen but not intended. To be clear, arguing for such an exception does not mean a prenatal child conceived in sexual violence has any less value than other children. Thomson isn't arguing that that violinist matters less than other people—she's arguing instead that if you are attached against your will to the violinist by violence you do not have a strong duty to stay attached.

What might be the response from supporters of the CLE who reject an exception for sexual violence? They would be deeply concerned that children conceived in sexual violence are an unimaginably vulnerable population, but claiming that a woman has responsibility to support a child conceived through sexual violence—who did not make a choice that led to her pregnancy—is a high moral standard indeed. It is, however, a standard that Christian supporters of the CLE should take very seriously. In the parable of the Good Samaritan, Jesus didn't have Thomson's optional view in mind; instead he commands his listeners to imitate the foreigner's hospitality by saying, "Go and do likewise." Supporting the vulnerable, even if we are not responsible for their need, is a deeply serious moral obligation. Autonomy and freedom of choice do not excuse us. Whether it means supporting our parents in old age or caring for a man on the street beaten by robbers, the CLE insists that although we do not choose them, moral duties and obligations sometimes impose themselves in unexpected ways. A supporter of the CLE who argues against an exception for sexual violence would have a similar view about supporting children conceived through sexual violence. The radical hospitality and mutuality at the center of the ethic require it.

But especially given the ethic's call to consistency, we should not shy away from the implications of radical hospitality and mutuality when it comes to other issues. A mother's hospitality to her prenatal child may include significant risk—and those who consider such hospitality to be a moral duty should accept the risk, even if significant, in other practices hospitality demands. To be sure, the next chapter will build on these insights by discussing our moral duties to the poor, to the immigrant, and to the refugee.

Conclusion

Given what we have learned thus far, we should have expected the CLE to disrupt our incoherent political binary imagination concerning abortion. Addressing the complexity of this issue and refusing to set one vulnerable population against another means going beyond lazy labels like "left" and "right," "life" and "choice." It also upends many assumptions of the abortion wars by insisting on mercy—especially for women who have had abortions, but also for abortion providers. And, in a related story, it flips how we approach our perceived opponents in the abortion debate. Engaging them personally, in the spirit of hospitality and mutuality, means welcoming them into our communities. It means getting to know them. Breaking bread together. Having genuine dialogue. It means seeking common ground and working together on areas of common interest and concern. It means assuming their good will. Especially for pro-lifers, it means keeping in mind that many who argue most strongly for abortion rights have profound, painful experiences of abortion in their personal lives. Our first reaction should not be judgment but mercy—and, when and if the time presents itself, an offer to help seek healing.[295]

As we conclude the abortion chapter and move on to other concerns of the CLE, it should now be clear, despite the critique of some, that none of these other concerns minimizes the unique gravity and evil of abortion. On the contrary, the CLE helps us see that many of the other issues with which it is concerned (racism, poverty, sex, biotechnology, patriarchy, ableism, social support for women/mothers) are deeply entwined with abortion. Being consistent in applying our values across a range of issues makes a pro-life anti-abortion witness stronger, not weaker. And as Bernardin himself said, it is a misuse of the CLE to put abortion on the same level of importance as all the other issues:

> Not all values, however, are of equal weight. Some are more fundamental than others. On this Respect Life Sunday, I wish to emphasize

that no earthly value is more fundamental than human life itself. Human life is the condition for enjoying freedom and all other values. Consequently, if one must choose between protecting or serving lesser human values that depend upon life for their existence and life itself, human life must take precedence. Today the recognition of human life as a fundamental value is threatened. Nowhere is this clearer than in the case of elective abortion.[296]

Chapter Five

The Poor and the Stranger

Introduction

Especially if we were discussing complex and technical policy proposals, a single chapter on our duty to aid the poor and the stranger would be insufficient. But, again, this book does not seek to engage in arguments about law and policy—it focuses on the moral claims and vision that underlie the CLE. If we can understand those clearly (a big if), we can then move to even more complex matters such as a living wage or border control. One reason for the "big if," at least in the context of this project, is that pro-lifers sometimes find it difficult to expand their concern beyond protecting vulnerable populations from direct killing and other aggressive violence to addressing the needs of vulnerable populations. It is one thing to expand beyond abortion and euthanasia to the death penalty and war. It is another to include the duty to aid. At times I have experienced the controversy surrounding this move personally—most recently when, while writing this book, my op-ed in the *New York Times* urging pro-life groups to take a stand against child-separation at the United States-Mexico border was roundly criticized for betraying the fundamental moral concerns of those who are passionate about pro-life issues.[297]

Many who object to including the duty to aid the poor and stranger within their matrix of pro-life concerns also resist making an abortion exception for victims of sexual violence. But as the previous chapter made clear, rejecting indirect abortion for a woman in such exceptional circumstances requires claiming that she has a duty to aid—that is, to gestate—a prenatal child when she has no moral responsibility for that child's need. From a strict pro-life perspective, the woman's right to autonomy and freedom does not override her responsibility to provide such aid. She cannot detach from the child's body—say, via early induction of labor or c-section—without, at least in principle, being morally responsible for the child's death. (Though, again given what the previous chapter laid out, her personal moral responsibility would be mitigated substantially—especially because she is a victim of sexual violence.) Accepting a pregnancy rooted in sexual violence is a radical acceptance of hospitality and mutuality—one that a CLE vision applies to a range of issues, including our moral duties to the poor, to the immigrant, and to the refugee.[298]

Some pro-lifers will claim that, though issues like this are important, a hierarchy of moral truths means we ought to leave these kinds of issues out of a pro-life ethic. The moral gravity of the injustice done to the poor, the immigrant, or the refugee, from this perspective, are not comparable with the moral gravity of injustice present in abortion and euthanasia. But claims like this are difficult to defend, especially when often life itself is at stake. The massive numbers of people who die from absolute poverty call to mind the massive numbers who die from abortion. And those who die from, say, the violence that many refugees are fleeing greatly outnumber those killed by euthanasia. Furthermore, in Matthew chapter 25 Jesus himself was perfectly clear that failing to aid the vulnerable—in particular the stranger and those who lack basic human resources (food, drink, clothes, medical care, and so forth)—puts our very salvation at risk.

In chapter 1 we saw how *Evangelium vitae* invoked the earliest known tradition of the Church—which insisted that the "way of life" for Christians connects concern for abortion and infanticide with concern for the poor and those who mistreat them. Indeed, in his encyclical John Paul II insists that "the commandment 'You shall not kill'" is "more fully expressed in the positive command of love for one's neighbor." This requires "showing concern for the stranger, even to the point of loving one's enemy."[299] Such insights are at the heart of the US bishops' ministry, put in action through Catholic Relief Services and Migrant and Refugee Services, which are joined by other Christian aid groups, like Lutheran Immigration and Refugee Service. Significantly, the bishops' concern for religious freedom includes the Church's right to resist unjust immigration laws—and immigration dominates the topics about which the US bishops send out press releases.[300] Some bishops have even wondered if public figures who violate the Church's teaching on immigration should suffer "canonical penalties."[301] The bishops criticized the Trump administration's immigration policy so strongly that senior advisor Steve Bannon felt compelled to respond—suggesting that the bishops reacted this way because they "need illegal aliens to fill the churches."[302]

Pope Francis inherited a deep papal tradition of care about these issues—including the century-long practice of highlighting the issues on a World Day of Migrants and Refugees.[303] As my Fordham colleague Thomas Massaro points out in a new book on Francis[304] (released while I was writing this manuscript), the pope has taken dramatic steps to put this tradition into action. On the 2016 World Day of Migrants and Refugees, for instance, "[H]e welcomed to St. Peter's Square a diverse group of six thousand refugees and migrants from thirty nations around the world." About a year later, Pope Francis hosted an International Forum on Migration and Peace that, Massaro notes, "was perhaps less spectacular but afforded an opportunity for deeper and more profound reflection" on the conference theme of integration. But perhaps Francis's most dramatic decision was making his first papal trip to what Massaro calls an "unlikely destination": the Mediterranean island of Lampedusa. The pope visited this "island of tears" that lies "along one of the world's deadliest migration routes" not only to share meals with the migrants and listen to their stories, but to mourn those who died while attempting to flee violence in their native lands. Massaro notes several of Francis's deeply symbolic and poignant gestures, including celebrating a memorial Mass using an altar and Eucharistic vessels carved from the wood of shipwrecks that had cost so many lives.[305]

In this introduction I have set the stage—and cleared the necessary conceptual space—to consider the issues raised in this chapter within a pro-life perspective. In what follows I will make the case in more detail via a now-familiar process. First, I will take a closer look at the current situation of vulnerable populations, use the CLE to critique how they are being treated, and then answer objections to such a critique.

The Stranger and the Poor Today

Readers may be familiar with the realities of those burdened with poverty (locally and globally)—we will examine their plight below—but might be less familiar with the realities of immigrants and refugees. I would first highlight their huge numbers: Massaro notes that over 240 million people currently live in a country other than the one where they were born. Remarkably, 64 million of those are refugees— people "whose dislocation is by and large involuntary."[306] Pope Francis is right to exclaim that such numbers are "unprecedented" and "beyond all imagination."[307] Multiple forces cause so many to leave their homeland, but Massaro points out that Francis understands the two that are most significant. The first is climate change. We are just beginning to understand how it generates refugees—and will return to it later in this chapter and at the beginning of the next. The second is violence. We underappreciate its power because, as Massaro reminds us, although we have learned to recognize how formally-declared wars create refugees, we "have been slow to broaden the categories of protection to include those fleeing other types of violence." He goes into impressive and sobering detail:

These include the types of periodic and "low-intensity conflict" associated with paramilitary insurgents, murderous drug cartels, heavily armed rival gangs, warlords in lawless regions, bands of modern-day pirates, and other unscrupulous non-state actors. Some victims are specifically targeted by armed assailants, some are simply caught in the crossfire, and still have to suffer the victimhood of profound and prolonged fear of attack.[308]

Thousands of refugees fleeing such violence have drowned while trying to cross the Mediterranean into Europe. Both Francis and Massaro drive home the fact that people take such risks—in poorly made boats, for a nearly-unaffordable fee—only because of their dramatically vulnerable and desperate situations.

For US Americans, the primary debate over immigration and refugees comes out of a similarly heartbreaking situation: a large flow of Mexicans and Central Americans over our southern border. An infernal combination of unstable governments and police forces, economies dominated by multi-national corporations, and merciless drug cartels has produced brutal violence and turmoil that pushes huge numbers of people to flee their homeland. Though Latin America comprises only 8 percent of the world's population, roughly one third of murders worldwide take place there.[309] It also accounts for forty-three of the fifty most murderous cities, including the entire top ten. The violence is particularly intense in the so-called "Northern

Triangle" of Honduras, Guatemala, and El Salvador. In 2014 tens of thousands of children fled that triangle—*by themselves*—to escape the violence. To put the violence in perspective, the murder rate in Honduras was 30 percent higher than the civilian casualty rate during the Iraq war.[310] Firearms are pervasive: "There is an armed security guard at every Dunkin' Donuts," according to a US missionary who spent considerable time there. "When you enter a pharmacy, the guard with a shotgun slung across his chest will considerately hold your pistol while you wait for your prescription to be filled."[311] *Vox* has reported on the particular brutality of gang violence: forcing boys to join and girls to become "girlfriends"—a euphemism for non-consensual sexual relationships. If these children refuse, they face kidnapping, rape, and murder. Many schools and bus routes are unsafe because they run through known gang territory.

The gangs finance themselves through dealing drugs, but also through human trafficking and selling illicit weapons. Catholic priests who step out of line by criticizing gangs and their practices are often murdered.[312] The hapless police forces, for the most part poorly funded and organized, are infiltrated by gang members. The government finds itself in a similar situation, unable to create and maintain stable institutions. Many parents seeking safety for their families feel they have little choice—even when they know that fleeing to the United States will be equally dangerous. Again, *Vox* reports a disturbing picture:

> Routes north are increasingly under the control
> of Mexico's Los Zetas cartel, according to a recent

report from the US Conference of Catholic Bishops, which means that child migrants are at risk of "violence, extortion, kidnapping, sexual assault, trafficking and murder" during the journey. Sending a child to the United States is also extremely expensive. "Coyotes" (people smugglers) charge $5,000 to $7,000 to bring a child to the US, according to the same report — an amount that can represent more than 18 months of earnings for an entire family.[313]

Even the US policy of child-separation at the border does not deter families. During the summer of 2018, for instance, Piedad De Jesús Mejía, a thirty-one-year-old mother from Honduras, took her four children to Reynosa, Mexico. She had heard about the policy of family separations at the US border, but her situation was so desperate that she "had to leave without caring about that."[314]

The Obama and Trump administrations have not welcomed migrants. Obama deported more than any president in history—so many that in some circles he became known as the "Deporter in Chief."[315] As I write this chapter, the fallout from Trump's child separation policy—designed to deter future migrants from trying to enter the United States by separating children from their parents—is uncertain. As of December 2018 there were 15,000 such children being held in nearly full shelters.[316] Despite the violence that many are fleeing, the Trump administration has made it difficult to claim asylum successfully. In 2017, six in ten asylum cases were rejected—the highest rate in a decade.[317]

In Philadelphia, one heartbreaking story of deportation unfolded even as proceedings were underway to give a five-year-old special needs juvenile immigration status. Pennsylvania Senator Bob Casey, Jr. drew the attention of reporters by live-tweeting the deportation as it took place.[318] He noted that the boy and his mother fled Honduras after she witnessed gang members killing her cousin and so became marked for death herself. But as he tweeted, the two were already on the plane back the Honduras—a trip, Casey noted, that would lead to their likely execution.

Now, it would be naïve to assume every claim of asylum is legitimate. Some do try to game the system. Homeland Security Secretary John Kelly, for instance, insisted that the case Senator Casey brought to the world's attention might not have been as he characterized it:

> The vast majority of people who come up here, that's a, the overwhelming number, say exactly the same words because they are schooled by the traffickers to say certain words, to give certain scenarios, which, generally speaking, will get you to remain in the United States, in the system, because of a credible fear claim. So she did that.[319]

It is reasonable to be sympathetic regarding families and children fleeing actual threats of violence, but also be disturbed at thousands making up stories to get into the United States. But recall the raw peril of the trip for these migrants. If not real threats of aggressive violence, what desperation would cause a family to uproot themselves from their homeland and take such a journey?

The cause, or at least a big part of it, is poverty. Many of the undocumented immigrants come from countries with some of the lowest GDPs in the Western hemisphere.[320] And despite recent gains, global poverty continues to be a massive problem on a massive scale. Consider these disturbing statistics:[321]

- Nearly 800 million people live on less than $1.90 per day.

- Children are twice as likely as adults to live in poverty.

- Nearly 400 million people in sub-Saharan Africa live in poverty.

- In the Central African Republic, the poorest country in the world, the yearly per capita GDP is $656.

- The richest eight men in the world have as much wealth as the poorest half of the world.

And this poverty is often deadly. Huge numbers of vulnerable people, including many millions of children, die of easily-preventable diseases like polio and diphtheria.[322] Given these facts, it is not surprising that in other parts of the world, being poor can take decades off your life expectancy.[323] But it is unexpectedly surprising that something similar is true in the United States—a male US American in the richest one percent lives over fourteen years longer than one in the lowest one percent.[324] Living in the wrong neighborhood could, on average, take two decades off your life. In fact, though the US rich live longer and longer, over the last three years the life expectancy of the US poor has declined.[325] A remarkable outcome for easily the richest nation in history, especially when elsewhere around the world life expectancies are rising.

Another important fact contributing to a fuller picture is the effect of poverty on women. We've already established how our culture's patriarchal expectations concerning sex, contraception, and abortion put many women in highly compromised situations—situations that force them into poverty because of their openness to welcoming a child into the world. The extra burden women bear has led to the so-called "feminization of poverty." Consider the following:[326]

- In the United States, nearly two-thirds of minimum-wage workers are women.

- More than 70 percent of low-wage workers get no paid sick days at all.

- Forty percent of all households with children under the age of eighteen include mothers who are either the sole or primary source of income.

And there's more.[327] Forty percent of US women who head up households live in poverty. In every US state, women are poorer than men. Each year, eight billion days of paid work are lost due to domestic violence against women. In part because they have little or no family leave, financially out-of-reach child care, and still rampant discrimination due to pregnancy and family status, 43 percent of women leave the workforce after they have children. Personal and structural racism also remains a significant factor, as households headed by African American and Latina women are more impoverished than those headed by white women.[328]

Debate concerning the plight of the stranger and the poor jumps to policy even faster than the debate on abortion does. Should we have more energetic and better-funded government programs or lift restrictions on economic freedom? Should we build a border wall or have unfettered immigration? And so on. Often the debate over these policies isn't about the good of the stranger and the poor themselves, but about the political advantages of using such rhetoric in public discourse. This is what Pope Francis had in mind, I think, when launching World Day of the Poor. He contrasted "empty words so frequently on our lips" with the "concrete deeds against which we are called to measure ourselves." We are called to love the stranger and the poor, he says, as Jesus loved: in both word and deed.[329]

Our typical responses, often based on a binary, polarized politics not geared toward those with the most need, are inadequate. We need to set aside (at least for the moment) policy debates and make space in our hearts for these populations, focusing on the meaning of our most cherished principles in light of the harsh realities described above.

The CLE Response

It is obvious how the issues just described affect particularly vulnerable populations, to whom we must give priority. To be poor is to be vulnerable, and many millions of migrants find themselves in highly vulnerable situations. Beyond this, however, the CLE insists upon attention to other factors that lead to even deeper vulnerability. In addressing these issues, we must direct our moral attention to age, gender, and race.

Our throwaway culture, however, works overtime to conceal the dignity of these populations behind a curtain of consumerism. Appealing to our strong sense of autonomy and privacy—something Pope Francis has described on numerous occasions as the "globalization of indifference"—our culture tempts us to reduce our concern to mere empty words. Even worse, the culture encourages us to use dehumanizing words and images to describe the poor and the stranger. People with their children fleeing violence are called "illegals." They are "swarms" of "undesirables" and "parasites." Sometimes they are even referred to as "rapists" and "animals." The poor are "takers" and "welfare queens."

As each chapter will demonstrate, the CLE must call attention to language that reduces the dignity of marginalized populations to mere catchphrases. Otherwise we can objectify the vulnerable and allow ourselves to discard them at will—often at the service of consumerist culture, and often in the face of terrible violence. What does the popularity of proposals to engage in mass deportation of migrants indicate?[330] Daniel Flores, bishop of the border community of Brownsville, Texas, says this:

One cannot in conscience countenance a program of mass deportation. It is a brutal proposal. In some instances, particularly dealing with the Central American mothers and children, and deportations into some parts of Mexico, we are dealing with placing them in proximate danger of death. I consider supporting the sending of an adult or child back to a place where he or she is marked for death, where there is lawlessness and societal collapse, to be formal cooperation with an intrinsic evil. Not unlike driving someone to an abortion clinic.[331]

As a group, the US bishops increasingly tend to see immigration and migration as a right-to-life response to deadly violence. Cardinal Daniel DiNardo, the head of the conference, spoke during the tumultuous summer of 2018, when the United States was changing its asylum policy:

At its core, asylum is an instrument to preserve the right to life. The Attorney General's recent decision elicits deep concern because it potentially strips asylum from many women who lack adequate protection. These vulnerable women will now face return to the extreme dangers of domestic violence in their home country. . . . We urge courts and policy makers to respect and enhance, not erode, the potential of our asylum system to preserve and protect the right to life.[332]

The US policy of separating children from their families is another example of how the throwaway culture reduces the dignity of a vulnerable population, treating them as a mere means to some other end. Again, here's Bishop Flores: "Separating immigrant parents and children as a supposed deterrent to immigration is a cruel and reprehensible policy. Children are not instruments of deterrence, they are children."[333] Asked about what will happen to the children after they are separated from their parents, White House Chief of Staff John Kelly, one of the architects of this policy, responded that they would be put into "foster care or whatever."

Refusing to aid the vulnerable poor and stranger not only violates our most solemn duty but is also a kind of violence. Building on a tradition that goes back to the very beginnings of the Church, Pope Francis does not mince words in describing what happens when economic forces marginalize and exclude the vulnerable. He says, "Such an economy kills." [334] We saw above that John Paul II taught that "You shall not kill" is "more fully expressed in the positive command of love for one's neighbor." The Catechism of the Catholic Church frames our response to poverty within the fifth commandment, which forbids killing:

> The moral law prohibits exposing someone to mortal danger without grave reason, as well as refusing assistance to a person in danger.

> The acceptance by human society of murderous famines, without efforts to remedy

them, is a scandalous injustice and a grave offense. Those whose usurious and avaricious dealings lead to the hunger and death of their brethren in the human family *indirectly commit homicide* [emphasis added], which is imputable to them. [335]

Unintentional killing is not morally imputable. But one is not exonerated from grave offense if, without proportionate reasons, he has acted in a way that brings about someone's death, even without the intention to do so.[336]

And the Second Vatican Council's *Pastoral Constitution on the Church in the Modern World* says something similar:

Since there are so many people prostrate with hunger in the world, this sacred council urges all, both individuals and governments, to remember the aphorism of the Fathers, "Feed the man dying of hunger, because if you have not fed him, you have killed him," and really to share and employ their earthly goods, according to the ability of each, especially by supporting individuals or peoples with the aid by which they may be able to help and develop themselves.[337]

Again, the CLE places concern for the poor and stranger at the center of "the way of life" and our personal failure to aid can be construed as a kind of violence that can be understood as killing.

Using others as a mere means, of course, does not always result in their death. Our consumerist throwaway culture uses and discards the poor and the stranger in many other ways—beyond what can be listed in a single chapter of a single book. Migrants are trafficked as sex workers, a particularly twisted and evil example of using a human being as a mere thing or object. More broadly, undocumented immigrants are used and exploited for their cheap and (often) regulation-free labor. More than one-third are paid less than minimum wage and most never get mandated overtime pay.[338] Essentially, privileged US citizens use and exploit economically vulnerable populations to get cheaper goods and services. Because their undocumented status prevents them from making legal challenges, migrants often work in inhuman, dignity-killing conditions. Especially in light of topics to be considered in the next chapter, consumers have access to unreasonably cheap meat because it is prepared by exploited migrants subjected to abusive and even sub-human conditions in factory farms and slaughterhouses.[339] The poor and marginalized, even those with proper documents, are still used and discarded in ways beyond what we can address here. Big banks exploiting the poor and the vulnerable helped bring on the Great Recession of 2008.[340] "Pay-Day Loan" companies use and then discard the desperate poor by trapping them in unreasonable debt from which many never escape.[341] And, of course, our binary politics and arguments use the poor as pawns to justify or deny government programs.

The CLE can provide an antidote to the throwaway culture's treatment of the poor and the stranger. Its vision demands more than not killing. It demands more than voting a certain way. It means each of us taking seriously the stories and realities of these Christ-bearers. It means cultivating a genuine encounter and allowing that encounter to transform us. Pope Francis notes that such encounters can offer an irreplaceable opportunity for human growth and dialogue—which can then "dissipate distorted fears and ideologies, and help humanity to grow, and help give space to feelings of openness and the building of bridges."[342] The pope has led the way in doing this by visiting the United States-Mexico border and listening to the migrants' stories.[343] This follows up on similar visits from Pope John Paul II, whose encyclical on the Gospel of Life said that welcoming the stranger means becoming a neighbor to a person in need—even to the point of "taking responsibility for his life."[344]

Having been transformed by the encounter, we need to take action. Mutuality and hospitality require it. Our salvation depends on it. Pope Francis emphasizes mercy over justice, a most important distinction. However, we should act on behalf of these populations not only out of mercy, but even more out of justice. St. Thomas Aquinas insisted that whatever we have "in superabundance" is "due, by natural law" to the poor. If the poor's needs are "manifest and urgent" then "it is lawful for a man to succor his own need by means of another's property, by taking it either openly or secretly: nor is this properly speaking theft or robbery."[345] It is not theft or robbery because we owe our excess resources to the poor as a matter of justice. If we do not give the poor our excess resources, we keep for ourselves something that is rightfully theirs.

But in this regard our duties to aid are sometimes a matter of justice in another sense. We owe the poor and the stranger resources and other aid particularly when we are responsible for their need. For example, when consensual sex results in pregnancy, the prenatal child's need has been created by the parents—in which case the duty to aid (at least on the mother's part) is stronger than if the pregnancy were the result of sexual violence. We can draw similar conclusions about many of the issues considered above. Global climate change, to which the rich world in particular contributes, is already starting to create refugees, and by 2050 the World Bank expects over 140 million of them.[346] US military interventions in Iraq and Syria displaced hundreds of thousands. The United States has aided Saudi Arabia and the UAE in their war against the Iran-backed rebels in Yemen, making the United States complicit in the famine and other atrocities to which civilians in that country are subject—a situation the UN calls "The world's worst humanitarian crisis."[347] Children in particular are at risk: US-made bombs have been dropped on schools and, as Nicholas Kristoff notes, "Starving Yemeni children are reduced to eating a sour paste made of leaves. Even those who survive will often be stunted for the rest of their lives, physically and mentally."[348] In the Northern Triangle, US interventions in those countries' affairs and our deep, unhealthy relationship with drugs have caused instability and violence.[349]

Facts like these demonstrate at least partial US responsibility for the need that drives many of those fleeing the Northern Triangle. But we are becoming even less welcoming and hospitable to these undocumented immigrants—as evidenced by the American response to the so-called "caravan" that arrived at the US border in November of 2018.[350] In a very real sense, we are responsible for the need of children and other vulnerable populations in Yemen. But our major media do not even bother to cover this story. In a very real sense, we are responsible for migrants fleeing climate change. But most US Americans refuse to change their carbon-addicted lifestyles. In a very real sense, we are responsible for the refugee crisis in Syria. But we continue to limit the already paltry number of refugees that the United States takes in.[351] Mercy requires that we aid all these populations, particularly because in a special way they bear the face of Christ. Given our responsibility for the common good, focusing particularly on the most vulnerable, justice requires that we come to their aid. But justice also requires that we come to their aid in a special way because we are responsible for creating their need in the first place.

Objections

> Objection #1: *Doesn't God reward the faithful? Doesn't God want us to flourish and be happy with the financial resources given to us? Why should the CLE insist that we have a*

moral duty to give away the resources God has given for our benefit?

Contemporary consumerist culture claims wealth brings happiness and prosperity, not Christ and his Church. Jesus says, "woe to you rich," who risk failing to enter the Kingdom of God. And as Charles Mathewes reminds us, many ancient and medieval traditions were clear about the consequences of wealth—it harms your character, warps your behavior, and corrupts your soul.[352] He also highlights obvious but often-ignored contemporary research. The rich, for example, are more likely to

- cheat on their taxes

- cheat on their spouse

- shoplift

- drink too much

- run stop signs and cut off other motorists

- refuse to share in a group.

This doesn't apply to every rich person, of course, but numbers are numbers. And if this list isn't bad enough, the rich also have less compassion and empathy, and proportionately give less to charity. They seem to have difficulty enjoying life's simple pleasures and—because they often lack compassion and empathy—miss out on the delight that can come from aiding another person. Rich people also isolate themselves from the close relationships within networks of interconnected and interdependent people—and such isolation produces yet more unhappiness.

And what happens to those who are faithful to our duty to aid? They are made happier by resisting the trap of consumerism and following the CLE with respect to the poor and the stranger. Notorious B.I.G. had it right: more money means more problems.[353] A new LinkedIn study found that "[s]even in ten (68 percent) people making more than $200,000 a year reported feeling stressed at work, compared to less than half (47 percent) of those making $35,000 to $50,000, and just 38 percent of those earning between $50,000 and $75,000."[354] Furthermore, consider a US household in which each parent has a job that nets $50,000. Once they start making more than that amount, the happiness of the household begins to decline.[355] So while it is certainly true that God wants us to be happy, and sometimes gives us substantial resources, it is by following God's command to aid the poor and stranger—and resisting the consumerist race to become rich—that we attain true happiness. Just as explicit violence like sexual manipulation and abortion has disastrous effects upon those who perform such acts, an agent of the violence this chapter considers is also negatively affected.

> *Objection #2: I'm willing to help those who help themselves and follow the law. But I'm not willing to help those who aren't deserving of my help. CLE fails to make this important distinction.*

This objection concerns a category of poor people that is remarkably small: about 2 percent of those below the US poverty line elect not to work or seek work.[356] And as Elizabeth Bruenig points out, "87 percent of able-bodied adults covered by the Medicaid expansion are already working, in school or seeking work," and "about 75 percent of those not working are full-time caregivers."[357] But how should we think of the tiny group of people who prompt this objection? Bruenig offers an important insight into what underlies this question:

> The intention is to shape poor people into the kind of people we want them to be, not to help them flourish as they are, or as they intend to be. Market labor, productivity and self-sufficiency are all aspects of that reformed person welfare ought to create, in this transformative framework.[358]

We cannot create a society where all are valued equally, Bruenig says, by trying to transform those we don't value into the kind of people we do. The CLE pointedly makes sure to value even the most vulnerable as equal in dignity to those who are not. Especially when our biases make it difficult for us to do so.

> Objection #3: *Maybe it is bad to refuse to aid, but could it really be—as the* Catechism of the Catholic Church *says—on par with homicide? How is that possible? Isn't directly killing the innocent intrinsically evil whereas failing to aid*

someone is not? And what about the distinction between local and global poverty? While we have seen some dramatic facts about local poverty in the United States, the more dramatic numbers come from developing countries. Can our duties of justice to the common good really mean we owe the same to those in countries far away living on less than two dollars a day as we do to our fellow US citizens?

From the perspective of Catholic moral theology, "intrinsic" does not mean "very." Catholic tradition considers masturbation, usury, and even lying to be intrinsically evil acts. But acts that are not intrinsically evil may be morally grave. Abandoning a homeless person who freezes to death is not an intrinsically evil act, but it is much more morally serious than lying to a child about Santa Claus. Suppose the homeless person was abandoned to die because you just couldn't be bothered to get up off the couch and open the door. How should we describe such a callous moral choice? It is not aiming at the death of an innocent person, but it is gross negligence regarding one's duty to aid, which (as we saw above) is a kind of violence. US law, for example, defines reckless and negligent behavior that leads to someone's death as homicide—and persons convicted of "negligent homicide" can be punished with a decade in prison. The CLE resists appeals to autonomy and freedom that override or obscure our duty to aid the poor and the stranger. If the vices of greed, sloth, or luxury lead us to abandon this solemn duty, and this leads to someone's death, the *Catechism* correctly refers to such a moral choice as homicide. Thinking about it from this angle helps us understand why Christ insisted that our failure to aid the most vulnerable can, again, threaten our very salvation.

The issue of how to think about our duties to local victims of poverty as opposed to victims of global poverty, by contrast, is difficult to resolve. On the one hand, all human beings are children of the same God, and therefore brothers and sisters. Furthermore, as Pope Francis insists, the Eucharist unites Christians all over the world as the body of Christ.[359] As a transnational community the Church rejects the idea that we limit our aid for the poor and the stranger to our nation state. On the other hand, the tradition supports a hierarchical order of charity in which we have a duty to our parents, children, friends, and neighbors that we do not owe to random people who live far away. How to resolve these two insights (that seem in tension)?

In some ways, genuinely asking the question puts us already in a good place. St. Thomas Aquinas wrestles with this tension and, from my perspective, offers a persuasive response. We should put those who are close to us first only if the needs in question are roughly comparable. Resurfacing a local tennis court in Kenosha, Wisconsin, doesn't compare, say, to saving children dying of easily treatable diseases in Bangalore. While it illustrates the general point, this extreme example doesn't offer much help with the hard choices in many readers' actual lives. How, for instance, do we weigh our child's college education against the need to fund children's literacy programs in developing countries? Where there is no obviously right answer,

Thomas suggests we cultivate the virtue of prudence in making decisions about the best way to resolve such difficult questions. Again, if we are genuinely struggling with the tension, we are already in a very good place regarding our duties to aid the poor and the stranger.[360]

Conclusion

Some may feel frustrated that this chapter does not argue for or against particular government policy proposals. For some, the obvious solutions to these massive, sweeping problems must involve energetic, broadly effective government programs. For others, such programs are inefficient, disconnected from the people, and often unintentionally extend the problem and even make it worse. Besides the fact that these policy questions and debates are too complex to engage here, let us recall that we must avoid jumping into binary left/right political debates and instead focus on the underlying values. In the previous chapter we did this with abortion, another issue in which the discussion is often limited to what the law should be. In both contexts, our current moment calls instead for a disciplined focus on the values before moving on to public policy. A focus on such values, among other things, is likely to highlight common ground that transcends the right/left divide over the size and scope of government. We can and should start with our own duties as individuals, families, churches, and other local communities. Again, our very salvation depends on it.

Chapter Six

Ecology and Non-Human Animals

Introduction

Is the CLE ethic limited to concern only for human life? For most of its history, the answer would have been yes. Clerics like Cardinal Bernardin, formed by the humanism of the Second Vatican Council, weren't attuned to the value of non-human creatures as Church leaders might be today. For example, searching for the term "animal" in *Gaudium et spes*—Vatican II's major work on the Church in the modern world—yields zero results. Furthermore, the first chapter of the document begins with a statement that betrays its anthropocentrism: "According to the almost unanimous opinion of believers and unbelievers alike, all things on earth should be related to man as their center and crown." In today's context, such words seem quaint—or even dangerous. Beginning in 1987 Pope John Paul II made ecological concern a central part of his ministry; Pope Benedict XVI was so concerned with care for God's creation that he was called "the Green Pope"; and Pope Francis wrote *Laudato si'*, the first ecological encyclical. After two generations of intense focus on these concerns, mainstream Catholic theology now acknowledges the intrinsic value of God's creation, as well as the mutuality and interrelatedness of the human and non-human.

The value and place of God's creation lies at the heart of Pope Francis's concern about throwaway culture. In *Laudato si'* he demonstrates, for instance, that the logic of this culture "generates so much waste" because of "the desire to consume more than what is really necessary."[361] As we will see in detail below, Catholic teaching is clear: non-human creation has value, not only because of its relationship to human beings, but also because God created it good—full stop—without reference to human beings. Creation belongs to God, not to us. We are its caretakers, under a mandate to cooperate in ordering creation according to God's design and intentions.

A traditional Christian understanding of the hierarchy of being places angels above humans, who are above non-human animals, who are above plants, which are above minerals.[362] Life has a special value, but a hierarchical continuum assigns some lives a higher value than others. Some might make a binary distinction between "human" and "the environment," but there is no theological basis for doing so. Non-human animals, for instance, are far closer to us (and to God) than are rocks. The CLE acknowledges that all life does matter in some sense, but within God's creation non-human animals have a special value.

This position is strongly affirmed in scripture. The conclusion to Genesis chapter 1 makes it clear that human beings may eat plants, but not animals. Genesis chapter 2 recounts how God created animals and brought them to Adam because it is not good that he should be alone. The prophet Isaiah, in a familiar image of the New Eden in the Kingdom of God, places the peaceable relationship between non-human animals (and between humans and non-human animals) at the center:

> The wolf shall live with the lamb,
>> the leopard shall lie down with the kid,
> the calf and the lion and the fatling together,
>> and a little child shall lead them.
> The cow and the bear shall graze,
>> their young shall lie down together;
>> and the lion shall eat straw like the ox.
> The nursing child shall play over the hole of the asp,
>> and the weaned child shall put its hand on the
>> adder's den.
>
> (Isaiah 11:6-8)

The *Catechism of the Catholic Church* also notes the special duties of justice we owe to non-human animals: we "owe animals kindness" and we must not cause them to "suffer or die needlessly."[363] The Church is developing this aspect of the teaching in more detail and specificity, and examining these issues through the lens of the CLE may help.

This chapter, though clear about the intrinsic value of all God's creation, will focus particularly on non-human animals. As with other chapters, we will explore the practices of our throwaway culture, subject those practices to a CLE critique, and then answer objections. Also, as with other chapters, readers may be concerned that our project avoids political and policy-related questions, focusing instead on personal responsibilities. But Pope Francis has been explicit on this question: "We should not think that political efforts or the force of law will be sufficient to prevent actions which affect the environment because, when the culture itself is corrupt and objective truth and universally valid principles are no longer upheld, then laws can only be seen as arbitrary impositions or obstacles to be avoided."[364] Before discussing carbon credits, the square footage a farm must have for each chicken, or the effect of global capitalism on the nature and purpose of farming, we must first engage some foundational issues.

What's Happening?

We are indeed facing an ecological crisis, though not everyone who accepts this truth lives as if it were so. According to a UN report issued as I was writing this manuscript, our inaction regarding climate change has brought us much closer to existential devastation than previously estimated.[365] For some time the Catholic Church has been raising the alarm on this issue: in 1990, for instance, Pope John Paul II described the problem as "urgent" and called for a new solidarity and set of lifestyles to address it.[366] In 2007, responding to widespread inaction, Pope Benedict XVI founded a Pontifical Council on Climate Change and Development, describing the issue as a "matter of grave importance for the entire human family."[367] Pope Francis's 2015 encyclical, *Laudato si'*, raised the alarm in great detail, however, and is worth quoting at some length:

> Warming has effects on the carbon cycle. It creates a vicious circle which aggravates the situation even more, affecting the availability of essential resources like drinking water, energy

and agricultural production in warmer regions, and leading to the extinction of part of the planet's biodiversity. The melting in the polar ice caps and in high altitude plains can lead to the dangerous release of methane gas, while the decomposition of frozen organic material can further increase the emission of carbon dioxide. Things are made worse by the loss of tropical forests which would otherwise help to mitigate climate change. Carbon dioxide pollution increases the acidification of the oceans and compromises the marine food chain. If present trends continue, this century may well witness extraordinary climate change and an unprecedented destruction of ecosystems, with serious consequences for all of us. . . . [Climate change] represents one of the principal challenges facing humanity in our day.[368]

Addressing skepticism about this concern from some quarters of the pro-life movement, the pope's right-hand man on Catholic social teaching, Cardinal Peter Turkson, insists that the struggle to combat climate change is an essential part of protection of human life. He notes that "[T]he present state of the climate is a menace to human life itself. It's not sustainable, and if we continue on this path, it won't be possible anymore to have human life on this planet. In that sense, the message on climate change coincides perfectly with any pro-life activism, or any belief in human life. The two are not separable."[369]

As we will explore in more detail, the problem is rooted in an out-of-control consumerist culture. We, especially in the developed West, seem unable to limit our wants and perceived needs. We exhibit a near insatiable desire to consume. When future generations or God's creation get in the way of living as we wish, we ignore those realities. We put the short-term growth and gain of those currently living above all other concerns. For instance, though many now realize that consuming cheap meat and other products from factory farms contributes to global climate change (as will be explored in more detail below), most people—even some who consider themselves deeply concerned about climate change—cannot bring themselves to change how they live. The consumerist trap is powerful.

Factory farms also torture and kill almost unimaginable numbers of animals. Of the ten billion killed in the United States each year, most are subjected to brutal conditions and practices. Here are just a few:[370]

- In windowless sheds broiler hens are raised like crops, their reshaped bodies causing them to reach slaughter-weight as quickly as thirty-five days, suffering because their immature legs cannot support their prematurely large bodies.

- Billions of chickens, "living" in tightly confined, stacked wire cages, are pelted with excrement from the cages above them; ammonia from the build-up of excrement on the floor is often so thick that, in addition to causing chronic respiratory disease, it makes some go blind.

- About four billion "redundant" male chicks are macerated, gassed, suffocated, or thrown away.

- Pregnant sows are moved to a farrowing pen in which a metal frame restricts almost all movement. They resist, sometimes spending hours trying to chew through the iron bars.

- Pigs being trucked to slaughter are crammed into a trailer that leaves them exposed to the elements. Some die of heat in the winter or of cold in the summer, while others suffocate in the tightly packed truck.

- Intensive dairy operations keep cows indoors without access to pastures, perpetually hungry, pregnant 3/4 of the time, their calves removed before they can meet their mothers. After three or four lactations, when their productivity falls below the optimum, they are culled for beef.

In the developed West, animals that have what our secular culture considers "high" moral capacities—like autonomy and self-determination—are treated with more dignity and respect. TV documentaries like CNN's *Blackfish*, movies about human exploitation of great apes, and news stories about the illegal hunting of elephants have drawn attention to these sophisticated animals. And it is easy to make a case for treating them better, especially given our cultural obsession with autonomy and self-determination. But more and more—especially in the context of medical research—rather than using animals like monkeys or chimpanzees, experimentation is done on the less sympathetic rat and mouse. And using such animals has coincided with game-changing advances in biotechnology. As I and my co-author Susan Kopp (a professor of veterinary medicine) recently wrote, both inbreeding and direct manipulation of genes at the nuclear level allow for the creation of brand-new, never-before-seen animal "lines":

> By targeting individual genes along an animal's chromosome, scientists are now able to produce animals that will be born with or develop diseases, such as diabetes, neuromuscular dystrophy and breast cancer. . . . Scott A. Armstrong, head of the Memorial Sloan Kettering Leukemia Center, was recently honored with the Paul Marks Prize for Cancer Research based in part on special lines of mice he engineered to develop leukemia. Similarly, rat lines engineered for a multiple sclerosis-like illness have been fundamental in the advancement of promising human therapies. The developments needed for creation of genetically altered animals in research have come rapidly over the past two decades—not only because of the promising horizons for medical advancement but also because of the enormous potential for profit. Biotech companies using these animals play a key role in the portfolios of top-shelf private and public investors.

These financial resources have paved the way for some disturbing practices:

Researchers, for example, are now able to modify pig embryos in the womb so that their pancreas never develops, in the hopes that these animals will be useful for future organ transplantation. Similarly, scientists studying dementia can purchase rat "Alzheimer models" from commercial laboratories. Prior to shipment, a slow release pump system is inserted into the rat's brain, injecting toxic compounds over four weeks. The resulting brain damage is said to mimic Alzheimer symptoms.[371]

Readers will react in different ways to these practices, but one fact is clear: these animals have become a pure commodity—designed, assembled, modified, and sold. Nor is this limited to the research lab: biotechnology is doing similar things to animals in factory farms. Turkeys are bred with breasts so large that they cannot have sex— and the show *Dirty Jobs* featured the disgusting process by which workers procure semen from males and "blast" it into females.[372] Many chickens are now genetically bred so that they never feel full and thus will eat as much and as quickly as possible. Their immature legs cannot support their huge bodies and thus they live with chronic pain, most unable even to stand up. And they are denied even the modest relief of a full stomach.

CLE Critique

The CLE is concerned that non-human animals are treated with extensive, appalling violence. The CLE involves itself because, as is true in other instances of violence, these abuses reflect how consumerism denigrates these living creatures' intrinsic value by reducing them to mere things used to generate a profit. Factory farms do not allow individual animals to flourish as God created them; the only concern is maximizing "protein units per square foot." Biotech and pharma companies manipulate animals for research without considering how these processes affect actual living creatures; they are concerned only with how new techniques will affect their bottom line. Acts chapter 15 recounts an important moment in the early Church when the various Christian communities were arguing about which precepts of Jewish law should be honored in their new movement. They decided to keep the prohibition of eating meat from animals that had been sacrificed to idols. This prohibition is still applicable today, as almost all meat consumed in the developed West comes from animals sacrificed to the idol of consumerism. Every time we buy meat purely on price, especially if we don't "need" it in any reasonable sense (more on this below), we participate in the idolatry.

In *Laudato si'* Pope Francis expresses concern with such consumerist practices:

> If we approach nature and the environment without this openness to awe and wonder, if we no longer speak the language of fraternity and beauty in our relationship with the world,

our attitude will be that of masters, consumers, ruthless exploiters, unable to set limits on their immediate needs. By contrast, if we feel intimately united with all that exists, then sobriety and care will well up spontaneously. The poverty and austerity of Saint Francis were no mere veneer of asceticism, but something much more radical: a refusal to turn reality into an object simply to be used and controlled.[373]

The population shift from rural areas to cities in the developed West has played a key role in rupturing our sense of intimacy and unity with God's creation, especially with non-human animals. The most common place many encounter non-human animals today is our dinner plate. The CLE, you may recall, pays close attention to how we use language that facilitates our throwaway culture. We eat "bacon" or "ham," not pig; or "hamburger" or "steak," not cow. Even the word "animal" is often used to marginalize—acting "like an animal" is an insult. It names base, dirty, irrational, thoughtless behavior. In today's era of smartphones and citizen journalism, we ought to be better at bringing to light the agony and suffering of marginalized creatures. But strong consumerist interests keep such practices hidden away, and powerful corporations hire the best lobbyists to get legislatures to pass "Ag-Gag" laws.[374] Such laws attempt to prevent journalists, activists, or even employee whistleblowers from documenting the reality inside factory farms, keeping helpless, voiceless creatures on the peripheries of the culture.

Supporters of the CLE have a duty not only to abstain from involvement in the consumerist idolatry of factory farms, but to speak up on behalf of the dignity of those who cannot speak for themselves. Genesis chapter 1 says that God created "living creatures of every kind" and Luke chapter 12 reminds us that "not one of them is forgotten in God's sight." As caretakers of God's creation, we are obliged to care for these animals because they are God's creatures. Again, they belong not to us but to God. The *Catechism* states that we owe animals kindness. This is the opposite of doing whatever we want with them; instead, the kindness we owe means treating animals as the creatures they are. We have no right to radically alter or change their basic make-up, especially for profit-making. We have no right to cause them to suffer or die without, again as the *Catechism* says, a reasonable claim of necessity. Animals have an intrinsic dignity and value independent of human beings. Were a rational alien race to come into contact with them long after human beings have passed out of existence (perhaps from catastrophic climate change), surely those rational beings would be bound by the same moral obligations toward these animals.

In addition, beyond their effect on non-human animals the CLE must also focus on what factory farms do to vulnerable humans. Such farms emit three times the amount of greenhouse gases than do all forms of transportation combined.[375] To address climate change, not supporting factory farms is far more significant than driving fuel-efficient cars or taking fewer trips on airplanes.[376] The previous chapter demonstrated how climate change has created many, many refugees—and, if unchecked, will create many more. But in *Laudato si'* Pope Francis highlights how climate change threatens everyone who might be considered vulnerable:

> Many of the poor live in areas particularly affected by phenomena related to warming, and their means of subsistence are largely dependent on natural reserves and ecosystemic services such as agriculture, fishing and forestry. They have no other financial activities or resources which can enable them to adapt to climate change or to face natural disasters, and their access to social services and protection is very limited. . . . Sadly, there is widespread indifference to such suffering, which is even now taking place throughout our world. Our lack of response to these tragedies involving our brothers and sisters points to the loss of that sense of responsibility for our fellow men and women upon which all civil society is founded.[377]

To the extent we bear responsibility for the needs of the poor, the CLE insists we give special priority to not consuming the products of systems primarily responsible for climate change. For those who have access to alternative sources of protein, taking climate change seriously means not eating animals raised and killed in factory farms.

And this leads us to another important theme of the CLE: not only must we refrain from killing; we must also support the vulnerable. We must *act*. We must change the way we live. Pope Francis, discussing how to resist throwaway culture, proposes a new lifestyle.[378] Instead of feeding our "self-destructive vices" while "trying not to see them, trying not to acknowledge them, delaying the important decisions and pretending that nothing will happen," we must instead make "bold decisions" to reject "our current lifestyle."[379] Pope Benedict XVI was also deeply concerned about lifestyles, arguing that [emphasis in the original] *"[t]he way humanity treats the environment influences the way it treats itself, and vice versa."* He invites contemporary society to review its lifestyle, which, in many parts of the world, "is prone to hedonism and consumerism, despite their harmful consequences." We require "an effective shift in mentality which can lead to the adoption of *new life-styles.*" We need a correct understanding of "human ecology" to help fulfill God's will for the broader ecological world.[380] To be sure, as the CLE points out, proper understanding of the human person is destroyed principally by consumerism. Pope John Paul II noted how contemporary "consumer attitudes and *life-styles*" can damage our "physical and spiritual health."[381]

The CLE is also concerned with the agents of violence and killing. Even if their behavior does not reach the truly ghastly conditions described above, the violence they do—whether to humans or non-humans—damages them, too. It especially affects those on factory farms, who have high rates of PTSD and PITS (perpetration-induced traumatic stress).[382] Witnessing and perpetrating violence and killing over and over again debilitates the workers themselves.

One noted that that pigs "have come up and nuzzled me like a puppy. Two minutes later I had to kill them—beat them to death with a pipe. I can't care." Another went into even more detail:

> The sheer amount of killing and blood can really get to you after a while. Especially if you can't just shut down all emotion and turn into a robot zombie of death. You feel like part of a big death machine. [You're] pretty much treated that way as well. Sometimes weird thoughts will enter your head. It's just you and the dying chickens. The surreal feelings grow into such a horror of the barbaric nature of your behaviour. You are murdering helpless birds by the thousands (75,000 to 90,000 a night). You are a killer.[383]

To do their jobs workers reduce the animals to mere objects. Sometimes they rip the heads off chickens, put them on their fingers, and do puppet shows. Other times they have "shit fights" in which they squeeze live chickens so hard that their excrement shoots onto a co-worker. Often, the violence against an animal migrates to violence against human beings—studies show that "slaughterhouse employment increases total arrest rates, arrests for violent crimes, arrests for rape, and arrests for other sex offenses in comparison with other industries."[384]

Many workers are illiterate, unable even to fill in the job application forms by themselves. They have little or no prospect of finding work elsewhere. After all, how desperate must you be to do a job like this? By taking advantage of such desperation, factory farms add another level of exploitation and violence, which we support when we buy their products. For example, consider Case Farms: this prominent company, according to a report in *The New Yorker*, "produces nearly a billion pounds for customers such as Kentucky Fried Chicken, Popeyes, and Taco Bell. Boar's Head sells its chicken as deli meat in supermarkets. Since 2011, the U.S. government has purchased nearly seventeen million dollars' worth of Case Farms chicken, mostly for the federal school-lunch program."[385] Case built its empire on the backs of desperate refugees from—you guessed it—the Northern Triangle.

But they didn't start there. Case built its first factory farm in Ohio Amish country, but the Amish refused to work there. The company then turned to nearby rustbelt cities, but even with those desperate populations the turn-over rate was too high. Next, Case scoured the United States for "Latino workers" and bussed them in to live near the factory farm and work there. But the subhuman working and living conditions led these workers to reject such employment too. Then Case human resources manager Norman Beecher heard about Guatemalan refugees who had fled the violent civil war and were housed by Catholic parishes in Florida. He drove a large passenger van there and at Sunday Mass recruited workers. He was so success-ful that Beecher made several more trips to the Florida par-ish. "I didn't want [Mexicans]," he said. "Mexicans will go back home at Christmastime. You're going to lose them for six weeks. And in the poultry business you can't afford that. You just can't do it. But Guatemalans can't go back home. They're here as political refugees. If they go back home, they get shot."[386]

Besides being sites of human manipulation and violence to non-human animals, factory farms are primary contributors to global climate change. In his homily on a recent World Day of Prayer for Care of Creation, Cardinal Tagle of the Philippines (a country of islands at extreme risk because of rising sea levels) warned that by violating God's will for creation we risk destroying ourselves as well.[387] It is easy to despair in the face of such huge problems, but their magnitude may push us, as Pope Francis suggests, "to take an honest look at ourselves, to acknowledge our deep dissatisfaction, and to embark on new paths to authentic freedom."[388] The throwaway culture is strong, but the CLE's counter-culture is stronger.

Those living in urban areas may deceive themselves that they can live apart from the rest of creation, but whether we recognize it or not, none of us can escape being in relationship with the natural world. Our relationship can be shaped by the violent, destructive consumerism a throwaway culture generates, or it can be shaped by a culture of encounter and mercy. Levels of depression and anxiety continue to rise in the developed West, and (although correlation doesn't equal causation) it appears that this trend corresponds with increased urbanization. Those who grew up in rural areas know intuitively what research also demonstrates: human beings flourish when they live in touch with nature. Recent studies show that such encounters can counteract the negative psychological aspects of living in a city.[389] Living around trees reduces stress, and the more trees the better.[390] In light of the positive relationship between human beings and trees, the Japanese practice of "forest bathing"—which lowers heart rate and blood pressure, reduces stress hormone production, and boosts the immune system—is becoming more and more popular.[391] Walking or running in rural areas is 50 percent better for one's mental health than doing the same exercise in a gym.[392] Some physicians are now even formally prescribing a year-long set of outdoor activities to improve their patients' health.[393]

Those who have pets know intuitively that mutual relationships with animals contribute to human flourishing. Data supports that intuition: these relationships relieve stress, anxiety, and depression.[394] For many years now service dogs, long essential for the blind and others with disabilities, have become essential companions for veterans who fought in Iraq and Afghanistan and have PTSD and PITS. Research supports this, too.[395] "Psychiatric Service Dogs" have been shown to:

- help patients avert panic attacks

- wake patients from nightmares

- in public situations create personal space comfort zones by standing in front of the patient

- remind patients to take their medications.

Especially as rates of anxiety and depression rise, more and more hurting humans turn to "Emotional Support Animals." Though not (yet) considered service animals under the Americans with Disabilities Act, more and more they have become formal parts of medical and therapeutic intervention for people with several kinds of disorders.[396]

A culture of encounter between humans and non-human animals should also inform our eating practices. If we are going to eat meat, we should make every effort to avoid factory farm products by getting to know the local farmer and/or butcher. We should be able to look in the eye the animals we are paying to have killed. Ideally, we should even form a relationship with them. We should make sure that farm or shop employees are treated well and paid a fair wage. And, escaping the consumerist cycle of buying purely on price—a practice that led to the creation of factory farms in the first place—we should willingly pay significantly more for our meat. (At the very least, meat should become a relatively rare party food, as it was in our relatively recent past.) Finally, such encounters may provoke a merciful reaction, and this mercy may lead us to a realization: no need or desire to eat animals can justify their suffering or death. It may even provoke a reaction of hospitality, taking non-human animals into our homes and homesteads where yet more profound and lasting encounters can take place.

This focus on mutuality and encounter is deeply theological. *Laudato si'* cites Bonaventure's invitation to encounter God by encountering God's creatures.[397] The *Catechism* calls us to recognize the solidarity and interdependence between all creatures.[398] Pope Benedict's *Caritas in veritate* speaks of a "covenant between human beings and the environment."[399] As noted above, Benedict invokes the concept of human ecology, explaining that getting this ecology right is essential for being in right relationship with the broader ecological world. Francis takes this even further by making "integral ecology" a central focus of *Laudato si'.* Using the image of St. Francis of Assisi, the Holy Father invites us to adopt his namesake's profound concern for the whole of creation. Reiterating what Pope Francis says, by understanding that we are "intimately united with all that exists" we can have the relationship with creation that God demands of us. We will refuse to turn creation into another component in a consumerist culture that we can use and throw away. Focusing instead on a culture of mutuality, encounter, and mercy will "broaden our vision" and lead to a "non-consumerist model of life, recreation and community."[400]

And ecological mutuality—or integral ecology—does not concern only those living today. The CLE calls for a mutuality that transcends time. Just as we rely on the wisdom and prayers of the holy men and women who have gone before us, future generations rely on us. Pope Benedict's ecological concern calls us to "intergenerational" solidarity and justice with precisely this concern in mind.[401] In *Laudato si'* Pope Francis mentions his concern for "future generations" at least eleven times. Because God's creation does not belong to us, we must preserve it for future generations. This, the Holy Father argues, is "a basic question of justice."[402] And for the CLE, this basic question of justice especially concerns the most vulnerable future populations. This is yet another reason for deep concern about each practice of ours that contributes to ecological degradation, particularly those that contribute to global climate change. We owe future generations a profound change in lifestyle.

Objections

> Objection #1: *Who are we to judge? After all, isn't one's relationship with the ecological world—and especially one's food—a personal, private matter? Why impose a point of view onto someone else's autonomous life when it comes to these matters? We should resist moral judgment and let everyone make up their own mind.*

It would be surprising to hear this objection from those who, in other contexts, have a profound concern for vulnerable populations. After all, when we err on the side of autonomy and freedom of choice, we ignore the claims (and even the existence) of the vulnerable. If we truly care about protecting and supporting those who our consumer throwaway culture puts at risk, we had better get comfortable with recognizing when certain behaviors have become immoral and often unjust. Especially given the gravity of our ecological concerns, Pope Francis makes no excuse for relativism.[403] As always, we should approach people with mercy, but no one should hesitate to judge as immoral the practices under scrutiny in this chapter when so much is at stake—not only for billions of helpless and voiceless animals, but for nearly the whole human family, including generations yet to come.

> Objection #2: *The CLE claims that it wants to protect and support vulnerable populations by curbing climate change, but once again fails to address overpopulation. There are too many people, and they are destroying the earth by emitting carbon at rates never seen before in human history. The climate crisis is a reproductive crisis.*[404] *The CLE is hamstrung in its ecological concern by its Catholic commitments with respect to contraception and abortion. As a result, it can't meaningfully address the climate crisis.*

This is a widely held view, at least part of which was addressed in chapter 2. Recall what that chapter demonstrated:

- Population rates are going down all over the world, and the United Nations predicts that in two generations the world's total population will actually begin to decline.[405]

- Many of the richest countries in the world are suffering now from lower population rates and even depopulation.

- From ancient Rome to late twentieth century China, human beings have a terrible record in manipulating population rates intentionally.

- Academics and climate activists have been predicting an overpopulation catastrophe for generations, and all of them have been wrong.

In the context of this chapter, it is important to know the countries and people that are responsible for the global climate crisis. The richest 10 percent are responsible for nearly half the world's carbon emissions—while the poorest 50 percent are responsible for about 10 percent of the world's carbon emissions.[406] And in which direction is the population rate for the world's richest countries going? You guessed it: lower. Even the United States, long thought to be an outlier with respect to typical population rates for rich countries, now has the lowest fertility rate in its history.[407] And like other rich countries, our population rate has declined even as our carbon emissions have increased.[408]

Pope Francis has an important—and, perhaps, counter-intuitive—explanation for this phenomenon:

> To blame population growth instead of extreme and selective consumerism on the part of some, is one way of refusing to face the issues. It is an attempt to legitimize the present model of distribution, where a minority believes that it has the right to consume in a way which can never be universalized, since the planet could not even contain the waste products of such consumption.[409]

The problem cannot be primarily one of population growth, for countries with such growth are generally quite poor and contribute the least to climate change.[410] Meanwhile, the countries with the lowest population rates are, nearly without exception, ruled by a consumeristic throwaway culture that leads to lower numbers of children and disproportionately large carbon emissions. Far from being a hindrance to the CLE's ecological concerns, being open and hospitable to new life (regardless of its impact on our self-centered lifestyle) is a significant part of the anti-consumerist culture we must cultivate in order to make the changes necessary to head off the climate crisis.

> Objection #3: *Concern about non-human animals takes attention and energy away from concern for human life. Indeed, this is a broader problem with the CLE. While issues x, y, and z might be important, the pro-life movement shouldn't dilute its focus on abortion (and maybe euthanasia) by giving them sustained attention. Mission creep—especially on an issue like animals—makes us more diffuse and less effective on the issues that really matter.*

I've already responded at the end of chapter 4, claiming that applying our principles consistently makes us not less effective, but more. (Especially with the people we most need to get onboard.) But a different version of the objection goes something like this: "It is one thing to give equal weight to human beings under threat from abortion and human beings under threat from gangs. Maybe we can get on board with that, but we could never get on board with giving the same kind of priority to non-human animals. Yes, we treat them badly, and maybe we should try to treat them better, but it is not the pro-life movement's main concern. We have, as it were, bigger fish to fry." In responding to this objection, we should first agree that human animals are more important than non-human animals, but also note just how close many of them are to us. Great apes use a 500-word vocabulary to express complex ideas, third order reflection, the love they have for their pet, and musings about anticipation of future holidays. Whales and elephants understand death and appear to engage in mourning rituals when someone close to them dies. Pigs are more social and intelligent than dogs and can even play simple video games.

But the majority of non-human animals, though perhaps more sophisticated than we care to know, are significantly lower on the hierarchy of being than are human beings. And we agree that issues which threaten the life of non-human animals are not as morally serious as issues which threaten the lives of human beings. But we focus on the evil of factory farms not only because they kill billions of vulnerable animals, but as the most important contributors to global climate change, they pose a grave threat to human beings. Even someone with no concern for the moral status of non-human animals at all should still refuse to support factory farms on that basis alone.

But what about the very idea of concern for non-human animals? Does it belong in the pro-life movement? Recall that very few active pro-lifers focus on a single issue.

Almost all focus on abortion, and nearly as many focus on euthanasia. A good number focus on human trafficking and the death penalty. Suppose a rare single-issue pro-lifer argued that it is inappropriate to focus on the relatively tiny number of deaths by euthanasia or the death penalty (when compared to the fifty million-plus killed via abortion in the United States since *Roe v. Wade*). Especially because prenatal children are innocent, cannot speak up in their own defense, and are killed without consent, these other issues—while important—don't rise to the level of seriousness of abortion. Surely pro-lifers would agree that abortion is the gravest of life issues, but also note that they can walk and chew gum at the same time. Their concern for life issues is not a zero-sum game. Pro-lifers of various stripes can be called to work on many different issues without weakening their abortion witness.

And again, broadening one's pro-life stance often makes such witness stronger. The well-known pro-life conservative Mary Eberstadt, for instance, wrote an article for *First Things* titled, "Pro-Animal, Pro-Life." In it she links concern for non-human animals with concern for prenatal children and abortion.[411] Though she notes that for decades conservatives have bashed animal activists, Eberstadt says that arguments on behalf of non-human animals are not easily dismissed and can easily be connected to abortion. In a remarkable passage, she suggests that animal activists and pro-lifers "are strangers to one another for reasons of accident rather than essence, and they also, furthermore, have a natural bond in moral intuitionism that should make them allies." No serious person who knows her public anti-abortion witness and activism believes Eberstadt is watering them down by writing this piece, or that she was equating these two issues. Rather, as a serious pro-lifer, following her principles wherever they lead her, she became an even more authentic and powerful pro-life presence.

Conclusion

Mary Eberstadt is not the only Christian thinker to reflect seriously on the moral status of non-human animals. Giants in the Christian tradition like William Wilberforce and C.S. Lewis, for instance, took concern for animals more seriously than you may have realized. And before the modern theological era, which has focused on the human in ways that exclude the non-human, much more serious reflection was given to the question. Rejecting the "it's all about us" view, through the Middle Ages and even in the late nineteenth and early twentieth century manualist tradition, moral theology has taken a more scriptural position on animals. Indeed, the manuals took animals seriously in a way that the humanism of the post-Vatican II era does not. But the lack of contemporary Christian voices on this set of issues is beginning to change. Russell Moore, head of the Ethics and Religious Liberty Commission, has joined other Evangelical leaders in assigning this issue serious moral and spiritual weight.[412] Along with the faith outreach office of the Humane Society of the United States, I've convened a meeting of US bishops to discuss theological and moral matters related to non-human animals. It is one of the hottest topics in academic Christian theology, regardless of political or theological bent. Pro-lifers need to become a more consistent part of this conversation. Not just because we have much to contribute. Not just because it will offer strategic partnerships. But ultimately because this is where consistent application of our principles takes us.

Euthanasia and the Margins of Human Life

Introduction

We didn't touch on euthanasia of non-human animals in the previous chapter but discussing it here may provide a helpful bridge to the current chapter. Generally, it is wrong to kill a non-human animal without a specific need to do so, but it is not *always wrong* to kill such an animal. It is not an exceptionless moral norm. We ought not to use euthanasia to discard non-human animals merely because they are no longer useful or convenient. That is throwaway culture. But at times euthanasia is the best option for a non-person—especially when, say, the animal's intense and irreversible suffering cannot be controlled. By contrast, the CLE claims that it is always wrong to radically reduce the dignity of persons by aiming at their death (which should be distinguished, as we will see below, from removing life support when death is not the aim), and herein lies the distinction. As we will see below, the debate over euthanasia of human beings revolves around what we think human dignity implies.

Much like his predecessors, Pope Francis has strongly criticized euthanasia. Tying it directly to throwaway culture, he claims that it "casts aside the sick, the dying, and those who do not satisfy the perceived requirements of a healthy life."[413] Dismissing "alleged" compassion in favor of killing such populations, Francis argues true compassion "does not marginalize, humiliate or exclude, much less celebrate a patient passing away." He insists we must resist "the triumph of selfishness, of that 'throwaway culture' that rejects and despises people who do not meet certain standards of health, beauty or usefulness." As we will see below, the Holy Father also has a deep concern about the effect of a euthanasia-friendly culture upon our capacity to encounter, welcome, and show true compassion to people with disabilities.

The debates over euthanasia and assisted suicide are closely tied to questions of the moral status of human beings at what I call the "margins of life." In this chapter, I will focus on human beings at "the margins of life" because they have disabilities related to profound brain injuries and diseases—injuries and disease so profound, in fact, that our consumer throwaway culture simply discards them, often as human non-persons. As with other chapters, we will begin by examining current practices about euthanasia and those at the margins of human life, subject those practices to a CLE critique, and then attempt to answer objections.

Brain Injuries and Moral Status

Post-Christian cultures in the developed West generally have difficulty including those with profound disabilities—both in the day-to-day activities of the culture, and in our moral imagination. Our obsession with autonomy, independence, and being a "productive member of society" leaves little room for dependent people who are considered a burden—both to us and (in the view of able-bodied people) to themselves. Our consumerist throwaway culture will even modify fundamental concepts like the definition of death to serve this view. Down through human history a person was considered dead because breathing ceased and the heart stopped beating—but during the last two generations a series of events has led to dramatic changes in that way of thinking:[414]

- The first organ transplants came in the late 1960s. But for a transplant to be successful, most vital organs need to be viable and so must be removed from a body very soon after death. Therefore, the need to obtain such organs to save the lives of desperate and dying patients on long wait lists became closely connected to our definition of death.

- The invention of the ventilator helped many permanently or persistently unconscious patients to continue breathing. Given the shortage of transplant organs, it became tempting to take them from such patients. But a barrier seemed to prevent doing this: removing a vital organ in this way looks a lot like killing the "donor."

- Henry Beecher, chairman of a Harvard University committee that oversaw the ethics of experimentation on human beings, wrote to the dean of his medical school suggesting that "the time has come for further consideration of the definition of death. Every major hospital has patients stacked up waiting for suitable donors."

Beecher formed the Ad Hoc Committee of the Harvard Medical School to Examine the Definition of Brain Death. Its report began this way:

> Our primary purpose is to define irreversible coma as a new criterion for death. There are two reasons why there is a need for a definition: (1) Improvements in resuscitative and supportive measures have led to increased efforts to save those who are desperately injured. Sometimes these efforts have only a partial success so that the result is an individual whose heart continues to beat but whose brain is irreversibly damaged. The burden is great on patients who suffer permanent loss of intellect, on their families, on the hospitals, and on those in need of hospital beds already occupied by these comatose patients. (2) Obsolete criteria for the definition of death can lead to controversy in obtaining organs for transplantation.

Princeton philosopher Peter Singer noted that the committee didn't argue for a new definition of death "because hospitals have a lot of patients in their wards who are really dead, but are being kept attached to respirators because the law does not recognize them as dead." Instead, as Singer highlighted, "with unusual frankness, the committee said that a new definition was needed because irreversibly comatose patients were a great burden, not only on themselves (why to be in an irreversible coma is a burden on the patient, the committee did not say), but also on their families, hospitals, and patients waiting for beds."[415] But even as frank as this might seem, an earlier draft of the report contained even more revealing language. It said, "[T]here is a great need for tissues and organs of, among others, the patient whose cerebrum has been hopelessly destroyed, in order to restore those who are salvageable." Upon seeing this draft, the dean of the medical school insisted that Beecher change this language because "it suggests that you wish to define death in order to make viable organs more readily available to persons requiring transplants."

Let us be clear about the revolution in thinking that these documents reveal. To procure more vital organs for transplant, a whole class of living, profoundly disabled human beings (brain-dead humans can gestate children, fight off disease, respond with an increased heart rate to bodily trauma, maintain homeostasis, and more), previously classified as living, were now deemed to be dead. It was no longer merely being a human creature that mattered but having certain brain functions. This brand-new standard would go on to become the law in all fifty US states, with only New Jersey and New York offering limited religious exceptions (mostly on behalf of Orthodox Jews) for those with a different understanding of death.

And it has become increasingly clear that the new standard logically need not stop with brain death. A 2009

Nature editorial noted that brain death is not a "clear, unambiguous boundary," and argued that "the law should be changed to describe more accurately and honestly the way death is determined in clinical practice." The current law requires that brain death be established, but "what if, as is sometimes the case, blood chemistry suggests that the pituitary gland at the base of the brain is still functioning? That activity has nothing to do with the person being alive in any meaningful sense." Not having a clear boundary means laws could be established that push physicians to be dishonest. Instead of requiring them to declare as dead "someone who will never again be the person he or she was" it would at least be honest to focus instead on the "value of giving a full and healthy life to someone who will die without a transplant."[416]

Understanding death in the slippery terms of brain function has since filtered down to human beings with less serious brain injury or disease. Patients seem to be classified in such medical categories almost haphazardly, but there is now a fairly strong sense that people determined to be in a (broadly defined) "persistent vegetative state" (PVS)—because they will never again be the people they once were—also do not have a moral status equal to that of a "normal" person. Maryland's state legislature has gone so far as to allow removing non-vital organs from PVS patients without their consent, and even discussed removing vital organs.[417] For more than twenty years respected medical ethicists have been arguing that there are strong arguments in favor of taking vital organs from PVS patients.[418] And why should PVS be the boundary? Someone with profound dementia will also "never again be the person he or she once was." Plus, they are no longer autonomous, independent, productive members of society. If our current trajectory continues, it is just a matter of time before human beings with late-stage Alzheimer's disease will also be used and discarded as human non-persons.

Physician-Assisted Suicide

Much of our discussion of euthanasia—often in the form of physician-assisted suicide (PAS)—concerns a patient who everyone agrees is a person like you or me. Arguments in favor of PAS are based on respecting patients' autonomous, free, rational decision to end their lives precisely because of their dignity as persons. Many are sympathetic to end-of-life cases where someone is wracked with unceasing pain, but data from Oregon's public health department on the reasons why people ask for PAS shows that physical pain doesn't even make the top five:[419]

1. loss of autonomy (91.4 percent)

2. decreased ability to engage in enjoyable activities (86.7 percent)

3. loss of dignity (71.4 percent)

4. loss of control of bodily functions (49.5 percent)

5. becoming a burden on others (40 percent).

A study of Canadian practices found something similar. People who requested PAS "tended to be white and relatively affluent and indicated that loss of autonomy was the primary reason for their request. Other common reasons included the wish to avoid burdening others or losing dignity and the intolerability of not being able to enjoy one's life. Few patients cited inadequate control of pain or other symptoms."[420]

It is one thing to read the studies and see the numbers, but it is another to hear the stories. Consider this one, told in the pages of the *New York Times* by a physician (who supports PAS), about her first experience with a request from one of her patients:[421]

> When I walked into his room, he glared at me. "Are you here to help me with this aid-in-dying thing?" he asked. He was in his early 60s, thin and tired, but in no obvious distress. . . . When I asked why he wanted to end his life early, he shrugged. "I'm just sick of living.". . . I probed further and the floodgates opened. He felt abandoned by his sister. She cared only about his Social Security payments, he said, and had gone AWOL now that the checks were being mailed to her house. Their love-hate relationship spanned decades, and they were now on the outs. His despair had given way to rage. "Let's just end this," he said. "I'm fed up with my lousy life." He really didn't care, he added, that his sister opposed his decision. His request appeared to stem from a deep family wound,

not his terminal illness. I felt he wanted to punish his sister, and he had found a way to do it. At our second meeting, with more trust established, he issued a sob, almost a keening. He felt terrified and powerless, he said.

This man met all the requirements (in California, where this took place) for assisted suicide, but unless an inquisitive physician had tried to care for his whole person, he would have killed himself out of anger, fear, and spite; instead he began taking antidepressants and months later died of natural causes.

People of privilege often cite their fear of being a burden on others, not their own deaths, as a reason for supporting PAS. And countries that have allowed euthanasia for many decades, like the Netherlands (a country in which a shocking 25 percent of deaths are induced via PAS or palliative sedation[422]), are coming to terms with the fact that they don't want to limit PAS to when they are dying. In one case, PAS was offered as a means of treating a Dutch victim of sex abuse.[423] In neighboring Belgium, PAS was offered to a woman who was devastated by breaking up with her boyfriend.[424] One might not even have to be physically or mentally ill; the Dutch are now considering to allow PAS for people over seventy-five who have simply decided that their life has come to an end.[425] (Why that would be the age limit, no one has said. Surely a reasonable person could come to the same conclusion even earlier in life.) With stigma for the procedure removed, and emphasis shifted to the autonomous choice of the patient, many in the Netherlands now see no way to stop the slide to PAS for virtually any reason at all.[426]

Yet more, the push for death is so strong that it is no longer required that patients be fully autonomous in deciding to end their life. People with a (largely) non-functioning or profoundly injured brain, even without an advanced directive or designated health care proxy (and thus without their consent), can be killed via euthanasia. The state, hospital, physician, or family member no longer needs to claim that treatment has become so burdensome as to outweigh its medical benefit; they can claim that the patient either is already dead in a legal sense (more on this confusing use of language follows below) or that he or she wouldn't have wanted to live with such a profound disability. Thus, they can decide to allow biological death by removing life-sustaining treatment.

But what about patients who likewise cannot consent but have no such life-sustaining treatment to remove? Six million US Americans currently have Alzheimer's disease, a number expected to jump to fourteen million by 2050.[427] Before the end of their lives, most of these human beings will lose their autonomy and even self-awareness, and thus (at least according to the definition we use in the post-Christian developed West) any sense that they are persons like the rest of us. Many have concluded that the lives of human beings in this state are not worth living.

A good number of those who make such conclusions are physicians. In the Netherlands, some offer euthanasia based on a written declaration made earlier in the patient's life—even when it seems clear that the patient does not meet the country's current requirement of unbearable suffering. Some Dutch euthanasia regulators have resigned in disgust because of the slouch toward a broadly expansive interpretation of what it means for someone with dementia to be "autonomous" in choosing PAS.[428] And Dutch physicians do not limit themselves to sketchy interpretations of written directives; some kill demented patients without consent of any kind. Fortunately, from a CLE perspective, it seems authorities in the Netherlands want to stop at least this practice.[429] Similar practices in Belgium (family members requested and received PAS for a demented patient who never made any such request), however, are not being treated as unlawful.[430] For the moment, US states that have legalized PAS have excluded degenerative diseases like Alzheimer's, but constituencies in Oregon and California are pushing to bring their laws more in line with those in Belgium and the Netherlands.[431]

Another group of human beings are also generally considered incapable of consent to medical procedures—children. For instance, my own children, who are in middle and high school, need parental permission to take even the most common medicines. It should go without saying that children lack the brain development or life experience to make an informed and consensual decision about something as huge and unalterable as PAS. Yet both Belgium and the Netherlands permit assisted suicide for minors. Recently, Belgian physicians even killed children nine and eleven years old. The eleven-year-old had cystic fibrosis—the modern treatment for which, as Charles Lane points out in *The Washington Post*, may "enable many patients to enjoy high quality of life well into their 30s or even beyond. Median life expectancy for new CF cases in the United States is now 43 years."[432]

It is important to mention how discussion has become normalized where PAS has been in effect for many years and among people who are long-time supporters. Such normalization can and does lead to ideas and practices that opponents of PAS find abhorrent. For example, in 2010 an engineer named Julijonas Urbonas designed a "Rollercoaster of Death" as part of a project in graduate school. It exists only as a scale model, but he argued that his proposed invention would allow those who choose assisted suicide to die "humanely with elegance and euphoria."[433] The patient would have a slow, very long climb up to more than 1600 feet, three times the height of the world's tallest coaster today. Once at the top, "there would be time to say a prayer or blow a kiss to relatives (or bail) before pressing the 'fall' button and plummeting into the long steep plunge followed by the first 360-degree loop." According to Urbonas, the speed would make the patient pass out from lack of oxygen, which can sometimes create a sense of euphoria. If the patient doesn't die in the first fall, "six more consecutive loops would finish the job." Urbonas has said it "would be a meaningful death: For the faller, it is a painless, whole-body engaging and ritualized death machine." According to Urbonas, his "ritual adapted to the contemporary world" could help overcome the separation between death and communal life that has opened up in the West.

Whatever one might say about this proposal, it clearly proceeds from the assumption that PAS is completely normal and does not take seriously what it means to have a dignified death in true relationships with others. Urbonas is correct, however, that in the West death has been disconnected from communal life and we need rituals to reconnect us with death and dying. Surely, the slouch toward assisted suicide in the West is caused in great part by isolation from the community and lack of rituals around death and dying.

CLE Response

The CLE begins with a moral prohibition, without exception, against radically reducing the irreducible dignity of innocent human persons by aiming at their death—especially if a person is disabled (including from profound brain injury or disease) or in an otherwise vulnerable situation. This prohibition applies to everyone, of course, but it is particularly important for medical professionals. They have taken an oath to heal and accompany patients yet wield unmatched (sometimes corrupting) power over life and death. Moreover, they generally operate with disproportionately privileged and ableist assumptions. Every so often media stories encourage us to "die like a doctor,"[434] but the attitudes behind such choices are often deeply problematic. Physicians consistently rate their disabled patients' quality of life lower than do patients themselves.[435] The same has been found with disabled or sick adolescents and their families.[436] And when confronted with the fact that patients generally prefer length of life to quality of life, physicians find themselves "surprised" and admit "we think we know what is best for a patient, but this is often wrong."[437]

Such bias is exemplified by the case of Amelia Rivera. Today she is healthy but in 2012, without a renal transplant, she faced death.[438] Amelia's mother wanted to donate a kidney to save her daughter's life, but their doctor at the respected Children's Hospital of Philadelphia (CHOP) did not approve. He considered Amelia a poor candidate for transplant because she was "mentally retarded." Amelia has Wolf-Hirschhorn syndrome, a rare genetic condition that brings with it substantial intellectual disabilities. But the syndrome is not fatal and having the transplant would save her life. Amelia's parents exposed the doctor's recommendation on a website dedicated to people affected by Wolf-Hirschhorn and opposition to the doctor's recommendation went viral. Fifty thousand people signed a Change.org petition and numerous newspaper stories and blog posts criticized the doctor and the hospital. Under such public pressure, CHOP apologized and approved the transplant, and Amelia's life was saved.

Sometimes, however, ableist physicians will attempt to circumvent the decisions of parents by "show coding" or "slow coding" children with profound disabilities, like Trisomy 18.[439] In their defense, critical care medical teams have disproportionately high levels of burnout and PTSD.[440] Being around (and especially participating in) so much trauma and death—as has been discussed throughout this book—changes a person. This is especially true when it comes to the emotional and psychological effects on physicians who participate in PAS, who say they are "profoundly adversely affected" by their experiences.[441] The CLE insists that medical professionals practice health care nonviolently and refuse to make ableist judgments about their patients. A professional commitment to healing is not compatible with caving to a throwaway culture that is ready to discard these vulnerable populations.

The consumerist culture pressures medical professionals to turn their practice from a relationship into a transaction of goods and services, but many are resisting the West's cultural slide into PAS. In the United Kingdom, an overwhelming number of professional medical associations teamed with disability activist groups to defeat assisted suicide.[442] Despite white-hot pushback from activists, as this book goes to press the American Medical Association rightly claims on its website that PAS is "fundamentally incompatible with the physician's role as healer, would be difficult or impossible to control, and would pose serious societal risks. Instead of engaging in assisted suicide, physicians must aggressively respond to the needs of patients at the end of life."[443] The American College of Physicians claims that PAS "fundamentally alters" the patient-physician relationship and the medical profession's role in society. Instead, physicians should focus "on efforts to address suffering and the needs of patients and families, including improving access to effective hospice and palliative care." This recommendation is significant because nations that legalize PAS tend to use hospice at lower rates, and palliative care lower yet.[444]

But we must not romanticize this kind of response. Honoring the dignity of patients at the margins of life is hard—especially because consumerist social pressure tries to reduce everything to an exchange of goods or services.

Under such pressure, it is difficult to witness to the dignity of a patient being claimed by a devastating disease. Indeed, when we hear of the "burden" on patients—especially in the face of the data noted above—we ought to ask first whose burden it is. Misleading language may mask who really has that burden; quite often it is not the person with the illness, but those who are witnesses and supporters. This brings to mind the high percentage of people who request PAS because they are worried about being a burden on others. Such linguistic misdirection, as we have seen throughout this book, is a symptom of a throwaway culture that ever more easily discards vulnerable people. By convincing ourselves that the burden is on the sick, injured, and disabled—rather than on us, the healthy and able-bodied who are made uncomfortable by encountering and supporting them—we feel justified in discarding them. If we convince ourselves that respecting their dignity means helping them die—rather than suffering and bearing their malady with them—we can claim that discarding someone is a sign of our virtue. We've already seen how the term "dead" has been twisted to allow patients with profound brain injury or disease to be used for their organs and then thrown away. In the post-Christian West, it is thought that the capacity to order one's life rationally requires autonomy, yet it is also thought that we are bound to respect the decision of a person who has lost autonomy and so requests PAS.

Such (mis)use of language can feel like gaslighting. Instead of being used consistently and plainly, words are twisted to hide or obscure the dignity of the vulnerable so they can be thrown away. A human being who anyone can recognize as being alive is instead described as obviously dead. The burden on healthy person X is instead described as being on sick or injured person Y. Autonomy is said to be necessary for being a person, but arguments claim that persons who have lost their autonomy ought to have their autonomous requests for PAS respected. Dignity no longer signifies the goodness of each individual person's existence. When pro-PAS activists speak of "death with dignity," it means precisely the opposite. And, of course, it is claimed that assisting in a patient's death is consistent with working toward his or her health.

The CLE helps us avoid the confusion of slippery language that simplifies and facilitates discarding vulnerable people. And the CLE gives first priority to those who cannot speak in their own defense: those who are brain dead, in a PVS, have late stage Alzheimer's disease, and so forth. Vulnerable populations who can speak up on their own behalf need to be listened to. Note that the overwhelming majority of those who request PAS are white.[445] Fifty-three percent of whites support legal PAS but, significantly, only 32 percent of Latinos and 29 percent of African Americans do. The motivation for these views needs to be studied in more detail, but it is likely that the well-placed distrust among US racial minorities for the medical community plays a significant role.[446] Even more significantly, Georgetown professor Patricia King notes that in these medical contexts, racial minorities fear becoming "throwaway people."[447]

Disabled communities have led nearly every successful resistance to PAS and we would do well to hearken to their voices.[448] For instance Jamie Hale, a UK artist and poet, an activist with Not Dead Yet, says the following:

- Society's priority should be to assist us to live, not to die. Provide a free social care system funded by progressive taxation that allows us to be productive, active community members.

- Root out the [dis]ableism that leads two-thirds of people with disabilities to think that we're seen as a burden on society. Only then can you come back to me and tell me that assisted suicide is no risk to disabled people.

- I can envisage no safeguards that would prevent people being pressured into ending their lives, by interpersonal, financial or social means. All I see is a system which divides lives, offering suicide prevention to some, and euthanasia to others . . . Yes, my suffering is sometimes unbearable, but the faith my loved ones have in me makes me able to bear it. Don't take that away, by legitimizing assisted suicide as the right, and gracious choice. [449]

A culture that distinguishes between acceptable and unacceptable reasons for PAS sends the clear message that some people think their lives are so bad they might want to kill themselves. It is difficult to imagine a more pernicious example of throwaway culture: instead of finding a way to accompany vulnerable and marginalized populations, we seek to make it easier for them to kill themselves.

It is not a coincidence that most of those in Oregon who request assisted suicide consider themselves a net burden on the consumer economy. They do not consider themselves autonomous "productive members of society." On the contrary, a consumerist standard has been used to measure their value, at least implicitly, and it was found wanting. It is also no coincidence that, in addition to being ableist, the throwaway culture is ageist. Ageism plays out dramatically at the beginning of life with abortion, but it also plays out with the elderly—a population who comprise the loneliest generation the United States has ever seen.[450] Pope Francis puts it this way:

> When the elderly are tossed aside, when the elderly are isolated and sometimes fade away due to a lack of care, it is an awful sign! ... [W]e throw away the elderly, behind which are attitudes of hidden euthanasia. They aren't needed and what isn't needed gets thrown away. What doesn't produce is discarded."[451]

In *Amoris laetitia*, Francis begins to address this issue by invoking Psalm 71, "Do not cast me off in the time of old age; do not forsake me when my strength is spent," then identifies this with the plea of today's elderly "who fear being forgotten and rejected." He explains that, just "as God asks us to be his means of hearing the cry of the poor, so too he wants us to hear the cry of the elderly."[452]

In a throwaway culture like ours, obsessed with youth and ability, it is reasonable to ask what it would take for disabled and elderly people to make "autonomous" decisions to kill themselves. We've already seen how family members can push a person toward PAS, but an ageist and ableist culture can also creative a coercive feeling of being a burden on society at large—especially in the context of limited health care resources. Unsurprisingly, given the cost associated with profound disability and illness, big institutions like insurance companies and government agencies see recourse to PAS as financially beneficial. For example, when a Nevada physician found that a local hospital would not do a certain treatment, he tried to have his patient transferred to a California or Oregon facility. The insurance company declined to cover the procedure and the transfer, and brazenly inquired whether the patient might consider assisted suicide instead.[453] And as crass as that example is, sometimes the coercion is even more direct, as happened with a chronically ill Canadian patient who had requested his hospital to provide a home medical care plan. When the plan was denied, the patient produced a recording of himself saying that he wants to end his life because of how he was treated by the hospital.[454] The hospital staff's response, which the patient also recorded, was that he "apply to get [your death] assisted, if you want to end your life."[455] Had either of these patients actually undertaken PAS, their decisions could not reasonably be called "autonomous."

Practices like these are woven into the fabric of the throwaway culture's consumerism. People are reduced to mere objects or products, and as with all consumerist processes, some products have more worth than others. Pope Francis laments the growing cultural demand for euthanasia, in which the value of human life lies primarily in its "efficiency and productivity."[456] Exemplifying what Catholic social teaching calls a "social structure of sin," the practice of PAS has a pernicious capacity to change culture. For decades we've known that some suicide leads to more suicide, for instance, and now we know that PAS also leads to more suicide overall.[457] A study in *Southern Medical Journal* found that, controlling for many other factors, legalizing PAS "was associated with a 6.3% increase in total suicides." In Oregon, where PAS has been legal for a generation, the overall suicide rate is more than 40 percent higher than in the rest of the United States.

Supporters of PAS focus on the individual's choice to request it, but a host of social and structural forces shape and even coerce that choice. Once unleashed, these social and structural forces may have unintended consequences. Beyond the examples just presented, it is also well-documented that giving some people the choice to die leads them to believe they have a duty to die. The philosopher John Hardwig argues, for instance, that because the "lives of our loved ones can be seriously compromised by caring for us" and "the part of you that is loved will soon be gone or seriously compromised," many have a moral obligation to use PAS.[458] Unfortunately, the duty to die is not just a topic of discussion in the ivory tower, but is being enforced by physicians—some of whom have even called patients who do not opt for PAS "selfish."[459] In addition, the choice to die can lead to a duty to kill. In Ontario, for instance, Catholic hospitals and individual health care providers are coming under fire for refusing to provide PAS.[460]

So, through the lens of how choices shape a culture at large, what may at first seem like relatively harmless support for individual autonomy may appear quite different. As previous chapters have made clear, the CLE emphasizes that supposedly autonomous individuals cannot make decisions in a moral vacuum. Instead, it reveals and calls attention to the great power of relationships and social context. Autonomy or freedom of choice cannot absolve us of the moral concerns that relationships raise. The CLE insists we can and should create a positive counter-culture of encounter and hospitality, one capable of resisting the consumerist relationships formed by throwaway culture. The CLE calls us to go well beyond mere refusal to participate or otherwise support PAS—it goes to the very heart of how we relate to those who are sick, elderly, and disabled. If we care about the vulnerable being discarded, we must be outraged that anyone could consider PAS their only option.[461] And then that outrage must make us commit to take action.

People formed by a culture of encounter and hospitality will accompany and bear with vulnerable populations at the margins of life. This counter-culture has a moral vision in which, far from a burden, aiding such people is nothing less than the privilege of aiding Christ himself. We must be willing to engage openly and seriously with death and dying—but not by creating deadly rollercoasters. We should create (or, in many contexts, recover) nonviolent practices and rituals that honor each and every person's existential goodness and inherent dignity. In this regard Anna Keating offers cogent and powerful suggestions, and I incorporate some of her examples in the following list:[462]

- Tell stories about good deaths. Do not hesitate to think of and speak openly and thoughtfully about one's own death.

- Return to the practice of being cared for and dying at home. This doesn't make as much money for health care providers and may not maximize the hours or days someone has to live, but it may be the most dignified and relational way to spend one's remaining time on this earth. Plus, again, it can help us reconnect to the witness of a good death.

- If possible, don't drift too far away from one's extended family. A particular job may seem important but being around to aid one's parents and other family as they age, decline, and die may be more important. Mothers and fathers, in particular, should expect to be honored this way and refuse to speak and act as if it is a burden (rather than a privilege) for their children to care for them.

- Resist ableism in all its forms. Bring and welcome disabled children and adults to church and other public activities. Demand that schools (including colleges and universities) and other institutions spend significant resources to make their communities fully inclusive for those who are not able-bodied.

- Support nonviolent medical interventions designed to treat the pain and suffering of patients without killing them, especially traditional and perinatal hospice programs.

- Consider careers and intense service projects at the service of the elderly, mentally ill (especially with dementia), disabled, and terminally ill. Given levels of depopulation in the developed West, we are on the verge of having way more people in need of this care than family members and others capable of caring for them. These who bear the face of Christ deserve better than robot caregivers.[463]

The CLE envisions a culture of genuine encounter and hospitality that resists the fear and denial of death and dying rampant in a culture that embraces PAS. Rather than slouching toward discarding these vulnerable populations, the CLE counter-culture will welcome them in the spirit of genuine encounter and hospitality—prepared to change ourselves and our expectations rather than capitulate to the throwaway culture and put these Christ-bearers at risk.

That said, let us turn to three objections to the CLE approach.

Objections

Objection #1: *Especially when it comes to people who are considered brain dead, or in a persistent vegetative state, isn't it disingenuous for the CLE to lump all these populations together? The elderly person who has been abandoned by his family is a good example of a victim of throwaway culture, to be sure, but how can we compare him to*

> *someone who is brain dead or in PVS? This just
> seems like a bad mistake, and, again, part of the
> CLE's Roman Catholic limitations. It is far from
> violence against a person with a disability; these
> individuals have brains which are so damaged
> that it doesn't make sense to refer to them as living
> persons in the first place. After all, they are only
> being kept "alive"—in some artificial sense—by
> machines.*

This objection is similar to the one made against seeing prenatal human children as vulnerable populations, and the response here will also be similar. Living human beings walking around today are kept alive by machines, including those with an artificial heart. So it can't be said that anyone who is kept alive by a machine doesn't count as a person. We need to go deeper. Is someone with a dead brain by definition non-human? This is an odd claim, not least because a prenatal child before she develops a brain is clearly a living member of our species who seems to share our nature. Someone who is brain dead can do lots of things that all human beings do: gestate children, fight off disease, respond with increased heart rate to bodily trauma, maintain homeostasis, and so forth. Clearly those who are brain dead—though clearly damaged and assisted by technology—are living human beings.

But might they be human non-persons? As we discussed in the abortion chapter, it might demonstrate speciesism to focus simply on the fact that a brain-dead individual is a member of the species *Homo sapiens*. In the chapter on abortion I pointed out my longer version of the argument elsewhere, and the same is true here. If you want to explore the full version, see the second chapter of my *Peter Singer and Christian Ethics*.[464] Many who say brain-dead individuals are not persons do so because these individuals lack certain traits and abilities: to feel pain, move around, engage in relationships, engage in rational thought, express self-awareness, and so forth. But the problem with a "Trait X" approach, as we saw in chapter 4, still looms large here. Picking a trait like pain, motion, and engaging in relationships risks making animals like mice and rats the equal of human persons. But picking traits like rationality or self-awareness risks excluding human beings with dementia. By describing brain-dead human beings as non-persons based on their not being rational and self-aware—at least if we are consistent—we are surely forced to conclude that many millions of demented human beings are non-persons as well.

In this regard, one thinker is consistent—Peter Singer. Among other things, he publicly argues that, considering our health care resource crisis, we should withhold medical treatment from human non-persons who have lost their rationality and self-awareness. Singer is aware this may sound harsh, but he says it is only because our secular culture is still hanging on to an outdated religious point of view about the fundamental equality of all human beings. But then his mother became precisely the human non-person he was talking about. In her late 60s Cora Singer, like many millions of others, developed serious dementia and lost her rationality and self-awareness. Singer is famous for following his stated moral positions consistently (he is, for instance, a very serious vegan and gives away more than 40 percent of his after-tax salary to alleviate global poverty) but in this case he could not do so. Despite a stated ethic to the contrary, he put substantial financial resources into his mother's care. When pressed on this, in a *New Yorker* profile he simply but movingly said, "Perhaps it is more difficult than I thought before, because it is different when it's your mother."[465]

Indeed. Followers of the CLE are not surprised that people like Singer cannot follow a different ethic and instead choose to engage in hospitality when facing their own mother's situation. Our mother does not cease to be our mother when she gets dementia. Or if she is in a persistent vegetative state (PVS). Or if she is brain dead. Those are accidental qualities. She remains the same substance with the same nature. As we saw in the abortion chapter, this is why we talk about people in these situations as having a disease or injury—the disease or injury is frustrating one's ability to fully express who they are (and remain until their cardiovascular death, and their body begins to break down and decay). Vagus nerve stimulation, for example, can mitigate the injury or disease of those in PVS and help them express their conscious self—even after fifteen years.[466] PVS patients were once thought to be wholly unconscious, but studies have now shown that a fairly high percentage are conscious but merely unable to express it.[467] To be sure, using the term "vegetable" might allow us to discard such patients more easily, but there is no good reason to refer to these people with such an offensive term. One of the most important secular medical ethicists of our time, Joe Fins, describes the fight for the dignity of PVS patients as "the civil rights fight of our times."[468]

Far from dismissing brain-dead individuals and those with PVS from the community of persons, those who adopt the CLE will strive to speak up for these marginalized, extremely vulnerable populations who cannot speak for themselves. And in doing so, we can join our Orthodox Jewish brothers and sisters who have refused to abandon these populations and who continue to fight for their rights to treat them as the living human beings they are.[469]

> Objection #2: *The CLE claims to be critiquing the killing of vulnerable populations, but in the overwhelming majority of US cases that's a poor description of what's actually happening. People who are brain dead or in PVS are not killed. Rather, treatment which is burdensome (like a ventilator or feeding tube) is removed. In some rare circumstances direct killing via assisted suicide happens for people with a terminal illness, but many more times burdensome and/or painful life-sustaining treatment (chemotherapy or dialysis) is withdrawn. Furthermore, if we acknowledge that we live in a world with limited resources (medical and otherwise) we then realize that we simply can't give a single patient unlimited access to those resources without being unjust.*

To respond, we first need to define more precisely what it means to reduce the dignity of a person radically by intending their death. Does it necessarily involve direct action? A classic bioethics thought experiment asks us to consider a murderous husband who wanted to kill his wife while she was bathing. He crept into the bathroom with the toaster but, much to his delight, found that she was already drowning in the tub. And so, though he easily could have saved her, instead he gleefully watched her die. Is there any significant moral difference between the omission of watching her die and the action of dropping the toaster in the water? Not from the perspective of Catholic moral theology, which describes euthanasia this way: "an action or an omission which of itself or by intention causes death."[470] If one's intention is to kill, then whether your decision constitutes an act or omission is of no moral difference.

This is different, of course, from removing life-sustaining treatment when one is not aiming at the death of a patient. In the abortion chapter we examined this distinction when we discussed indirect abortion of pregnancy. Direct killing of an innocent child, because it aims at her death, is never permitted. But this is different from an indirect abortion of pregnancy—say, removing a cancerous uterus before the child is viable—which can be done as long as one is not aiming at the child's death and there is a proportionately serious reason for permitting the death. In such a case the parents would be overjoyed if, say, there was a mistake about the age of the child and she ended up living through the procedure. Clearly, they are not aiming at death. Do they have a proportionately serious reason? Catholic teaching allows individuals plenty of leeway for a prudential judgment in this context, but almost everyone would agree that the mother saving her own life (which, again, is permitted—not mandated) would be just such a reason.

Similar reasoning should be done at the margins and end of life. The dignity of the person can never be violated by aiming at their death, but one may—for proportionately serious reasons—stop or refuse treatment in a way that will result in someone's death. Thus, PAS is never permitted, but giving someone a very large dose of medication to control their pain but which also (unintentionally) speeds their death could be morally acceptable. Given the CLE's insistence on supporting and caring for the vulnerable (not just refusing to kill them) in some circumstances it certainly may be morally required to give a patient such high doses of pain medication. For similar reasons chemotherapy could be withdrawn or not started at all. Same with dialysis and a host of other life-sustaining interventions. I've even written in some detail about heartbreaking situations in which a medical system or family may not be able to offer a patient life-sustaining treatment because doing so would unjustly take those resources from someone else.[471] Jesus and the martyrs showed us in no uncertain terms that holiness, while it requires non-violence (both with regard to others and ourselves), does not require us to do everything possible to preserve our lives. At times even holy persons are required to proceed in such a way that they foresee, but do not intend, that death will be the result.

How does this analysis work with regard to brain-dead patients or those in PVS? First, judgments need to be free from ableism. If life-sustaining treatment is stopped because of the disabled individual's quality of life, then the clear intention is death. I like to ask my students to do what I call the "pissed test." Would the moral agent be pissed or frustrated if withdrawing or refusing treatment didn't result in death? If yes, then it is almost certain that the agent was aiming at death and engaging in euthanasia. If on the other hand the agent was just aiming at removing or avoiding burden and/or painful forms of medical treatment, and foresaw but did not intend death, then they would obviously be thrilled if the patient lived. The following two cases may help illustrate the difference:

1. Parents remove a ventilator from a brain-dead child because the child's brain injury has made her life not worth living.

2. Parents stop chemotherapy on their child because it is so painful, and she is likely to die soon anyway.

In (1) we find a clear example of aiming at death by omission. If, for some reason, their child started breathing on her own their intentions would be thwarted. They wanted to end the life of the child by omission. But in (2) we find a clear example where the parents wanted to end not their child's life, but her suffering due to a particular form of treatment. They would be thrilled if the cancer suddenly left her and she continued to live. The decisions made in (1) and (2) may both result in hastening a child's death, but from the perspective of the CLE they are totally different moral acts.

Objection #3: *If an autonomous right to our bodies means anything, it means we can choose to check out of our broken and dying body. Why can't we decide how we will die? How can we judge other people's private and difficult decisions in this regard?*

Many objections we have considered in this book come from the different ways we look at the person. If we take an individualist approach whereby we imagine ourselves cut off from entangling relationships, then this objection could make a great deal of sense. But if we have a more accurate anthropological vision, then it quickly falls apart. Our lives don't belong to us. First, they belong to God. Second, the reality is that most of us are in such tight-knit relationships with others that it is misguided to imagine ourselves making such a decision apart from these relationships. Our lives also belong to our spouse or partner, our parents, our children, our other relatives, our neighbors, our Church community, and more. As we've seen above, our decisions about PAS impact others—and not just those close to us. If we choose it, then it becomes much more likely that someone else will choose it. If we choose it because we have (or fear having) disability X, then those who have disability X feel that much less valued in the culture.

One cannot pretend to decide to pursue PAS in ways that affect only ourselves or our immediate family. Furthermore, as we have also seen above, it is often a stretch to think that the vulnerable people driven to consider PAS are making fully autonomous decisions. Many feel lost, frightened, and abandoned. Many have considerable mental illness. Many don't know where else to turn, and some are even presented with PAS as the only option. "Decisions" made in these contexts are not autonomous. Certainly, PAS often seems attractive to people—as seen in the Oregon study—precisely because they have lost their autonomy and feel like they are out of options. There is a double standard at play here in our culture: at a time when increased efforts are directed toward suicide outreach, psychological treatment, and even public health campaigns for those who are lonely and depressed, we see precisely the opposite impulse when it comes to physician-assisted suicide. Why do we so lament deaths like those of Robin Williams or Anthony Bourdain? Answering that question should lead us to a deep skepticism about physician-assisted suicide.

Conclusion

It is significant that almost all traditional pro-lifers are concerned not only about abortion, but also about euthanasia as pro-life issues. As has been said multiple times, almost no pro-lifers are "single issue" people who care only about life before birth. On the contrary, many spend countless hours advocating and fighting for change on the issues presented in this chapter. And, in so doing, they follow their principles consistently on an issue other than abortion. This methodology, of course, is at the heart of the CLE. But notice also how many principles in play in this chapter—particularly those about protecting and supporting the disabled—tend to lead in directions traditionally perceived (in US American politics at least) as on "the left." Yet another example of the CLE dissolving our incoherent right/left binary.

Another set of issues traditionally considered "on the left" involves suspicion of nuclear weapons, the death penalty, and other state-sponsored violence. Our final chapter turns to these issues.

Chapter Eight

State-Sponsored Violence

Introduction

The first major threat Jesus faced in his postnatal life came from state-sponsored violence. On the Feast of Holy Innocents, the Church recalls Herod the Great's brutal attempt to kill the Christ child by ordering the slaughter of all male children under two years old within the vicinity of Bethlehem (Matthew 2:16-18). It is one thing for the state to permit violence (often in ways, as we saw in previous chapters, that coerce violence), but it is another when the state is the direct agent of violence. This latter category deserves its own chapter, especially because it was a primary concern for the originator of the CLE. Recall that the *New York Times* headline which launched the CLE ("Bernardin Asks Catholics to Fight Both Nuclear Arms and Abortion") highlighted something novel on the US political scene precisely because the Cardinal's proposed ethic connected concern with abortion and concern with state-sponsored violence. As the newspaper described it, Bernardin opened "a broad attack on a cluster of issues related to the 'sanctity of life,' among them nuclear arms, abortion, and capital punishment."[472]

Pope John Paul II also made this connection in *Evangelium vitae*—an encyclical deeply concerned not only with many of the issues mentioned in the previous chapters, but also with war and the death penalty. Pope Benedict XVI called for abolition of capital punishment and denounced the "pointless slaughter" of war.[473] Pope Francis has also spoken out in strong opposition to war and has developed Catholic teaching to the point that the death penalty is now described as "inadmissible."[474] Cardinal Bernardin's particular focus on nuclear weapons in the CLE was consistent with the witness of the broader Church. All the way back in 1948, Pope Pius XII condemned them as the "most horrible weapons the human mind has ever conceived."[475] In 1981, at Hiroshima, John Paul II said "to remember Hiroshima is to abhor nuclear war." In the 2006 World Day of Peace message, Benedict XVI wrote that in a nuclear war, "there would be no victors, only victims."[476] Concerning nuclear weapons Francis said, "The threat of their use as well as their very possession is to be firmly condemned."[477]

There are so many possible examples of state-sponsored violence (especially when the nation-state under scrutiny is the United States) that no single chapter could even mention them all. Many examples—like torture and police violence—will not be discussed below. But as I mentioned in the introduction, others might apply the principles and framework of the CLE laid out in this book to issues I have not been able to include. This chapter will focus on two issues that are classic examples of the CLE and one that is not. We will spend significant time on war (especially the so-called "war on terror" and the proliferation of nuclear weapons) and the death penalty, but also focus on the violence involved in mass incarceration—even with the modest federal reform that was signed into law at the end of December 2018, a blight on the character of the United States, which has the highest rate of incarceration in the world.[478] As always, we will use the CLE to critique these practices and to attempt a response to objections.

One quick note before proceeding, however. Given that by its very nature state-sponsored violence is a question of public policy, I had considered omitting this chapter altogether. By now readers realize that I'm committed to making moral arguments and not proposing specific public policies—the prudential issues of which divide many of us politically in ways that limit the central goal of this book. But, for two reasons, I ultimately decided to include the chapter. First, critiquing state-sponsored violence is absolutely central to the history of the CLE; I could not claim to be working within this tradition without devoting at least a chapter to it. (Certainly, some would have preferred separate chapters on war, nuclear weapons, and mass incarceration.) Second, although previous chapters did not prescribe particular solutions, certain policies came under moral scrutiny. We saw that legal euthanasia causes many vulnerable populations to feel as if their lives are not worth living. We saw that child separation policies at the border (itself a kind of state-sponsored violence—but one which fit better within a chapter on immigration) causes devastation for the kids no longer with their parent(s). We saw that laws make it difficult to come to terms with the violence in factory farms and in abortion clinics. This chapter aims to focus the lens of moral scrutiny on policies of state-sponsored violence and critique them in light of the CLE. Ultimately, however, I will not propose particular policies to replace what we are doing now.

The "War on Terror"

In the mid-1990s, *New York Times* columnist Thomas Freidman argued that as the world becomes profoundly interconnected, especially with more and more mutual foreign investment, we would see dramatically less war.[479] This has not been true for the United States, currently engaged in the longest war in its history. The disastrous "war on terror" began more than seventeen years ago, and there is no end in sight. By the end of fiscal year 2019, the United States will have spent nearly six trillion dollars on this conflict, causing between 480,000 and 507,000 deaths in Afghanistan, Pakistan, and Iraq.[480] This doesn't include the hundreds of thousands of deaths from the war in Syria, a conflict that the United States fostered directly by supporting a rebel and jihadi uprising—and indirectly by unwittingly allowing the emergence of ISIS, a group formed in opposition to our occupation of Iraq.

A great number of those directly killed have been civilians, though we do not know the full total because the numbers of civilian deaths from the US military are notoriously inaccurate.[481] (And those who die indirectly— say, from health conditions caused by the war, hardships due to travel as a refugee, and so forth—are not included.) Furthermore, the reports after US air strikes often do not distinguish between combatant and non-combatant deaths.[482] Later we will examine in more detail the CLE's concern about the effect on soldiers of extended fighting in war, but here we will consider one story, of decorated medic and Navy SEAL Edward Gallagher.[483] Considered special even by the very high standards of his cohort, Gallagher was broken and reshaped by the violence he saw and performed when fighting ISIS militants in Iraq. As I write these words, he is in a naval brig waiting to face charges that during his eighth deployment he "shot indiscriminately at civilians, killed a helpless teenage Islamic State fighter with a hand-made custom blade, and then performed his re-enlistment ceremony posing with that teenager's bloody corpse in front of an American flag." Prosecutors offered testimony from colleagues in his platoon that he "fired into civilian crowds, gunned down a girl walking along a riverbank and an old man carrying a water jug, and threatened to kill fellow SEALs if they reported his actions."

Navy prosecutors described Gallagher's actions as "propaganda manna from heaven" for ISIS—a group, once thought defeated, that always seems to be resurgent in Iraq.[484] A detailed report from the independent Center for Strategic and International Studies states that the outcome of the "war on terror" is opposite to its intended goal, and that "nearly four times the number of Sunni Islamic militants" exist today than there were on September 11, 2001. Though the report insists that "Americans should understand that terrorism won't end," we continue to behave as if we can make that happen. Even after seventeen years, our government seems intent on continuing action that makes the problem only worse. In 2018 the US military dropped a record number of bombs on Afghanistan[485] without seeming to have any impact upon the ideology that leads our perceived enemies to plan their attacks.

Proxy Wars, Arms Sales, and Drone Strikes

Chapter 5 presented some disturbing details about US participation in the war in Yemen. To oppose the forces in that country backed by Iran and Al Qaeda, we wage a proxy war by aiding Saudi Arabia and the UAE in their direct action against the rebels. In part because of the disastrous Iraq war, the United States now (rightly) has little stomach for any more of its soldiers getting killed. That reluctance, as well as the difficulty in getting Congressional approval for new wars, makes our intervention in Yemen the model for how we currently wage war. According to the Center for Strategic and International Studies, the United States has provided aerial targeting assistance, intelligence sharing, and mid-flight aerial refueling for Saudi and UAE aircraft.[486] We also continue to sell weapons—including hundreds of millions of dollars' worth of precision-guided bombs—to the same Saudi leadership that ordered the "bone-saw execution" of a US-based journalist who criticized their regime.[487]

Chapter 5 mentioned that US precision bombs, which cause devastating damage, have been used even on a schoolhouse. The children killed in that blast comprised just a fraction of the tens of thousands of innocent people who have died (many by starvation[488]) in a war enabled by the United States. Others have been killed by drone strikes, a major part of US "warfighting" strategy over the better part of two decades. Drone strikes have been used in Yemen since at least 2002.[489] President Obama ratcheted US drone strikes up to unprecedented levels—so much so that ABC News described him as going from being a Nobel Peace Prize winner to "Drone Warrior in Chief."[490] President Trump has gone even further than Obama in using drones—including giving the CIA broad permission to use them. Often these strikes occur in countries where the United States is not at war. For instance, in 2017 over thirty-five took place in Somalia—two and a half times Obama's fourteen in 2016, eclipsing the thirty-three in that country during Obama's eight years as president.[491] And the current administration and military leadership are even less transparent about the number of civilians killed in these strikes.

Nuclear Weapon Proliferation

Those who grew up during the Cold War probably don't feel the threat of nuclear weapons today as acutely as they did then. And to a certain extent that reduced sense of threat is justified, especially given that an enemy superpower isn't currently aiming thousands of nuclear weapons at the US homeland. But given the possibility of nuclear weapon proliferation to unstable states and non-state actors, the threat might be even more dangerous—especially from rogue nations that mean to harm the United States. An international Non-Proliferation of Nuclear Weapons Treaty exists, but non-state actors and several countries are not signatories. One is North Korea, which now has built missiles that can carry its nuclear weapons to the US Pacific Coast, and perhaps even farther, to Chicago.[492] As this book goes to press, despite the Trump administration's efforts at negotiation, North Korea appears to be ramping up its nuclear weapons technology.

Some studies of the geopolitical landscape suggest that, as bad as the threat is from North Korea, the one from Pakistan is worse. An often unstable country that has had nuclear weapons for three decades, by 2020 Pakistan may have 200 nuclear warheads.[493] A decade ago the Obama administration was deeply concerned that the country was not stable enough to keep such weapons out of the hands of terrorists, and back then the relationship between the United States and the Pakistani government was more or less positive.[494] Today that relationship has unraveled to the point that President Trump has stopped $300 million in aid promised to that country. This deteriorating situation raises enormous concern because the country appears to have become even more friendly to terrorist organizations and other non-state actors.[495]

Other countries remain threats, though perhaps not so immediate. The Obama administration joined a coalition to try buying the United States (along with the rest of the world) a decade-long pause in Iran's likely march toward nuclear weapons, but the Trump administration has undone that agreement. Will Iran now resume what many intelligence agencies believe is its goal of having nuclear weapons? No one knows for sure, but a nuclear-armed Iran causes deep concern—especially for Israel, a country Iran is determined to wipe off the map. China, the United States' most significant long-term geopolitical competitor, is ramping up its attempt to compete with the United States and Russia when it comes to nuclear weapons. Russia has also been increasing its nuclear capacity in recent years, and the Trump administration responded by cancelling a thirty-year bilateral treaty.

According to former Soviet President Mikhail Gorbachev, the United States has "taken the initiative in destroying the entire system of international treaties and accords that served as the underlying foundation for peace and security following World War II."[496] Rather than continuing to reduce its nuclear weapons, the United States now seeks to build up a modernized arsenal with which it can fight and "win" a nuclear war with Russia or China or both of these powers—though doing so requires almost unsustainable spending.[497] This should sound familiar. The Cold War forced the former Soviet Union to overspend vastly on its military, even though the huge cost weakened the rest of its economy. The United States faces the same fear because of its own inflated debt (due to the cost of a decades-long "war on terror"), future unfunded entitlements, and a new, low-key nuclear arms race with China and Russia.[498]

The Death Penalty and Mass Incarceration

The United States is unique in many ways, including our justice system. Our lawyers and judges laud the right to a speedy jury trial, the presumption of innocence, and state-supported legal counsel for poor defendants. Less often, however, do they speak about our world-leading rate of incarceration. And they avoid mentioning that, although more than 170 countries have abolished the death penalty, we and a handful of other countries (Iran, China, and Saudi Arabia) retain it. Some of the following facts may be familiar, but it is worth reminding ourselves of US death penalty practices:

- Of those who are given the death penalty, 76 percent of the time their victim is white.[499]

- Someone who kills a "high status" person is six times more likely to get the death penalty than someone who kills a "low status" person.[500]

- Although 13 percent of the population is African American, they comprise 42 percent of those on death row.[501]

- The executed are almost all economically vulnerable; those who can afford their own legal counsel almost always avoid capital punishment and are often acquitted.[502]

- Sometimes executed prisoners have very low IQ and by many reasonable measures are intellectually disabled.[503]

- In part due to the cost of legal safeguards built into the process, executing a convicted criminal actually costs more than keeping him or her in prison for life.[504]

- Hundreds of people convicted of capital crimes later have been exonerated through DNA evidence—61 percent were African-American and 70 percent involved witness misidentification.[505]

For example, given how many death row inmates in Illinois were being exonerated via DNA evidence, in 2003 Governor George Ryan decided to commute all the death sentences in his state, keeping 167 inmates from execution. Observing that the judicial process was "haunted by the demon of error," he must have come to the reasonable but deeply troubling conclusion that before DNA tests became available it is likely that Illinois had executed innocent people.

In 2011 Illinois joined nineteen other states in banning the death penalty, but recently it has begun a resurgence. Fifty-four percent of US Americans now support it, up from 49 percent in 2016.[506] In the 2016 elections strong majorities in both Nebraska (61 percent) and Oklahoma (66 percent) undid their bans on capital punishment. Even liberal California saw a ballot measure to repeal its death penalty, but it failed.[507] Ohio reinstated the death penalty in 2017. Although capital punishment has public support, there is no way to—as *The New Republic* puts it—"set [it] apart from the heinous crimes it is used to punish." Even with our supposedly sophisticated technology, too often executions are quite cruel. Consider the recent killing of Kenneth Williams, who was "coughing, convulsing, lurching, [and] jerking"[508] during his execution by lethal injection. Some death row inmates are now choosing the electric chair because of their fears over lethal injection, even when it goes "right."[509]

That is a remarkable choice, especially because some executions by electric chair have resulted in the inmate catching fire, filling the chamber with smoke and the stench of burning flesh. Before that, gas was a preferred method, but more than 5 percent of those cases "were botched when the gas did not produce rapid loss of consciousness and witnesses watched as the condemned suffered an agonizingly slow asphyxiation." That was preceded by the firing squad; "in one of its first uses, the condemned stiffened up in the chair in which he had been placed, which caused the bullets to miss his heart. He died 27 minutes later, having bled to death." Even so, some death row inmates (particularly in Utah) see death by firing squad as their least bad option.[510]

Given that we continue to allow executions despite their innate cruelty, it may come as little surprise that the United States also has the highest incarceration rate in the world.[511] It fits our nation's throwaway culture. Those countries with the next-highest rates are Rwanda and Russia, respectively. A shocking 2.2 million people are incarcerated in the United States, a 500 percent increase over the last 40 years. Gender and race are important predictors of who is most likely to end up in jail or prison. Here are the relative chances for those born in 2001:

- all men: 1 in 9

- White men: 1 in 17

- Black men: 1 in 3

- Latino men: 1 in 6

- all women: 1 in 56

- White women: 1 in 111

- Black women: 1 in 18

- Latina women: 1 in 45.

This trend reflects the "tough on crime" approach of the "war on drugs" in the early 1980s. Whites and blacks use illegal drugs at similar rates, but the imprisonment rate of blacks for drug use is six times that of whites.[512] The high number of incarcerated people who are addicted to drugs could be helped much more with rehabilitation than incarceration.[513] Huge numbers of prisoners have psychological problems—such that our prisons now serve essentially as warehouses for the mentally ill. It is a fact that US prisons and jails house ten times more mentally ill people than do state psychiatric hospitals.[514] Many of these inmates could be more accurately described as victims of disease, not willful perpetrators of crime.

Furthermore, many of those who are incarcerated have never been convicted of a crime. Almost two-thirds of those in local jails are there because they cannot afford bail.[515] Because they are poor, they just sit, unable to work or provide for their families. Or they are exploited by bond-lending agents who earn more than $2 billion annually off those who otherwise would be in jail. Both options often contribute to the spiral of debt that hurts the poor disproportionately and makes future crime more likely. And as with capital cases, those with money can avoid jail time while waiting for their court date, and often avoid jail time altogether.

What is incarceration like? *America* magazine recently reviewed *Refuge in Hell* by a prison chaplain, Rev. Ronald Lemmert. He writes, "Perhaps nowhere in our contemporary culture in the United States is the contrast between Christian love and hellish indifference more stark than in our prison system."[516] He describes prison as "the closest thing to hell on earth." (Though things were even worse for those held at a Brooklyn dentition center, where in late January 2019, 1,600 inmates, were forced to endure temperatures as low as two degrees Fahrenheit for nearly a week.[517]) Moreover, part of the hellish nature of prison comes from the way prison workers are discouraged from helping inmates flourish. The prison is a business, Lemmert says, "that makes money by turning out a bad product." Prison workers "deliberately go out of their way to make sure that most of the prisoners they release will come back to prison."[518] In other words, prisons have a perverse financial incentive to turn out people who will end up back behind bars.

The Agents of State-Sponsored Violence

The CLE's concern about violence can be applied in this chapter more clearly than in any other. Unlike the topics of other chapters, almost no one questions whether warfare, nuclear weapons, the death penalty, and incarceration are forms of violence. The question is whether these forms of violence are justified. Incarceration, perhaps, is different from the others, but we should remember the act of incarceration relies on explicit force or the threat of force. Sometimes people are dragged out of their homes in the middle of the night and forced into a police car and then into a jail cell. Some are forcibly led down death row. And the source of this violence, as well as the institution that supports it, is the state.

Agents of the state are affected profoundly by the violence they witness and inflict. The public has heard of PTSD among soldiers, but prison workers have rates similar to or higher than those among the troops coming home from Iraq and Afghanistan.[519] Women, African-Americans, and those who have worked in prisons over ten years are most at risk. Almost all have witnessed beatings or sexual assault. Many have witnessed an inmate's death. They live with near-constant stress, always on alert for battle. Ninety-five percent of their job is mundane, but they can never anticipate when the unexpected and violent 5 percent will come. As one officer put it, on any given night he could be "dealing with inmate violence, coming home with faeces smeared all over [my] uniform, trying to stop suicide attempts." It is no wonder that the suicide rate among corrections officers is twice that of police officers.[520]

Ron McAndrew, now a death penalty abolitionist, had been a prison warden who supervised executions. They haunted him. "I started to have some horrible nightmares. It was the faces of the men that I executed. I woke up and saw them literally sitting on the edge of my bed."[521] John Hurlbut started out as the prison electrician before performing 140 executions via electric chair. Over that time he was "emotionally, slowly deteriorating," but his wife was chronically ill and he felt that he had no choice but to continue in the job.[522] One day, before three back-to-back executions, Hurlbut collapsed and was taken to the prison hospital. One year later he quit (after getting "tired of killing people"), but the damage was done: haunted and broken, he committed suicide only three years later. Today, when states like Ohio bring back the death penalty, the family members of former executioners take to the pages of their local newspapers, warning what this will do to the corrections officers who have to perform state-sponsored violence.[523] Given the debilitating effect of violence on those who inflict it, it is clear why the American Medical Association forbids physicians from participating in legally authorized executions.[524]

As mentioned above, what soldiers do and witness in war makes them suffer terribly. The experience leaves many of them broken. Each day twenty US American veterans of war kill themselves; more soldiers have died by suicide than have been directly killed in the entire Middle-Eastern conflict.[525] My maternal grandfather, who fought in WWI in France, regularly told my mother "war is hell." During the last two decades the reality of that hell has come home to the United States, even though we've tried to use technology to keep us at a distance from the flames. The very nature of drone technology, one might think, could do this—but it turns out that even being separated from the actual violence by thousands of miles cannot spare its agent from substantial damage. After years of killing via drone, twenty-nine-year-old Christopher Aaron had a nervous breakdown. Even after getting his symptoms under control, his days were filled with a fog of gloom. According to the *New York Times,*

> [H]e dreamed that he could see — up close, in real time — innocent people being maimed and killed, their bodies dismembered, their faces contorted in agony. In one recurring dream, he was forced to sit in a chair and watch the violence. If he tried to avert his gaze, his head would be jerked back into place, so that he had to continue looking.[526]

Interviews with 141 military personnel involved in remote violence reveal that they did not feel a sense of detachment from the violence. Instead, more than 75 percent "reported feeling grief, remorse, and sadness" and "disruptive emotions" for a month or more after their kills. Drone operators—given their regular exposure to graphic violence on a large scale in high definition—may be at even more risk than traditional soldiers.

Dehumanizing the Objects of State-Sponsored Violence

Their training teaches soldiers how to dehumanize the enemy. It does not come about by accident; they are shaped into ruthless and efficient killers. Ex-Marine Sergeant Michaiah David Dutt put it this way: "Before we could become effective killers, we had to die to ourselves . . . [we] had to become murderers."[527] He recounts the marching songs Marines sing during training:

> A drill instructor (DI) leads the cadence (chant). The platoon responds in unison with KILL. We chant KILL every time our left foot strikes the pavement.
>
> DI: I went to the church house where all the people pray. . .
>
> "KILL"
>
> DI: I pulled out my rifle and blew them all away. . .
>
> "KILL"
>
> DI: I went to the schoolhouse where all the kiddies learn. . .
>
> "KILL"
>
> DI: I tossed in a grenade and watched those f*ckers burn. . .
>
> "KILL"

DI: I went to the market where all the people shop. . .

"KILL"

DI: I pulled out my Ka-Bar and then began to chop. . .

"KILL"

Human beings do not naturally blast people into bullet-riddled pulp as they worship, watch children burn after tossing grenades into a school, or cut helpless shoppers into pieces with a large knife. Their training as killers requires that they themselves be dehumanized. As the CLE warns, those who are dehumanized use language that dehumanizes their victims. Dutt recalls another training exercise before being deployed to Iraq:

> "I'm gonna get me a f*cking dune coon!" our sergeant bellows. "I can't wait to put those ragheads in the dirt!" "Those filthy f*ckers want a war? We're going to bring it to them!"

> Racial epithets are common now. Everywhere I go marines are talking about killing hajis, dune coons, sand [n-word]s, ragheads.

Dehumanizing prisoners of war, as the graphic and disturbing pictures of inmates at Abu Ghraib made us see, is also something with which Dutt became familiar:

As a sergeant I should stop this abuse. Instead, I laugh and participate. Only later in reflection do I consider that he could just be some old guy who was rounded up and blamed for something he didn't do. That thought haunts me to this day. Lord Jesus Christ, Son of God, have mercy on me, a sinner. How I wish I could throw myself at the feet of this man and beg his forgiveness. I know what it's like to surrender my soul to darkness and to enjoy the abuse of human beings. Even now while writing I am reduced to tears. God forgive me.

Such dehumanization (as we saw above) allows soldiers to kill so many civilians. Despite the innocent being the most vulnerable—again, a center of concern for the CLE—the hellish logic of war turns them into objects that can be discarded. Often the victims are children. Even if fortunate enough to avoid death, children of war suffer from a malady that the Syrian-American medical society calls "human devastation syndrome."[528]

Those given the death penalty are also described with dehumanizing language. They are called "monsters," "less than human," are compared to animals taken to slaughter. Similar things are said of the incarcerated, as Rehumanize International points out.[529] Their welfare is not important, for they are reduced to objects that can be discarded without much thought. Of course, many given the death penalty are also members of vulnerable groups. Most are poor and could not pay bail or afford adequate representation

They are often people of color and victims of explicit and structural racism. Many have a mental illness and/or are addicted to drugs or alcohol. Some are innocent but lack the resources to prove it.

Consumerism

Many rich people make lots of money from war. Sometimes war buoys entire economies. The United States, for instance, became a twentieth-century economic powerhouse by destroying its competitors' economies in the course of winning World War II. Back in 1961 President Dwight D. Eisenhower, who had commanded all Allied forces during WWII, warned the country about the danger of our country's appetite for weapons, machines, and institutions of war, but we have not heeded his warning. Today, the US military-industrial complex is vast and secretive, much of it operating without democratic oversight or control. Based on what appears to be on the books, at least, US military spending equals that of the next ten countries combined. When we choose to fight an elective war, such as the one in Iraq, we somehow manage to find the money even if it means going deeper into an already monstrous debt. Beyond what we spend on our own military, our arms sales to other countries are so important that the current administration, as noted above, refuses to curb them even to countries with egregious human rights violations. Few investments are safer than those made in US companies that manufacture weapons of war.

Pope Francis has pointed out that powerful people benefit financially from war and thus do not seek peace. "It's the industry of death, the greed that harms us all, the desire to have more money." The system "revolves around money and not around the person, men and women, but money—so much is sacrificed and war is waged in order to defend the money."[530] And as other chapters have demonstrated, the violence of consumerism reduces people to objects that can be used then discarded. Whether the victims are Syrian or Yemeni children or soldiers with PTSD or other mental illness, war has "collateral damage" built into its very nature. We are told to expect these things because that's what war requires. "We're at war," after all, so what do you expect?

The prison industrial complex also reveals the violence of consumerism, especially with the advent of private prisons. The *Huffington Post* notes that "imprisoning Americans in private prisons run by mega-corporations has turned into a cash cow for big business."[531] As states try to save money by outsourcing incarceration to the private sector, the logic of the market has taken over. We've already seen two examples of this—private lending companies profiting from inmates who cannot afford bail and the perverse incentive within the penal system to ensure that released inmates end up returning. "And this is where it gets creepy," said Joe Weisenthal, a reporter for *Business Insider*, "because as an investor you're pulling for scenarios where more people are put in jail."[532] Eric Schlosser describes the prison industrial complex as "a set of bureaucratic, political, and economic interests that encourage increased spending on imprisonment, regardless of the actual need."[533] In fact the prison industrial complex is cultivating exploited labor—a type of modern day slavery. (Disturbingly, many more African-American men are now in US jails and prisons than were enslaved in 1850.[534]) In North Carolina, for instance, inmates are paid between sixteen and twenty-six cents per hour for their labor—a windfall for big businesses who exploit them via lucrative prison labor contracts.[535] Much like the consumerism beneath the reality of war, the consumerism of the prison industrial complex dehumanizes people, making them objects to be used for profit. Jonathan Kay writes that this is essentially a "human-warehousing operation that combines the worst qualities of government (its power to coerce) and private enterprise (greed)."[536]

Nuclear Weapons and Throwaway Culture

The only country ever to use nuclear weapons in war, of course, is the United States. Faced with a dilemma toward the end of World War II, President Truman decided to try forcing Japan's unconditional surrender by killing tens of thousands of innocent people (including very young children and elderly who were not contributing to the Japanese war effort) with nuclear bombs. Many hailed Truman for saving many millions of Japanese and US lives that would have been lost in an invasion. The University of Oxford even proposed to give him an honorary degree. In response, however, the well-known Catholic philosopher at Oxford, Elizabeth Anscombe, gave a stirring dissent.[537] She noted that in war one can never use the intended death of the innocent as a means to some other (even good) end. Innocent elderly and young people are not mere things to be used and discarded. In fact, she described the use of atomic weapons as a "covenant with death." Attending the bestowal of the honorary degree, she argued, would in a sense be cooperation with the murder of the innocent. She said she would not go "in case God's patience suddenly ends."

The CLE's first principle, as we have seen, forbids intentionally killing the innocent in any circumstance. We are not utilitarians, adding up the costs of life like accountants, as if their values can be compared with each other like goods or products. It is difficult to think of a single act more at odds with the CLE than using a nuclear weapon on innocent people. Catholic moral theology forbids even the intention to use such weapons against the innocent—even as a deterrent. It is also problematic for military leadership, even if it never intends to use such weapons, to compromise a soldier's integrity by expecting him to form the grossly immoral intention to use missiles or bombs to kill hundreds of thousands of people if so ordered. Any "peace" made possible by a willingness to slaughter the innocent is no peace at all—and mocks the Prince of Peace to whom Christians owe our ultimate allegiance.

The Commands of Christ

It should go without saying (but often does not), that the flourishing and survival of the United States is not a Christian's primary value. When the perceived need for state-sponsored violence and the life and commands of

Jesus do not agree, Christians have a duty to avoid the idolatry of the state by imitating the life and following the commands of the Son of God. We are to turn the other cheek. Refuse to live by the sword. Pray for one's persecutors and love one's enemies. Visit those in prison. These commands, which many in secular culture consider foolishness, are fundamental parts of the Gospel and at the heart of Christian faith.

The CLE, which takes Jesus' commands on these issues seriously, shows how a broader culture of mercy and encounter is built up by specific actions, like loving one's enemies and visiting those in prison. In many contexts the encounter with one's enemy creates conditions for the possibility of loving them. Dutt, for instance, recalled the post-war encounter between himself, a homeless veteran, and a homeless Iraqi man near St. Francis of Assisi Catholic Church on Portland's inner east side. The Iraqi, he learned, was from Ramadi, where the US military had acted with particular violence.[538] The man also revealed (through tears) that his wife and two sons were killed in US bombing runs. Dutt, the former US Marine sergeant, recalled his reaction:

> My heart sinks and my eyes begin to water. I ask for his forgiveness and begin to weep. He opens his arms and we embrace in a strong hug. Two homeless men broken by war weeping in a park. I a homeless veteran. He a homeless refugee in the land that murdered his family. We cry for minutes that seem like hours. Rain pouring over our broken bodies in the garden of Francis of Assisi.

Jesus' command to visit those in prison is also about encounter. Prisons maximize the chances inmates will return after being released by being factories of violence, fear, and hate. A culture of encounter that leads to seeing prisoners as human beings, worthy of attention and love, resists the objectifying throwaway culture that shapes our prisons and those in them.

Of course, creating such a culture requires Christians to take Jesus seriously and go to the peripheries (including the prisons) where, as Matthew chapter 25 reports his commands, we will visit (and definitely not kill) *him*. And we may be required not just to visit; we may be called to offer our skills in service of these Christ-bearers. Health care volunteers (especially in palliative and mental health) are especially welcome. One can join any number of prison ministries, and even become a mentor to an inmate.[539] Georgetown University runs a particularly impressive new program that educates inmates and helps them re-enter the outside culture. The CLE would find it worthy of support and even replication.[540] Don't have a prison ministry in your area? Think about working with your church's leadership in creating one from scratch.[541] Though encountering the most vulnerable on the peripheries carries some risk, the CLE insists we could make a significant difference (and even change a life[542]) merely by writing a prisoner. You can also donate your resources to many organizations that aid those charged with a crime as well as prisoners—like the Equal Justice Initiative or The Bail Project. You can even do your part to provide support for the children of incarcerated parents.[543]

There are similar options to serve veterans who have been damaged by the violence they've witnessed and perpetuated. The medical institutions designed to aid them, like VA hospitals, welcome volunteer help and donations.[544] You can work with organizations (such as Catholic Worker houses of hospitality) that house and feed homeless veterans, many of whom are mentally ill and addicted to alcohol or other drugs. The National Alliance for the Mentally Ill offers resources for those who want to help veterans in such situations.[545]

Christians who live out the CLE place their primary and ultimate loyalty in the commands of Christ, not in the state. Just war theory is an important part of the Christian tradition. Although the CLE does not require pacifism, we ought not excuse state-sponsored violence that puts the survival and flourishing of the state ahead of being faithful Christians. Some find Christian values reflected in the "Pax Americana," as it is sometimes described, but no Christian should support a false peace that flouts CLE principles. Instead of countenancing the US flag in Catholic church sanctuaries, uncritically praising our troops' success overseas, or putting "tough on crime" policies ahead of seeing Christ when we look into prisoners' faces, we must critique the secular state's violent practices through moral principles based upon the true source of our ultimate concern—Our Lord, the Son of God, the Prince of Peace.

Objections

> Objection #1: *While Christians should witness to the peaceable Kingdom of God as much as possible, we do not live in the fullness of that Kingdom just yet. It is unfortunate that violence sometimes is necessary, especially when protecting the vulnerable populations the CLE claims it wants to protect. Indeed, Jesus seems to say little or nothing about using deadly violence to protect the least among us. For this reason, Just War Theory, an important part of the Church's tradition, should be given its due as a counterweight to the concerns just presented.*

The CLE is not pacifist. In a sinful, fallen world deadly violence is sometimes necessary—such as when abortion is used to protect the life of the mother. But especially given our sinful proclivity to use violence far more often, we must take violent action only if we are sure the other requirements of the CLE are being fulfilled. There is a strong presumption against using violence, especially deadly violence, which must be the absolute last resort. When possible, and perhaps even sometimes when some believe it is not possible, our first impulse should be to show mercy. We should make every genuine effort to encounter (and even show hospitality to) our enemies before using deadly violence against them. Even if we must kill them—as St. Augustine reminds us—we are still bound by Christ's command to love them.

We should hold no illusions about what this means. If Christians follow the CLE, it may well make us (and perhaps our country) less safe. No one should be naïve about what it means to follow the nonviolent example and commands of Jesus: there may be times when we foresee (but do not intend) that a nonviolent approach will result in our death. As with other issues considered in this book, following the CLE is not always safe, and we should refuse to make an idol out of our own safety—and even out of concern for our own survival. There may be extremely rare times, however, when deadly violence indeed is our last resort to protect the most vulnerable among us.

However, it is difficult to see how any of this is consistent with stockpiling and using nuclear weapons. The bombings of Hiroshima and Nagasaki, in addition to targeting the innocent and using them as a means to an end, were not the last resort. The unconditional surrender of Japan was not an absolute moral requirement. And even if one thinks that it was, there is significant historical evidence that Russia's declaration of war on Japan had more to do with their surrender than our intentional mass slaughter of their innocent—a slaughter that, according to the Imperial High Command, was not much different from the fire-bombing the United States was already doing in other parts of the country.[546] (There is strong evidence, moreover, that the United States dropped nuclear bombs to deter the development of what would become the Soviet Union.[547]) It is not clear how using today's nuclear weapons—far more powerful than the ones used against Japan—could be consistent with the CLE and Just War Theory. Even if killing the innocent is not intended, Just War Theory requires the resulting deaths to be "proportionate." While Catholic moral theologians disagree about what "proportionate" means (including what, precisely, needs to be in proportion and how to measure it), it is well-nigh impossible to imagine a scenario when a mass slaughter of the innocent can be proportionate with the goals of any faithful follower of Christ.

> Objection #2: *The Church has a long history of accepting and even using the death penalty. Pope John Paul II explicitly justified its use (at least in principle) by public authorities defending society. The CLE prohibition of the death penalty—especially as articulated by Pope Francis's recent change in the Catechism's wording—seems to contradict this long tradition.*

Responses to this objection should begin by admitting that over time the Church's teaching on the death penalty has developed. The traditional Catholic philosopher John Finnis, for instance, strives to show just this—and even compares the development of this teaching to those concerning slavery and religious liberty.[548] He convincingly shows that, beginning with Pope Pius XII, a gradual shift has come about that to the present day continues to be clarified.

One central clarification in particular—made necessary by the popularity of weak arguments by Thomas

Aquinas (and even Pius XII in one lecture[549])—is articulated by Pope Francis in a new teaching which claims that "the dignity of the person is not lost even after the commission of very serious crimes."[550] Pius, at least at one point, apparently thought that a criminal who committed a capital crime forfeited the right to life, and so the state could not be responsible for violating such a right. Thomas Aquinas had gone further, claiming that such criminals had lost their dignity because they were like brute beasts, a position that Christopher Tollefsen strongly rebuts.[551] It might also be argued that retributive justice requires the death penalty as a just and proportionate response to truly awful crimes. But David Bentley Hart has the proper critique of such positions:

> The whole of the Sermon on the Mount . . . is a shocking subversion of the entire idea. Christ repeatedly and explicitly forbids the application of such punishment, even when (as in the case of the adulterous woman) this means contradicting the explicit commands of the Law of Moses regarding public order and divinely ordained retribution. According to Paul, all who sin stand under a just sentence of death, but that sentence has been rescinded purely out of the unmerited grace of divine mercy. This is because the full wrath of the Law has been exhausted by Christ's loving surrender to the Cross. Again and again, the New Testament demands of Christians that they exercise limitless forgiveness, no matter how grievous the

wrong, even in legal and public settings. And it insists that, for the Christian, mercy always triumphs over judgment.[552]

Those who defend the CLE agree: mercy triumphs. But does it always triumph over the protection of society, especially of the most vulnerable, as when deadly violence is used in a just war, or when particularly dangerous criminals are executed?

Pope John Paul II defends the death penalty only "in cases of absolute necessity." That is, "when it would not be possible otherwise to defend society."[553] Even back in 1995, however, the Holy Father acknowledged that "such cases are very rare, if not practically non-existent" given the capacities of most penal systems. More than two decades later, penal systems having been improved with even better technology and organization, Pope Francis made a similar point in his updated teaching: "[M]ore effective systems of detention have been developed, which ensure the due protection of citizens but, at the same time, do not definitively deprive the guilty of the possibility of redemption."

The new teaching, therefore, calls the death penalty "inadmissible." What does this word mean? Intrinsically evil? Is the norm against the death penalty the same as the norm against intentionally killing the innocent? The new teaching, frankly, is not clear. Even in the developed world, as seen above, we cannot prevent deadly violence, even in our prisons. What if we place ourselves in the place of public authority in a very poor society, one with virtually no resources to construct a penal system that can house capital offenders safely? Is the death penalty inadmissible there as well? It is difficult to reconcile this with the teaching of John Paul II in a way that (again, depending on what was meant by "inadmissible") obviously does not contradict the new teaching. It is probably better to think of the death penalty in terms similar to the other kinds of killing we've explored (killing to save the mother's life via abortion or killing in a just war): in almost all cases we must be ruled by the principle of mercy, with extremely, extremely rare exceptions.

> Objection #3: *Those advocating for the CLE, like the author of this book, generally live a life of safety and privilege precisely because of the practices criticized in this chapter. The global exchange of goods that has made them so wealthy is only possible with the US military ensuring peace. They are largely safe from nuclear war because of the deterrence factor of our own nuclear weapons. Especially if they live in urban areas, they can sleep soundly in their homes and travel safely to work and other places because the justice system has incarcerated and deterred criminals who would otherwise force them to live very differently. It takes a lot of chutzpah for someone to critique the very practices that provide you the capacity to live as you do.*

This objection is a version of the one offered by Col. Nathan Jessep, played by Jack Nicholson in the now-classic film *A Few Good Men*. In response to an objection from Lt. Kaffee (played by Tom Cruise) to the violent practices used to train Marines at his military base, Jessep castigates him as "a man who rises and sleeps under the blanket of the very freedom that I provide and then questions the manner in which I provide it." He tells his accuser, in a line that has become famous, that though he may find the Marines' violence grotesque, Kaffee "can't handle the truth" that these are the very practices that keep him safe at night. This, according to the unspoken critique, is rank hypocrisy.

But is it? Suppose a child benefits even more directly by ill-gotten resources provided by a father who, say, is a high-ranking member of the mafia. Is it hypocritical to live in that situation when one benefits from violence and injustice and still criticize the violence and injustice? Not at all, especially when there are no real short-term options to live in a context where one wouldn't benefit. Like such a child, we can work toward the day when we can live in a different context, but for now there is little we can do. And if in fact we are living in a situation where we benefit from violence and injustice, it is important to keep that at the front of our minds as, again, we work toward a different culture.

But do these practices lead to safety and other flourishing as much as those making this objection would have us believe? The evidence is mixed. Defenders of stockpiling nuclear weapons often claim that we need them to deter rogue states and other enemies who might use similar weapons against us; but this claim is coming from the only country in the world ever to use nuclear weapons (and in a case where it wasn't the last resort). Furthermore, it isn't clear that the deterrent effect of nuclear weapons, if they have any at all, outweighs the greater threat of nuclear proliferation. As for conventional military actions, it is true that there have been no more 9/11-level attacks on US soil and that the US military presence facilitates global trade. But as we saw above, the United States has spent trillions of dollars on the "war on terror," killed hundreds of thousands of people (most of whom were innocent noncombatants) and has created many more jihadi warriors than existed before 9/11. In US states that have the death penalty, murder rates are consistently higher than those that do not.[554] The United States is one of the few countries in the world with legal capital punishment, yet most developed countries have less crime without choosing to kill their prisoners. Some evidence shows that increased incarceration has made US cities safer, but there are also diminishing returns—especially when incarcerating people over forty years old.[555]

This book does not intend to explore the complex data and analysis necessary to reach even a provisional conclusion about accepting the Col. Jessep argument that (most) CLE supporters are safe and can flourish because of the very practices the CLE critiques. We should be open to whatever the data and a fair analysis can demonstrate—which means, perhaps, that we should be prepared to accept significant risk and possibly lead a very different kind of life. CLE supporters must acknowledge that our commitment may, in certain situations, make us (and our country) less safe.

Conclusion

As chapter 4 showed, the pro-life movement is rooted in the anti-war movement of the 1960s.[556] The CLE's deep concern with state-sponsored violence, therefore, conserves a foundational dimension of the pro-life activist tradition. It honors the movement's historical and ideological core. Single-issue pro-lifers who exclude state-sponsored violence from their pro-life concerns disconnect themselves from their own history.

Furthermore, though we'll return to politics and political philosophy in the conclusion of this book, it might be worthwhile to pause for a moment on this topic. When I started this project (things may be changing during the Trump realignment), many pro-lifers claimed to stand for a smaller, more accountable government. They claimed to be suspicious of big, slow, distant, bureaucratic, unaccountable, wasteful, corrupt governmental institutions. This critique seems to apply clearly to the prison and military industrial complexes—but, at least in my experience, most small-government pro-life conservatives do not apply their critique consistently. The US military, particularly, is not subjected to the small/accountable government critiques, and some pro-lifers even celebrate the military in a way that can seem to border on idolatry. "Supporting the troops" and "supporting our [wartime] president" become frequent public refrains. New saints and martyrs are created for the civil religion. Yes, it has become standard practice to laud their blood sacrifice at our great national liturgies—like at the president's state of the union address, where "the troops" always get the longest ovations, from both sides of the aisle.

So, among other things, the CLE may help push small-government conservatives to extend their pro-life concerns to practices of state-sponsored violence. And it may do so in a way that brings their important critiques of big, slow, distant, bureaucratic, unaccountable, wasteful, corrupt institutions to bear on all such institutions—not just those that fit the more comfortable half of our incoherent liberal/conservative binary politics.

Conclusion

Toward a Politics of
Encounter and Hospitality

As I suggested in the introduction, many of us need to take a long, hot, cleansing political shower. To retreat, at least temporarily, from the fray of national politics (especially online) and quiet our minds. Focus on real, local, physical things. Cultivate genuine encounters with others. Show hospitality—not just to our family, friends, and neighbors—but to many kinds of vulnerable populations on the margins of our communities. We should refuse to outsource what we owe these populations to disconnected and distant institutions (whether public or private); we should get up off the couch and do what we can ourselves.

As I also suggested in the introduction, this sentiment fits well with where many US Americans are right now. There is a clear "exhausted majority" that is unhappy not only with our national politics and government, but also with corporations, banks, and the whole public thing in general. Younger people, though keen on making social change, are particularly frustrated by big, slow, and unresponsive institutions; many are looking around for alternative ways to make a difference.

One of those ways has been the use of devices with glowing rectangles. And while they are undoubtedly important tools, the costs of using them regularly are sobering. It has a seriously detrimental effect on your well-being, especially if you are young:[557]

> Teens who spend more time than average on screen activities are more likely to be unhappy, and those who spend more time than average on nonscreen activities are more likely to be happy. There's not a single exception. All screen activities are linked to less happiness, and all nonscreen activities are linked to more happiness.[558]

Social media is even worse:

> Eighth-graders who spend ten or more hours a week on social media are 56 percent more likely to say they're unhappy than those who devote less time to social media. Admittedly, ten hours a week is a lot. But those who spend six to nine hours a week on social media are still 47 percent more likely to say they are unhappy than those who use social media even less. The opposite is true of in-person interactions. Those who spend an above-average amount of time with their friends in person are 20 percent less likely to say they're unhappy than those who hang out for a below-average amount of time.

And combining screens and social media with smartphones is actually toxic. On *60 Minutes*, industry insiders report that the smartphone is designed essentially as a kind of "brain hack."[559] In what they describe as a race to the bottom of the brain stem, smartphone designers are working with biologists and social scientists to keep us scrolling and tapping our phones as much and as long as possible. And they have been successful. Studies show that when regular users try to put down their phones, their bodies release cortisol, the same stress hormone released when early *Homo sapiens* confronted a predator in the wild. Normally, the release of small amounts of this hormone from time to time are insignificant, but its chronic release is so toxic to the human body that some experts refer to it as "public health enemy number one."[560]

Media consumption has inserted itself into our relationships, disconnecting us from real people and, as a result, increasing our loneliness. Social media isn't the only thing that is making us lonely, however. As Senator Ben Sasse points out in his book *Them*, our consumer lifestyles are geared toward an unrootedness that lacks the relationships of thick communities.[561] Many caught in consumerist culture have the goal to be "independent," in a large house (most often requiring the income of two full time workers), and self-reliant. And if that means hopping from job to job, city to city, then that's what will be done. Even if we could afford the children necessary to rebuild the extended family, many of us wouldn't stay long enough to take root in a community.

This loneliness has had predictable effects on our mental and physical health. Our children are now facing unprecedented rates of psychological problems (especially depression and anxiety).[562] Loneliness in the overall US population has become a public health crisis even more damaging than obesity.[563] More is being learned about the close correlation between loneliness and a dramatically increased rate of drug abuse.[564] The stakes involved in addressing these problems couldn't be higher: deaths due to drug overdose and suicide have increased markedly—so much, in fact, that from 2015 through 2017 US life expectancy has declined each year, the worst such drop since World War I.[565] We are a disconnected, lonely, anxious, stressed, despairing, and depressed people—a people who, in matter of fact, are killing ourselves.

Many have tried to distract themselves from these issues by focusing on the constant hum of national politics. As one *Atlantic* headline put it, "National Politics Has Taken Over America."[566] But engaging politics from a position of loneliness and despair often leads us to the angry, polarized, hate-driven politics described in the introduction.[567] Prominent political commentators, especially after the 2018 midterm elections, have begun to describe the United States as being in the middle of a "cold civil war."[568] On election day morning 2018, one West Virginia voter put it this way: "I'm so upset, I feel physically ill. Just the ugliness of it all. It's so heartbreaking that all we can do is bring each other down and cut into each other. I feel like I'm going to cry."[569] Politics, as Jonah Goldberg reminded us in the introduction, cannot fill the hole in our souls.[570]

Fr. Julián Carrón, leader of the Communion and Liberation Movement, repeats a familiar refrain when asked about the Holy Father: "If you don't think Pope Francis is the cure, you don't grasp the disease."[571] In *Laudato si'*, paragraph 128, Francis discounts the idea that "political efforts or the force of law" will be sufficient to create authentic, robust, life-giving social change. On the contrary, Francis's primary concern is to help create a culture of encounter and hospitality—precisely the counter-culture needed to help us face what is killing us. Rather than engaging via "screens and systems which can be turned on and off on command," Francis calls us to "face-to-face encounter with others, with their physical presence which challenges us, with their pain and their pleas, with their joy which infects us in our close and continuous interaction."[572]

Writing these words during the lead-up to Christmas 2018 made me begin to ponder the Christmas song I most enjoyed singing to my seven-month-old son, Thaddeus: "Good King Wenceslas." One day while singing, it struck me that the king's thinking and practices are a wonderful example of Pope Francis's culture of encounter and hospitality. First, it appears that the king was actively looking to encounter someone on the peripheries,

> Good King Wenceslas looked out
> On the Feast of Stephen,
> When the snow lay round about,
> Deep and crisp and even.
> Brightly shone the moon that night,
> Though the frost was cruel,
> When a poor man came in sight
> Gathering winter fuel.

For as soon as he saw the man, he wanted to know more about him:

> Yonder peasant, who is he?
> Where and what his dwelling?

After his page provides some details, though the king easily could have sent for a servant, he decides he will aid the man himself. In person. He will bring his hospitality to the peripheries and encounter the man where he is. Notice that "seeing him dine" is of particular concern to the king:

> Bring me meat and bring me wine,
> Bring me pine logs hither.
> Thou and I shall see him dine
> When we bear them thither.

And the drama of the song, of course, is that they encounter danger along the way. It is not a safe or comfortable way to respond:

> Page and monarch, forth they went,
> Forth they went together,
> Through the rude winds' wild lament
> And the bitter weather.

The page nearly dies of cold but is saved by literally (and figuratively) following in the footsteps of the great saint. The lesson, of course, is that:

> Ye, who now will bless the poor
> Shall yourselves find blessing.

In going out to the peripheries to serve the poor, the king engaged in a practice those around him probably considered below his station. This has deep resonances in what Pope Francis highlights in the Franciscans' title "friars minor"—a willingness to be "little" for the faith.[573] The pope reiterates that this is one of the central messages of Christmas:

> In order to discover him, we need to go there, where he is. We need to bow down, humble ourselves, make ourselves small. The Child who is born challenges us: he calls us to leave behind fleeting illusions and go to the essence, to renounce our insatiable claims, to abandon our endless dissatisfaction and sadness for something we will never have. It will help us to leave these things behind in order to rediscover in the simplicity of the God-child, peace, joy and the meaning of life.[574]

In the act of becoming small—by imitating Christ's becoming poor, though he was rich—Francis shows us the place for genuine encounter: with God, with all men and women, and with God's creation. The Didache's insistence that Christians "suffer with the suffering" should not hide the fact that such genuine encounters are often life-giving and push against our self-obsessed, self-loathing, lonely, depressed culture. We discover that one of the most important keys to leading a whole and healthy life is genuine encounters with others.[575]

Leading a life of consistency is also important for our flourishing. Inconsistency can lead to what psychologists call cognitive dissonance—something the human mind resists so strongly that we tell obviously false stories (to ourselves and to each other) just to make our life choices appear consistent.[576] And this book, of course, has attempted to show what it might look like to live fundamental principles consistently across a range of issues. Of course, refusing to follow our principles consistently leads to injustice, but it also diminishes our well-being.

But there is something else with which the CLE is concerned, something that perhaps isn't so easy to see given the way this book is organized. In the context of a genuine encounter we can avoid using the person we meet only as a means to the (admittedly good) end of trying to bring about social change on a given issue. It is throwaway culture, after all, that sees and uses people only as a means to an end. Instead, the CLE encourages encounters that help us see a fuller picture of an individual's situation and respond to that person's unique circumstances. It helps us dive into the thickness of their story; in so doing we often find several interconnected issues to be at play. Consider these two thought experiments as examples:

Thought Experiment Number One

As a four-year-old child, Joshua was brought without papers to the United States by his mother, who was fleeing violence in Honduras. They lived in a very poor area of Cleveland—an area with dysfunctional schools and lots of violence—in constant fear of deportation. Joshua's mother worked three jobs for less than minimum wage, including at a local restaurant. One day, when Joshua was fourteen years old, ICE officials raided that restaurant and deported his mother. Afraid of encountering ICE, Joshua decided not to stay at their house and instead lived on the streets where he became familiar with gang and drug culture. He did manage to finish high school, however, fulfilling a promise made to his mother. Without many options, especially as a non-citizen, a now eighteen-year-old Joshua joined the military. He was trained and then deployed to Iraq where he saw and did the most terrible things. He came back to Cleveland a US citizen, but also a broken, isolated, and desperately lonely man. He turned back to the gang life and to drugs and alcohol in order to cope and seek some kind of community. Selling pot in order to make ends meet, one day he sold to an undercover cop. He landed behind bars for ten years and this experience stripped him of even more of his humanity. In a desperate attempt to flee a life he knew was bad for him, upon his release Joshua moved to Pennsylvania to work for a meat company in one of their factory farms. The job involved all kinds of violence toward animals—which pushed him even further into inhumanity and despair. Defeated and not knowing what else to do, he eventually left that job and returned to his gang life in Ohio, where he rose through the ranks due to his familiarity with firearms and a new willingness to use them. One day, high on cocaine, in a hold-up gone bad, Joshua shot and killed an innocent man. With no money for a lawyer, he got a court-appointed attorney who was unable to keep him off Ohio's new death row. Especially with a governor trying to be tough on immigration, Joshua's history doesn't make it likely his appeal for clemency will be successful.

Thought Experiment Number Two

When she was eleven years old Larissa was first shown hardcore porn on a smartphone by a boy in her class. Over the next two years he sexually abused her by insisting they act out the scenes he made her watch. As a way of coping with her pain, Larissa dove into a sexually aggressive lifestyle. Sexual attention from boys was the only thing that distracted her from her self-loathing. This loathing was made worse because, as a charter member of iGen, she was constantly bombarded with photos and videos from other girls on social media who seemed to have lives much better than hers. Lonely, depressed, and full of anxiety, she stopped going to school and at sixteen moved in with a twenty-nine-year-old man. When she got pregnant, he became physically abusive, however, and she quickly left that relationship, soon after giving birth to a beautiful baby girl. Not long after that she met another man and moved in with him, in part because she wanted financial security and housing stability for her daughter. He insisted that she use the pill, but because it made her depression worse and even caused suicidal thoughts Larissa wasn't consistent in taking it. When she became pregnant again her boyfriend flew into a rage and insisted that she have an abortion, or he would kick her out of his apartment. Thinking primarily about supporting and protecting her daughter, but also about her own safety, Larissa went to one of several abortion clinics in her neighborhood. They didn't ask her if she was being pressured into the decision—they just wanted her to sign the forms and contribute to their monthly abortion quota. Though numb at the time, soon after Larissa came to the devastating conclusion that she killed her baby boy. Somehow gathering the strength to leave this second abusive relationship, she checked herself and her daughter into a homeless shelter.

These thought experiments demonstrate how a culture of encounter might resist taking a drive-by approach to vulnerable people that reduces them to the one or two issues we may have at the front of our minds or that primarily animate our activism. Authentically honoring our duty to aid someone in his or her fullness not only is necessary for engagement with them, it can change us as well. It can challenge our previously held assumptions and force us to take a harder look at ourselves to see how our views and actions might be contributing to the intersecting forces that push people into desperate and unhealthy situations.

Before returning to a focus on US politics we should live in this space—where we can be transformed by such encounters—for at least several months. Perhaps even years. It would be part of a cleansing political shower. We need the time not only to allow the change to take place, but to reflect on the new person we are becoming and envision new ways we might approach the public thing. Take walks without ear buds or drives without the radio or Bluetooth in the background.[577] Meditate. Pray. Adore the Blessed Sacrament. Be still and know that God is doing something new. And *then* go out and work toward a politics of encounter and hospitality.

And do it in dialogue with others, especially those who think differently. Steel man, don't straw man, their point of view. Resist with all your might the urge to define yourself by opposition to the other. Lead with what you are for, not with what you are against, in the hopes of finding unifying common ground. This may not seem like a lot, but we are in the midst of a political realignment; it may provide the fertile soil in which these small seeds will sprout and become the trees and forest of a new and healthy political ecosystem. Our culture is primed to reject the divisive political assumptions of the last fifty years. We are ready for a politics of encounter and hospitality to unify us.

But when I say "we" I obviously mean most people: the seven in ten of us who are part of the exhausted majority. I don't mean everyone. Many are still powerfully wedded to the divisiveness, the left/right narrative, and defining one's self by opposition to the other. Plus, too much power and too much money is at stake for the old guard to fade away without strong resistance. Undoubtedly, our current political turmoil at least in part is a reaction by those who have benefited from the binary culture wars and the uncertainty of our current moment. Those who wish to help usher in something new should be prepared for virulent resistance. Pope Francis, no stranger to such resistance himself, offers important resources for engaging the people who want to do us harm. Supporters of the CLE should keep them in mind. Going forward, we will need them if we are going to persevere through the suffering Jesus predicted would come if we followed him:

Panta hypoménei. This means that love bears every trial with a positive attitude. It stands firm in hostile surroundings. This "endurance" involves not only the ability to tolerate certain aggravations, but something greater: a constant readiness to confront any challenge. It is a love that never gives up, even in the darkest hour. It shows a certain dogged heroism, a power to resist every negative current, an irrepressible commitment to goodness. Here I think of the words of Martin Luther King, who met every kind of trial and tribulation with fraternal love: "The person who hates you most has some good in him; even the nation that hates you most has some good in it; even the race that hates you most has some good in it. And when you come to the point that you look in the face of every man and see deep down within him what religion calls 'the image of God,' you begin to love him in spite of [everything]. No matter what he does, you see God's image there."[578]

Appendix

Charts

1. It is always **wrong to radically reduce someone's inherent dignity for some other end**, especially by aiming at their deaths.

2. Use of **violence ought to be resisted at every turn**, not only because of the effect it has on the victim, but also because of what it does to the agent of violence. When protecting one's vulnerable neighbor it is permissible to use deadly force, but mercy requires that such violence must be strictly regulated and the absolutely last option used.

3. In every circumstance we must **give priority to both protecting and supporting the lives of the most vulnerable and especially those who cannot speak up in their own defense.** In some circumstances, such as gross neglect of our duty to aid, we may be morally responsible for the deaths of those we could have saved.

4. **Resist appeals to individual autonomy and privacy which detach us from our duty to aid** and

slouch toward a relativistic culture which rewards the powerful and discards the vulnerable. These vulnerable include not just those who are alive today—those marginalized due to their age, race, gender, level of ability, and more—but also generations to come.

5. **Resist language, practices, and social structures which detach us from the full reality and dignity of the marginalized**—especially as such dignity is hidden by the broader consumerist culture.

6. Focus positively on creating a culture of encounter, especially with those we find most difficult to show mercy and love. **Go to the peripheries, when there is risk, show hospitality and care for the stranger**, especially (but not only) if we are responsible for their need in the first place.

7. Acknowledge **mutuality, not only between human persons currently living, but also between current and future generations, and between human persons and the rest of non-human creation.** This includes a concern for those suffering, marginalized creatures who, though subjected to terrible violence, cannot speak up in their own defense.

Issues

	Sex Practices and Cultures	Reproductive Biotechnology	Abortion
Reduction of Inherent Dignity for Another End	Explicit goal of "hookup culture" is to use a person as a thing or object for sexual pleasure, social status, or some other good.	Embryo selection based on sex or health; social pressure on women to put off reproduction to be more productive at work; children reduced to product by consumerist culture.	Reduction of dignity by directly aiming at persons' deaths–often because a prenatal child simply isn't wanted (especially because of disability).
Violence and/or Discarding of the Vulnerable	Sexual assault and abuse, especially of economically unstable women, young persons, people with STIs. Hook-up "partners" used and discarded.	Forms of artificial reproduction discard vulnerable children, even simply because they are female or have disabilities.	Direct killing of vulnerable, voiceless children, often because they have disabilities. Vulnerable women who face violence expected to remain unpregnant in patriarchal culture.

Principles

The Poor and the Stranger	Ecology and Non-Human Animals	Euthanasia and the Margins of Human Life	State-Sponsored Violence
Dehumanizing language leads to lack of concern or to hostility. Children's suffering from separation used as deterrent. Undocumented immigrants used and abused, especially in service industry.	Inherent dignity of non-human animals and broader ecological world reduced to mere means for promoting consumerist culture. Sometimes by even radically altering animals´ God-given nature and way of being.	Radical reduction of dignity by directly aiming at death, especially when the person is burdensome or disabled.	Radical reduction of dignity by directly aiming at death. Dehumanization of those on death row. Using inmates for a kind of slave labor. Soldiers used as pawns for questionable military goals.
Premature death of vulnerable caused by poverty and forced migration. Refugees refused aid in face of a deadly threat, which is often an act of violence. Economy discards the poor.	Direct killing of vulnerable, voiceless creatures–often for consumerist reasons. Poor and other vulnerable human populations suffer in relation to climate change.	Direct killing and discarding of the elderly, brain-damaged, depressed, and those with other mental illness. Those who cannot afford good care are at particular risk.	Most wars, especially nuclear war, cause terrible deadly violence for the innocent. "Collateral damage" from drone warfare; mass incarceration and capital punishment, especially of vulnerable racial minorities.

Issues

	Sex Practices and Cultures	Reproductive Biotechnology	Abortion
Skepticism of Money-Making and Consumerism	Huge money made by "big porn" corporations. Huge money made off our sexual culture by purveyors of other media (music, movies, YouTube, etc.). Also money made by corporations convincing people to feel bad about their bodies.	Huge money made by the whole industry surrounding artificial reproductive technologies. Renting wombs, especially cheaply in the developing world. Buying gametes, especially from women with desirable genetic material.	Consumerist culture requires abortion so women can be equal to men in production of capital. Must reach consumer success before having children; need abortion as backup to contraception to control reproduction.
Suspicion of Individual Autonomy and Privacy	Critique of "staying out of people's bedrooms" in light of sexual violence and #MeToo. Choices must respect human dignity while resisting patriarchal, consumerist assumptions.	Critique of virtually unlimited reproductive autonomy. The good of especially vulnerable children must come first.	Autonomy and privacy must not hide the terrible violence done to prenatal children and our duty to come to their aid.

Principles

The Poor and the Stranger	Ecology and Non-Human Animals	Euthanasia and the Margins of Human Life	State-Sponsored Violence
Poor and under-class built into the expectations of unrestricted market capital-ism. Exploiting undocumented immigrants built into consumer economy, espe-cially for the rich.	Quest for market share and profit drives the exis-tence and practices of factory farms. Climate change driven by need for energy in the service of capital production and economic growth and efficiency.	Culture has a consumerist standard for the value of life. Must be a "productive" member of society. Not a burden on one's family or community. If one is the latter rather than the former, then it might be a good reason for killing yourself.	The huge monies involved in our military indus-trial complex is virtually the only unquestioned part of the US federal budget. For-profit prisons have perverse incentive to have inmates return.
Individuals cannot appeal to the autonomous right to spend in the marketplace however they wish. Needs of the poor and stranger, especially when poverty threatens death, makes a claim of justice on us.	Our food choices involve claims of justice–especially a duty to be kind to animals. There's no autonomous right to consume in ways which damage our eco-logical world and threaten future generations.	Suspicion of autonomy as standard for as-sisted suicide. Not only are patients often not making autonomous choices to die, but standard sends cultural message that those without autonomy do not have lives worth living.	The state's demand for autonomy and privacy when it comes to killing–especially in war–must be seriously contested by its citizens if the vulnerable are to be protected from violence.

Issues

	Sex Practices and Cultures	Reproductive Biotechnology	Abortion
Use of Language that Marginalizes the Vulnerable and Makes Them Easier to Discard	Words used to describe people in our pornified hookup culture are degrading (especially when they are women) and makes them easier to use and discard.	Consumerist practices with regard to artificial reproductive technologies language imply that children are "products" to be used and discarded. Even the word re-production sends this message.	When a prenatal child is wanted, we call her a baby, but when she is unwanted we call her a fetus, product of conception, parasite, or even cluster of cells.
Creating a Culture of Encounter (Especially on the Peripheries) and Hospitality	Resisting hook-up culture by requiring deep personal relationships which acknowledge inherent dignity of one's sexual partner. Welcome and hospitality for children as essential part of sex.	Radical acceptance of disabled persons, especially children. Welcoming children only through a genuine encounter in a sexual relationship.	Welcoming prenatal child in a spirit of hospitality, especially those who are unwanted and undesirable. Create a space for pregnant women and mothers, especially in the workplace.

Principles

The Poor and the Stranger	Ecology and Non-Human Animals	Euthanasia and the Margins of Human Life	State-Sponsored Violence
We refer to the poor and the stranger with dehumanizing language: welfare queens, takers, undesirables, illegals, criminals, animals, etc.	Factory farming reduction of non-human animals to consumerist object hides their true dignity. We eat "pork", not pig. We eat "burgers", not cow. Factor farms speak of "protein units per square foot."	Changing definition of death so certain people can be used for their organs. Using presence of autonomy as a threshold for euthanasia and lack of autonomy as a reason why euthanasia would be good for someone.	Objectifying and racist language used by soldiers to describe enemies and victims of war. Thinking of people on death row as "monsters." Dehumanizing language used for victims of mass incarceration.
Encountering and welcoming the poor and the stranger as individuals, families, churches, and local communities. Be willing to risk encountering and developing genuine relationships with those on the peripheries.	Encounter the natural world on a regular basis, questioning the norm of urban living. Culture of encounter and hospitality with non-human animals. Get to know the producers of meat and other products.	Encounter the sick and disabled in a spirit of hospitality and relationship. Welcome dying relatives and friends into one's home. Refuse to push them to the margins of the culture.	Visit and encounter those in prison, especially those who are suffering from our racist mass incarceration practices. Encounter and work to love enemies, showing them hospitality.

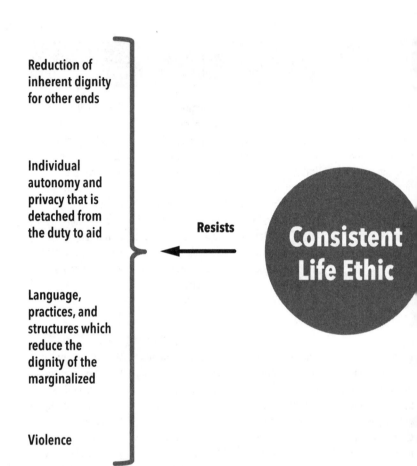

Promotes

Protection and
support of the
most vulnerable

Mutuality
between persons,
generations, and
non-human
creation

Movement
toward the
peripheries and
hospitality

Culture of
encounter

Endnotes

1. "Congress and the Public," *Gallup*, https://news.gallup.com/poll/1600/congress-public.aspx.
2. "Americans Prefer Hemorrhoids and Cockroaches to Congress," *NPR*, October 9, 2013, https://www.npr.org/sections/thetwoway/2013/10/09/231015154/americans-prefer-hemorrhoids-and-cockroaches-to-congress.
3. Lydia Saad, "Trump Sets New Low Point for Inaugural Approval Rating," *Gallup*, January 23, 2017, https://news.gallup.com/poll/202811/trump-sets-new-low-point-inaugural-approval-rating.aspx.
4. Abigail Geiger, "For Many Voters, It's Not Which Presidential Candidate They're for, but Which They're Against, http://www.pewresearch.org/fact-tank/2016/09/02/for-many-voters-its-not-which-presidential-candidate-theyre-for-but-which-theyre-against/.
5. Elizabeth Bruenig, "Kavanaugh Is One More Step in America's Cycle of Self-destruction," *Washington Post*, https://www.washingtonpost.com/opinions/kavanaugh-is-one-more-step-in-americas-cycle-of-self-destruction/2018/10/04/0afa7a3c-c819-11e8-b2b5-79270f9cce17_story.html?noredirect=on&utm_term=.b9c3657bd916 .
6. Alan Abramowitz and Steven Webster, "'Negative Partisanship' Explains Everything," *Politico*, September/October 2017, https://www.politico.com/magazine/story/2017/09/05/negative-partisanship-explains-everything-215534.
7. Ezra Klein, "The Single Most Important Fact about American Politics," *Vox*, last modified April 28, 2016, http://www.vox.com/2014/6/13/5803768/pew-most-important-fact-american-politics.
8. David Roberts, "Donald Trump and the Rise of Tribal Epistemology," *Vox*, May 19, 2017, https://www.vox.com/policy-and-politics/2017/3/22/14762030/donald-trump-tribal-epistemology.
9. Mark Hemingway, "While Truth Puts Its Shoes On," *The Weekly Standard*, December 15, 2017, https://www.weeklystandard.com/while-truth-puts-on-its-shoes/article/2010858.
10. Jim VandeHei, "How American Politics Went Batshit Crazy, Starting with Newt Gingrich," *Axios*, November 14, 2017, https://www.axios.com/how-american-politics-went-batshit-crazy-starting-with-newt-gingrich-1513306860-b5c49fe2-b406-4b41-82d4-b2cb74673b53.html.
11. David French, "We're Not in a Civil War, but We Are Drifting Toward Divorce," *National Review*, June 8, 2017, https://www.nationalreview.com/2017/06/americans-left-right-liberal-conservative-democrats-re-

publicans-blue-red-states-cultural-segregate/?utm_source=social&utm_medium=twitter&utm_campaign=french&utm_content=divorce.

12. "Party Affiliation," *Gallup¸* https://news.gallup.com/poll/15370/party-affiliation.aspx.

13. Paul Waldman, "What Howard Schultz's Ludicrous Candidacy Tells Us about the American Electorate," https://www.washingtonpost.com/opinions/2019/01/29/what-howard-schultzs-ludicrous-candidacy-tells-us-about-american-electorate/?utm_term=.eecd29cdc73e.

14. Sabrina Tavernise, "These Americans Are Done with Politics," November 17, 2018, https://www.nytimes.com/2018/11/17/sunday-review/elections-partisanship-exhausted-majority.html.

15. Yascha Mounk, "Americans Strongly Dislike PC Culture," *The Atlantic* October 10, 2018, https://www.theatlantic.com/ideas/archive/2018/10/large-majorities-dislike-political-correctness/572581/.

16. Chuck Todd, "Lousiana Points to Realignment for Democratic Party," *NBC News*, October 31, 2014, http://www.nbcnews.com/watch/nbcnews-com/louisiana-points-to-realignment-for-democratic-party-350468163560.

17. Michael Barone, "Another Impossible Thing May Happen: Change in Partisan Alignments," *National Review*, September 1, 2015, http://www.nationalreview.com/article/423314/donald-trump-hillary-clinton-partisan-realignment.

18. Eugene Robinson, "The 2016 Election was Not a Fluke," *The Washington Post*, September 18, 2017, https://www.washingtonpost.com/opinions/the-2016-election-was-not-a-fluke/2017/09/18/b45a8a0e-9cb4-11e7-9083-fbfddf6804c2_story.html?utm_term=.4a5c034202e6.

19. Karl Rove, *The Triumph of William McKinley: Why the Election of 1896 Still Matters* (New York: Simon and Schuster, 2015), http://books.simonandschuster.com/The-Triumph-of-William-McKinley/Karl-Rove/9781476752952.

20. "Tom Brokaw – Rising Tide of Independent Voters," *YouTube*, January 28, 2008, https://www.youtube.com/all_comments?v=zLLu9C6JMGo.

21. Peggy Noonan, "America Is So in Play," *Wall Street Journal*, August 27, 2015, http://www.wsj.com/articles/america-is-so-in-play-1440715262.

22. Thomas Kidd, "Donald Trump and the Coming Christian Political Realignment," *Patheos*, October 20, 2015, http://www.patheos.com/blogs/anxiousbench/2015/10/donald-trump-and-the-coming-christian-political-realignment/.

23. Jonathan Merritt, "Southern Baptists Call Off the Culture War," *The Atlantic*, June 16, 2018, https://www.theatlantic.com/ideas/archive/2018/06/southern-baptists-call-off-the-culture-war/563000/.

24.   Peter Jesserer Smith, "The Sleeping Giant of Pro-Life Latinos Awakens," *National Catholic Register*, January 22, 2014, http://www.ncregister.com/daily-news/the-sleeping-giant-of-pro-life-latinos-awakens/.

25.   Jane Coaston, "Tucker Carlson Has Sparked the Most Interesting Debate in Conservative Politics," *Vox,* January 10, 2019, https://www.vox.com/2019/1/10/18171912/tucker-carlson-fox-news-populism-conservatism-trump-gop .

26.   Chuck Todd, Mark Murray, and Carrie Dann, "Last Night Wasn't a Wave. It Was a Realignment," November 7, 2018, https://www.nbcnews.com/politics/first-read/last-night-wasn-t-wave-it-was-realignment-n933436.

27.   Ron Fournier, "The Outsiders: How Can Millennials Change Washington If They Hate It?," *The Atlantic*, August 26, 2013, http://www.theatlantic.com/politics/archive/2013/08/the-outsiders-how-can-millennials-change-washington-if-they-hate-it/278920/.

28.   Hannah Hartig and Stephanie Perry, "Millennial Poll: Strong Majority Want a Third Political Party," *NBC News*, November 29, 2017, https://www.nbcnews.com/politics/politics-news/millennial-poll-strong-majority-want-third-political-party-n824526.

29.   Fournier, "The Outsiders."

30.   Jonah Goldberg, "Politics Can't Fill the Holes in Our Souls," *American Enterprise Institute*, June 27, 2018, https://www.aei.org/publication/politics-cant-fill-the-holes-in-our-souls/.

31.   José H. Gomez, Twitter Post, August 26, 2016, 8:10pm, https://twitter.com/ArchbishopGomez/status/769326062467710976.

32.   "Confidence in Institutions," *Gallup*, https://news.gallup.com/poll/1597/confidence-institutions.aspx.

33.   Rhina Guidos, "Pollster: Religion Can Serve as Moderating Force in Politics," *Crux,* May 18, 2018, https://cruxnow.com/church-in-the-usa/2018/05/18/pollster-religion-can-serve-as-moderating-force-in-politics/.

34.   "Though Many, One: Overcoming Polarization through Catholic Social Thought," The Initiative on Catholic Social Thought and Public Life, June 4, 2018, https://catholicsocialthought.georgetown.edu/events/though-many-one-overcoming-polarization-through-catholic-social-thought.

35.   Maria Vultaggio, "Pope Francis Central Park Visit: Millennials Talk About His Effect on Catholicism," *International Business Times*, September 25, 2015, http://www.ibtimes.com/pope-francis-central-park-visit-millennials-talk-about-his-effect-catholicism-2111117.

36.   I owe the following narrative history to Thomas A. Nairn, O.F.M. "Introduction," in *The Consistent Ethic of Life: Assessing Its Reception and Relavance* (Maryknoll, NY: Orbis, 2008), xi-xiii.

37. Kenneth A. Briggs, "Bernardin Asks Catholics to Fight Both Nuclear Arms and Abortion," *New York Times*, December 7, 1983, https://www.nytimes.com/1983/12/07/us/bernardin-asks-catholics-to-fight-both-nuclear-arms-and-abortion.html.

38. Joseph Cardinal Bernardin, "Address at Seattle University," in *Consistent Ethic of Life* (Sheed and Ward, 1988). I focus in particular on pages 88-90.

39. John Paul II, *Evangelium vitae*, Vatican Website, March 25, 1995, http://w2.vatican.va/content/john-paul-ii/en/encyclicals/documents/hf_jp-ii_enc_25031995_evangelium-vitae.html, 3.

40. Benedict XVI, *Caritas in veritate*, Vatican Website, June 29, 2009, http://w2.vatican.va/content/benedict-xvi/en/encyclicals/documents/hf_ben-xvi_enc_20090629_caritas-in-veritate.html, 51.

41. Gerard O'Connell, "Avoid becoming Christians of 'the right or the left' urges Pope Francis during Pentecost Homily," *America*, June 4, 2017, https://www.americamagazine.org/faith/2017/06/04/avoid-becoming-christians-right-or-left-urges-pope-francis-during-pentecost-homily?utm_content=buffer49fa0&utm_medium=social&utm_source=twitter.com&utm_campaign=buffer#.

42. Ryan Teague Beckwith, "Transcript: Read the Speech Pope Francis Gave to Congress," *Time*, September 24, 2015, http://time.com/4048176/pope-francis-us-visit-congress-transcript/.

43. "Pope Francis Issues Marching Orders for New Pro-Life Leader," *Crux*, August 18, 2016, https://cruxnow.com/vatican/2016/08/18/pope-issues-marching-orders-new-pro-life-leader/.

44. Antonio Spadaro, "A Big Heart Open to God: An Interview with Pope Francis," *America*, September 30, 2013, http://americamagazine.org/pope-interview.

45. Charles Camosy, "Does Pope Francis have a 'Weak' Bioethic?–A Response to Mark Cherry," *Catholic Moral Theology*, February 9, 2015, http://catholicmoraltheology.com/does-pope-francis-have-a-weak-bioethic-a-response-to-mark-cherry/.

46. Philip Pullella, "Pope Compares Having an Abortion to 'Hiring a Hit Man,'" *Reuters*, October 10, 2018, https://www.reuters.com/article/us-pope-abortion/pope-compares-having-an-abortion-to-hiring-a-hit-man-idUSKCN1MK1E7.

47. Junno Arocho Esteves, "Pope: Euthanasia is Triumph of Selfishness, Not Act of Compassion," *Catholic News Service*, http://www.catholicnews.com/services/englishnews/2016/euthanasia-is-triumph-of-selfishness-not-act-of-compassion.cfm.

48. Francis, *Amoris laetitia*, Vatican Website, https://w2.vatican.va/content/dam/francesco/pdf/apost_exhortations/documents/papa-francesco_esortazione-ap_20160319_amoris-laetitia_en.pdf, 42.

49. "Pope Denounces 'Throwaway' Culture of Consumer Society," *Chicago Tribune*, July 9, 2015, http://www.chicagotribune.com/news/nation-world/ct-pope-bolivia-20150709-story.html.

50. Francis, *Evangelii gaudium*, Vatican Website, http://w2.vatican.va/content/francesco/en/apost_exhortations/documents/papa-francesco_esortazione-ap_20131124_evangelii-gaudium.html, 214; and Francis, *Laudato si'*, Vatican Website, May 24, 2015, http://w2.vatican.va/content/francesco/en/encyclicals/documents/papa-francesco_20150524_enciclica-laudato-si.html, 157.

51. Scott Neuman, "Pope Calls Abortion Evidence of 'The Throwaway Culture,'" *NPR*, January 13, 2014, http://www.npr.org/sections/thetwo-way/2014/01/13/262085456/pope-calls-abortion-evidence-of-the-throwaway-culture.

52. Diane Montagna, "Pope Condemns 'Throw-away Culture' That Sees Elderly as 'Baggage,'" *Aleteia*, March 14, 2015, http://aleteia.org/2015/03/04/pope-condemns-throw-away-culture-that-sees-elderly-as-baggage/.

53. Francis, "Visit to the Joint Session of the United States Congress," Vatican Website, September 24, 2015, https://w2.vatican.va/content/francesco/en/speeches/2015/september/documents/papa-francesco_20150924_usa-us-congress.html.

54. *Amoris laetitia*, 316.

55. Ibid.

56. *Evangelii gaudium*, 53-55.

57. "How Do Our Words Dehumanize?," *Rehumanize International*, https://www.rehumanizeintl.org/badwords.

58. *Laudato si'*, 105.

59. *Laudato si'*, 20.

60. *Evangelii gaudium*, 88.

61. John L. Allen, Jr., "Christ child is with refugees, child soldiers and abortion victims, pope says," *Crux*, December 24, 2016, https://cruxnow.com/vatican/2016/12/24/christ-child-refugees-child-soldiers-abortion-victims-pope-says/.

62. In my book on Peter Singer and Christian ethics, I recount a story of how this worked with Catholic Relief Services and their response to the Rwandan genocide. See *Peter Singer and Christian Ethics: Beyond Polarization* (Cambridge, MA: Cambridge University Press, 2012), 154.

63. Rick Noack, "If Pope Francis Had His Way, European Parishes Would House up to 500,000 Refugees," *Washington Post*, September 6, 2015, https://www.washingtonpost.com/news/worldviews/wp/2015/09/06/if-the-pope-had-his-way-european-parishes-would-house-up-to-500000-refugees/.

64. John L. Allen, Jr., "Pope Offers Cautious Yellow Light for US Airstrikes in Iraq," *Boston Globe*, August 18, 2014, http://www.bostonglobe.com/news/world/2014/08/18/pope-offers-cautious-yellow-light-for-airstrikes-iraq/wisPM9745VsDwx8uttZdJJ/story.html.

65. Francis, "Greeting of Pope Francis to the Synod Fathers During the First General Congregation of the Third Extraordinary General Assembly of the Synod of Bishops," Vatican Website, October 6, 2014, https://w2.vatican.va/content/francesco/en/speeches/2014/october/documents/papa-francesco_20141006_padri-sinodali.html.

66. *Laudato si'*, 241.

67. *Evangelii gaudium*, 241.

68. *Laudato si'*, 128.

69. Nairn, 88.

70. Charles Camosy, "Pro-Life Groups Have an Obligation to Call Out Trump on Immigration," *America*, June 22, 2018, https://www.americamagazine.org/politics-society/2018/06/22/pro-life-groups-have-obligation-call-out-trump-immigration.

71. Francis, *Amoris laeitita*, Vatican Website, https://w2.vatican.va/content/dam/francesco/pdf/apost_exhortations/documents/papa-francesco_esortazione-ap_20160319_amoris-laetitia_en.pdf, 153.

72. Lauren Petersen, "Wanting Monogamy as 1,946 Men Await My Swipe," *New York Times*, May 26, 2017, https://www.nytimes.com/2017/05/26/style/modern-love-wanting-monogamy-as-1946-men-await-your-swipe.html.

73. Sarah Hepola, "Ask a Former Drunk: It's Time to Talk About Alcohol and Sex," *Jezebel*, July 5, 2016, http://jezebel.com/ask-a-former-drunk-its-time-to-talk-about-alcohol-and-1783117457.

74. *Amoris laeitita*, 39.

75. Sandee LaMotte, "New STD Cases Hit Record High in US, CDC Says," September 28, 2017, http://www.cnn.com/2017/09/26/health/std-highest-ever-reported-cdc/index.html .

76. Tara Parker-Pope, "Love, Sex, and the Changing Landscape of Infidelity," *New York Times,* October 27. 2018, http://www.nytimes.com/2008/10/28/health/28well.html.

77. Elizabeth McCauley, "Beginning Pornography Use Associated With Increase in Probability of Divorce," press release, August 22, 2016,

American Sociological Association, http://www.asanet.org/sites/default/files/pr_am_2016_perry_news_release_final.pdf.

78. Elaine K. Martin, Casey T. Taft, and Patricia A. Resick, "A Review of Marital Rape," May 2007, https://www.researchgate.net/profile/Patricia_Resick2/publication/223831051_A_review_of_marital_rape/links/5506fdf70cf26ff55f7b6360.pdf.

79. Tara Parker-Pope, "An Older Generation Falls Prey to Eating Disorders," *New York Times*, March 28, 2011, http://well.blogs.nytimes.com/2011/03/28/an-older-generation-falls-prey-to-eating-disorders/?hpw.

80. Jason S. Carroll, et al. "Generation XXX: Pornography Acceptance and Use Among Emerging Adults." *Journal of Adolescent Research* 23, no. 1 (January 2008).

81. Ross Benes, "Porn Could Have a Bigger Economic Influence on the US than Netflix," Quartz, June 20, 2018, https://qz.com/1309527/porn-could-have-a-bigger-economic-influence-on-the-us-than-netflix/.

82. Conor Friedersdorf, "Porn Star James Deen's Crisis of Conscience," *The Atlantic*, May 1, 2017, https://www.theatlantic.com/technology/archive/2017/05/porn-star-james-deens-crisis-of-conscience/523347/.

83. Sarah Plake, "Children Abusing Children: Children's Mercy Sees Dangerous Trend Involving Children and Porn," November 30, 2018, updated December 26, 2018, https://www.kshb.com/news/local-news/children-abusing-children-childrens-mercy-sees-dangerous-trend-involving-children-and-porn.

84. Joe Pinsker, "The Hidden Economics of Porn," *The Atlantic*, April 4, 2016, http://www.theatlantic.com/business/archive/2016/04/pornography-industry-economics-tarrant/476580/#article-comments.

85. "An In-Depth Look at the Evolving Porn Searches in Every State," Fight the New Drug, July 20, 2017, http://fightthenewdrug.org/a-disturbing-look-into-the-most-popular-porn-searches-in-each-state/.

86. Carmine Sarracino and Kevin M. Scott, *The Porning of America* (Boston: Beacon Press, 2008).

87. Ibid., 157-158.

88. Elise Harris, "Internet Porn Is the 'Neon Colosseum' of the Digital Age, Expert Says," *Catholic News Agency*, October 4, 2017, https://www.catholicnewsagency.com/news/internet-porn-is-the-neon-colosseum-of-the-digital-age-expert-says-98780.

89. Fight the New Drug, "Russell Brand Talks Sex, Softcore & Hardcore Porn," YouTube video, 6:27, posted [February 2015], https://www.youtube.com/watch?v=5kvzamjQW9M.

90. Derek Lawrence, "Chris Rock Talks Porn Addiction, Cheating on His Wife in Candid Netflix Special," *Entertainment Weekly*, February 14, 2018, http://ew.com/tv/2018/02/14/chris-rock-porn-addiction-cheating-tamborine/.

91. Afza Kandrikar Fathima, "Online Porn Easy Too [sic] Access: Research; Cameron Diaz is a 'Porn Addict,'" August 20, 2014, http://www.ibtimes.com.au/online-porn-easy-too-access-research-cameron-diaz-porn-addict-1351162.

92. Sarracino and Scott, x.

93. David Smith, "David Simon: 'If You're Not Consuming Porn, You're Still Consuming Its Logic,'" *Guardian*, September 10, 2017, https://www.theguardian.com/tv-and-radio/2017/sep/10/david-simon-george-pelecanos-the-deuce-pornography-drama-interview-the-wire?CMP=share_btn_fb.

94. Hannah Roberts, "Pope Francis Warns of Dangers of Internet 'Filth' for Children," *Express* (London, UK), June 9, 2015, http://www.express.co.uk/news/world/583160/Pope-Francis-internet-children-bedrooms-porn.

95. Judith Shulevitz, "It's O.K., Liberal Parents, You Can Freak Out About Porn," *New York Times*, July 16, 2016, https://www.nytimes.com/2016/07/17/opinion/sunday/its-ok-liberal-parents-you-can-freak-out-about-porn.html?WT.mc_id=2016-KWP-AUD_DEV&WT.mc_ev=click&ad-keywords=AUDDEVREMARK&kwp_0=190474&kwp_4=754378&kwp_1=379551&_r=4&referer=http://m.facebook.com/.

96. Gail Dines, "Is Porn Immoral? That Doesn't Matter: It's a Public Health Crisis," *Washington Post*, April 8, 2016, https://www.washingtonpost.com/posteverything/wp/2016/04/08/is-porn-immoral-that-doesnt-matter-its-a-public-health-crisis/?utm_term=.fe2a8fa6cf84.

97. John-Henry Westen, "Want to Stop Sex Trafficking? Look to America's Porn Addiction," *Huffington Post*, January 28, 2015, last modified March 30, 2015, http://www.huffingtonpost.com/johnhenry-westen/want-to-stop-sex-traffick_b_6563338.html.

98. Marlo Safi, "The Porn Industry and Human Trafficking Reinforce Each Other," *National Review*, August 1, 2018, https://www.nationalreview.com/2018/08/porn-human-trafficking-reinforce-each-other/.

99. Emma Green, "Most People Think Watching Porn Is Morally Wrong," *The Atlantic*, March 6, 2014, http://www.theatlantic.com/politics/archive/2014/03/most-people-think-watching-porn-is-morally-wrong/284240/.

100. "Naked Ambition," *Economist*, April 20, 2013, http://www.economist.com/news/international/21576366-iCLEand-determined-outlaw-

worlds-oldest-business-can-it-succeed-naked-ambition; and Chris Mor-ris, "No Porn Please, We're British," July 24, 2013, https://www.cnbc.com/id/100907216.

101. Scott Christian, "10 Reasons Why You Should Quit Watching Porn," *GQ*, November 20, 2013, http://www.gq.com/blogs/the-feed/2013/11/10-reasons-why-you-should-quit-watching-porn.html?mbid=social_retweet.

102. Naomi Wolf, "The Porn Myth," *New York*, October 20, 2003, http://nymag.com/nymetro/news/trends/n_9437/#ixzz0bL6kgjYJ.

103. Mary Rezac, "The New Celibacy? How Porn May be Destroying the Impetus for Sex," *Catholic News Agency*, June 11, 2017, http://www.catholicnewsagency.com/news/the-new-CLEibacy-how-porn-is-destroy-ing-the-impetus-for-sex-93222/.

104. Adam Kirsch, "A French Novelist Imagined Sexual Dystopia. Now It's Arrived," *New York Times*, July 12, 2018, https://www.nytimes.com/2018/07/12/books/review/michael-houellebecqs-sexual-distopia.html.

105. Rachel Lu, "Sex is Cheap and It's a Buyer's Market—If You're a Man," *American Conservative*, September 14, 2017, http://www.theamerican-conservative.com/articles/sex-is-cheap-and-its-a-buyers-market-if-youre-a-man/.

106. Jon Zimmerman, "We're Casual about Sex and Serious about Consent. But Is It Working?," *Washington Post*, October 13, 2015, https://www.washingtonpost.com/news/in-theory/wp/2015/10/13/were-casual-about-sex-and-serious-about-consent-but-is-it-working/?utm_term=.c13aaca8a0b9.

107. Kate Julian, "Why Are Young People Having So Little Sex?," *The Atlantic*, De-cember 2018, https://www.theatlantic.com/magazine/archive/2018/12/the-sex-recession/573949/?utm_source=newsletter&utm_medium=email&utm_campaign=atlantic-daily-newsletter&utm_content=20181113&silverid-ref=NDQzNzU1OTA4NTYwS0.

108. Matthew Haag, "It's Not Just You: Americans Are Having Less Sex," *New York Times*, March 8, 2017, https://www.nytimes.com/2017/03/08/us/americans-less-sex-study.html.

109. Katie Sanders, "A Startling Stat That Checks Out: 46 Percent of Young Women in Japan are Averse, Uninterested in Sex," *Politifact*, June 23, 2015, http://www.politifact.com/punditfact/statements/2015/jun/23/aziz-ansari/startling-stat-checks-out-46-percent-young-women-j/.

110. Greg Wilford, "Young Japanese People are Not Having Sex," *Independent*, July 8, 2017, http://www.independent.co.uk/news/world/asia/japan-sex-problem-demographic-time-bomb-birth-rates-sex-robots-fertility-crisis-virgins-romance-porn-a7831041.html.

111. "More Adult Diapers than Baby Ones to Be Sold in Japan," *Tokyo Times, n.d.,* https://www.tokyotimes.com/more-adult-diapers-than-baby-ones-to-be-sold-in-japan/.

112. Felix Allen, "My Sex Doll is So Much Better Than My Real Wife," *New York Post,* June 30, 2017, http://nypost.com/2017/06/30/i-love-my-sex-doll-because-she-never-grumbles/.

113. Jenna Moon and Claire Floody, "North America's First Known Sex Doll Brothel Opening in Toronto," *The Star,* August 27, 2018, https://www.thestar.com/amp/news/gta/2018/08/26/north-americas-first-known-sex-doll-brothel-opening-in-toronto.html?__twitter_impression=true.

114. "We Need to Talk about Sex, Robot Experts Say," *Japan Times,* July 5, 2017, http://www.japantimes.co.jp/news/2017/07/05/world/science-health-world/need-talk-sex-robot-experts-say/#.WYxLqITyvIU.

115. Beth Timmins, "New Sex Robots with 'Frigid' Settings Allow Men to Simulate Rape," *Independent,* July 19, 2017, http://www.independent.co.uk/life-style/sex-robots-frigid-settings-rape-simulation-men-sexual-assault-a7847296.html.

116. Shivali Best, "Would You Date a Robot? More Than a Quarter of Millennials Say They Would Replace a Human Lover with a DROID," *Daily Mail,* December 8, 2017, http://www.dailymail.co.uk/sciencetech/article-5156943/27-millennials-say-consider-dating-robot.html.

117. "Contraceptive Use in the United States," Guttmacher Institute, July 2018, http://www.guttmacher.org/pubs/fb_contr_use.html.

118. David P. Gushee, *The Sacredness of Human Life: Why an Ancient Biblical Vision Is Key to the World's Future* (Grand Rapids: Eerdmans Publishing Company, 2013), 360.

119. And, even then, many times our human nature manages to sneak through. From *Jersey Shore* to the average college dorm room, one person often gets emotionally attached after the supposed disconnected hookup.

120. Hannah Smothers, "I'm Waiting Until Marriage — This is What My Dating Life is Like," *Cosmopolitan,* March 11, 2016, http://www.cosmopolitan.com/sex-love/news/a54884/im-waiting-until-marriage-and-this-is-what-my-dating-life-is-like/.

121. *Amoris laetitia,* 80, 125.

122. Daniel Bates, "Number of College Students Having Casual Sex on the Rise. . .But Virginity Makes a Comeback Too," *Daily Mail,* March 31, 2011, http://www.dailymail.co.uk/news/article-1372004/Number-college-students-having-casual-sex-rise--virginity-makes-comeback-too.html#ixzz1nJH8tQHm.

123. Kari-Shane Davis Zimmerman, "In Control? The Hookup Culture and the Practice of Relationships," in *Leaving and Coming Home: New Wine-*

skins for Catholic Sexual Ethics, ed. David Cloutier (Eugene, OR: Cascade Books, 2010), https://digitalcommons.csbsju.edu/theology_pubs/69/.

124. "The Most Surprising Demographic Crisis," *Economist*, May 5, 2011, http://www.economist.com/node/18651512.

125. Steven Lee Meyers and Olivia Mitchell Ryan, "Burying 'One Child' Limits, China Pushes Women to Have More Babies," *New York Times*, August 11, 2018, https://www.nytimes.com/2018/08/11/world/asia/china-one-child-policy-birthrate.html.

126. Associated Press, "Russia Marks Day of Conception," MSNBC.com, September 11, 2007, http://www.nbcnews.com/id/20730526/ns/world_news-europe/t/baby-car-russians-hold-conception-day/#.W-DSufZFz3V .

127. "World Population in 2300," Proceedings of the United Nations Expert Meeting on World Population in 2300, March 24, 2004, http://www.un.org/esa/population/publications/longrange2/longrange2.htm, 1.

128. Edward C. Green, "Condoms, HIV-AIDS and Africa— The Pope Was Right," *Washington Post*, March 29, 2009, http://www.washingtonpost.com/wp-dyn/content/article/2009/03/27/AR2009032702825.html.

129. One kind of contraception actually caused the HIV infection rate to double: Pam Belluck, "Contraceptive Used in Africa May Double Risk of H.I.V.," *New York Times*, October 3, 2011, http://www.nytimes.com/2011/10/04/health/04hiv.html?pagewanted=1&hpw.

130. Tim Allen and Suzette Heald, "HIV/AIDS policy in Africa: what has worked in Uganda and what has failed in Botswana?," *Journal of International Development* vol. 16, no. 8 (November 2004), http://onlinelibrary.wiley.com/doi/10.1002/jid.1168/abstract.

131 LaMotte.

132. "Melinda Gates Says She Is 'Optimistic' Pope Francis Will Change Teaching on Contraception," *Catholic Herald*, July 11, 2017, http://catholicherald.co.uk/news/2017/07/11/melinda-gates-says-she-is-optimistic-pope-francis-will-change-teaching-on-contraception/.

133. Mary Rezac, "Pope Francis was right about condoms and HIV," *Catholic News Agency*, December 13, 2015, http://www.catholicnewsagency.com/news/the-pope-was-right-about-condoms-and-hiv-49253/.

134. *Amoris laetitia*, 42.

135. *Laudato si'*, 50.

136. Rita Rubin, "The Pill: 50 Years of Birth Control Changed Women's Lives," *USA Today*, n.d., http://www.usatoday.com/news/health/2010-05-07-1Apill07_CV_N.htm.

137. Christopher Ingraham, "The Best Age to Get Married If You Don't Want to Get Divorced," *Washington Post*, July 17, 2015, last modified

December 30, 2015, https://www.washingtonpost.com/news/wonk/wp/2015/12/30/the-best-age-to-get-married-if-you-dont-want-to-get-divorced-2/.

138. For a particularly good example of this kind of argument, see Erika Bachiochi and Catherine R. Pakaluk, "The Pill is Not Good for Women," *National Review*, February 21, 2012, http://www.nationalreview.com/articles/291514/pill-not-good-women-erika-bachiochi?pg=1.

139. Bobbi Nodell, "Hormonal contraception use doubles HIV risk, according to UW study in Lancet," *UW News* (University of Washington), October 4, 2011, http://www.washington.edu/news/2011/10/04/hormonal-contraception-use-doubles-hiv-risk-according-to-uw-study-in-lancet/.

140. "Known and Probable Human Carcinogens," *American Cancer Society*, last modified November 3, 2016, http://www.cancer.org/Cancer/CancerCauses/OtherCarcinogens/GeneralInformationaboutCarcinogens/known-and-probable-human-carcinogens.

141. Dana Farrington, "Birth Control and Blood Clots: Women Still Weighing the Risks," *NPR*, February 9, 2014, http://www.npr.org/sections/health-shots/2014/02/09/273145327/nuvaring-contraceptive-settlement-leaves-women-weighing-risks?sc=17&f=.

142. Roni Caryn Rabin, "Birth Control Pills Still Linked to Breast Cancer, Study Finds," *New York Times*, December 6, 2017, https://www.nytimes.com/2017/12/06/health/birth-control-breast-cancer-hormones.html?emc=edit_tnt_20171206&nlid=58583175&tntemail0=y&mtrref=undefined&_r=0&referer=http://m.facebook.com/.

143. Charlotte Wessel Skovlund, Lina Steinrud Mørch, Lars Vedel Kessing, and Øjvind Lidegaard, "Association of Hormonal Contraception With Depression," *Journal of the American Medical Society Psychiatry* 73, 11 (November 2016), https://jamanetwork.com/journals/jamapsychiatry/fullarticle/2552796; and Charlotte Wessel Skovlund, Lina Steinrud Mørch, Lars Vedel Kessing, and Theis Lange, "Association of Hormonal Contraception With Suicide Attempts and Suicides," *American Journal of Psychiatry* 175, 4 (November 2017), https://www.ncbi.nlm.nih.gov/pubmed/29145752.

144. And the side effects have a disproportionately negative impact on poor women. The Affordable Care Act may cover contraception without cost to the user, but even after Medicaid expansion the poor (who are most at risk for depression even apart from these devices) risk not getting the mental health care they require. Even more disturbingly, the trend seems to be encouraging impoverished people to use high-dose IUDs and other long-acting contraception. For example, a recent *Forbes* headline wonders, "Can the IUD Prevent Poverty, Save Taxpayers Billions"

(Carrie Sheffield, *Forbes*, October 5, 2014, https://www.forbes.com/sites/carriesheffield/2014/10/05/can-the-iud-prevent-poverty-save-taxpayers-billions/#30e921c63291). Recently, Bayer said it would stop selling the Essure birth control device after thousands of women said that it "caused serious health problems" and "excruciating pain." See Daniel Arkin, "Bayer Says It Will Stop U.S. Sales of Birth Control Device Essure," July 20, 2018, https://www.nbcnews.com/health/health-news/bayer-says-it-will-stop-u-s-sales-birth-control-n893186. Many have also lodged similar complaints about the IUD Mirena and other long-acting contraceptive devices. One woman saw her IUD become dislodged, travel to her stomach, break into pieces and enter her liver. Though her life was saved after her organs began to fail and she was put on a ventilator, the ordeal cost her uterus, ovaries, and toes—which had to be removed. See Alexandria Hein, "Mom Loses Ovaries, Uterus, and Toes after IUD Ends up in Stomach," June 8 [no year given], https://www.foxnews.com/health/mom-loses-ovaries-uterus-and-toes-after-iud-ends-up-in-stomach.

145. January 2019 Fact Sheet: "Unintended Pregnancy in the United States," https://www.guttmacher.org/fact-sheet/unintended-pregnancy-united-states.

146. Helen Alvaré, "Contracepting Conscience," *Public Discourse*, July 25, 2011, http://www.thepublicdiscourse.com/2011/07/3577. Interestingly, Mahatma Gandhi made exactly this point in an extraordinary exchange with the founder of Planned Parenthood, Margaret Sanger. For details see *The Collected Works of Mahatma Gandhi*, v62 (Government of India: Publications Division, 1975), pp154-160.

147. George A. Akerlof. *Explorations in Pragmatic Economics*. (Oxford University Press, 2005), 135-140.

148. Helen M. Alvaré, "Beyond the Sex-Ed Wars: Addressing Disadvantaged Single Mothers' Search for Community," George Mason University, March 2010, http://works.bepress.com/cgi/viewcontent.cgi?article=1003&context=helen_alvare.

149. Of course, another vulnerable group to consider in this context is the children born into these situations. Social science shows overwhelmingly that they do worse than those born into a married household. More will be said about them in the next chapter.

150. Charles C. Camosy, "Is Fertility Awareness a natural alternative to the Pill?," *Crux*, April 19, 2017, https://cruxnow.com/interviews/2017/04/19/fertility-awareness-natural-alternative-pill/.

151. John Thavis, "Vatican Clarifies Pope's Reference to 'Male Prostitute' in Condoms Comment," *Catholic News Service*, November 23, 2010, http://

cnsblog.wordpress.com/2010/11/23/vatican-clarifies-popes-reference-to-male-prostitute-in-condoms-comment/.

152. "Kesha's note to her 18-year-old self: 'There is light and beauty after the storm,'" *CBS News*, August 10, 2017, http://www.cbsnews.com/news/kesha-note-to-self/?linkId=40804420.

153. "Emergency Contraception (EC)," *Center for Young Women's Health*, May 31, 2017, https://youngwomenshealth.org/2013/05/23/emergency-contraception/; "Which Kind of Emergency Contraception Should I Use?," *Planned Parenthood*, last updated 2018, https://www.planned-parenthood.org/learn/morning-after-pill-emergency-contraception/which-kind-emergency-contraception-should-i-use.

154. Daniel P. Sulmasy, "Emergency Contraception for Women Who Have Been Raped: Must Catholics Test for Ovulation, or Is Testing for Pregnancy Morally Sufficient?" *Kennedy Institute of Ethics Journal* 16, no. 4 (December 2006): 305-31, and Nicanor P. G. Austriaco, OP, "Is Plan B an Abortifacient? A Critical Look at the Scientific Evidence," *National Catholic Bioethics Quarterly* 7.4 (Winter 2007): 703–707.

155. *Ella* (United States: Afaxys, 2015), https://www.ellanow.com/downloads/ella-brochure.pdf, 3.

156. "FDA Approved Patient Labeling Patient Information," *FDA*, last updated August 2010, http://www.accessdata.fda.gov/drugsatfda_docs/label/2010/022474s000lbl.pdf, 9.

157. "Contraception and Insurance Coverage (Religious Exemption Debate)," *New York Times*, 2012, http://topics.nytimes.com/top/news/health/diseasesconditionsandhealthtopics/health_insurance_and_managed_care/health_care_reform/contraception/index.html.

158. Henry T. Greely, *The End of Sex and the Future of Human Reproduction* (Cambridge: Harvard University Press, 2016).

159. Aurora MacRae-Crerar, "Will Genetic Advances Make Sex Obsolete?," *NPR*, June 16, 2016, http://www.npr.org/sections/health-shots/2016/06/16/482189322/will-baby-making-move-from-the-bedroom-to-the-lab?utm_source=twitter.com&utm_medium=social&utm_campaign=npr&utm_term=nprnews&utm_content=20160616.

160. Gabriel Bell, "Study: Sperm Counts are Half of What They Used to be 40 Years Ago," *Salon*, July 25, 2017, http://www.salon.com/2017/07/25/study-sperm-counts-are-half-of-what-they-used-to-be-40-years-ago/.

161. Ariana Eunjung Cha, "U.S. fertility rate falls to record low, stoking fears of a demographic shift," *The Washington Post*, June 30, 2017, https://www.washingtonpost.com/news/to-your-health/wp/2017/06/30/the-u-s-fertility-rate-just-hit-a-historic-low-why-some-demographers-are-freaking-out/?utm_term=.a3acf726c427.

162. Liz Alderman, "After Economic Crisis, Low Birthrates Challenge Southern Europe," *New York Times*, April 16, 2017, https://www.nytimes.com/2017/04/16/business/fewer-children-in-greece-may-add-to-its-financial-crisis.html?smid=tw-share.

163. Barbara Lippert, "Inside Apple's New Campus: No Childcare (But You Can Freeze Your Eggs)," *AdAge*, July 6, 2017, http://adage.com/article/guest-columnists/childcare-apple-s-mothership/309650/.

164. In the story that follows, we see that she was under intense social and familial pressure to give birth a male heir: "Pictured: world's oldest mother, 70, lies dying with baby at her side after risking her life to beat stigma of being barren," *Daily Mail*, June 15, 2010, http://www.dailymail.co.uk/news/article-1286412/Worlds-oldest-mother-Rajo-Devi-Lohan-reveals-dying.html#ixzz0wjHTqJ9y.

165. "Couples any age to be allowed to apply for fertility treatment," *Scotsman*, November 3, 2005, http://www.scotsman.com/news/health/couples-any-age-to-be-allowed-to-apply-for-fertility-treatment-1-1102869.

166. Georgina M. Chambers, Elizabeth A. Sullivan, Osamu Ishihara, Michael G. Chapman, and G. David Adamson, "The economic impact of assisted reproductive technology: a review of selected developed countries," *Fertility and Sterility* Volume 91, Issue 6 (June 2009): 2281-2294, http://www.sciencedirect.com/science/article/pii/S0015028209008735.

167. "Stem cell research" is an enormous and complex topic, one to which we certainly cannot do full justice in a footnote, but it may be worth making some brief points specifically as it relates to IVF. Though some countries regulate embryonic stem cell research so they don't develop this problem (Germany, for instance, has required that all created embryos be implanted), the main sources for embryonic stem cell research are the many thousands of "excess" embryos "left over" from IVF. (When this isn't good enough, however, New York State has decided to pay women for their eggs to create embryos specifically for such research.) Embryos are essentially made of generic "pluripotent" cells that can be coaxed to become any cell in the body and possibly heal damaged tissue—from, say, a heart attack or even a spinal injury. Much debate about embryonic stem cell research comes from what one thinks about the moral status of the human embryo and the fact that an embryo is destroyed in the process of procuring its cells for research. We will engage this question below, but first we should lay out the research and medical facts. Embryonic stem cell research, as this book goes to press, has not developed a single widely available therapy or cure for a disease. This, despite the billions of dollars that have been put into such research worldwide. Happily for people with illnesses that could benefit from stem cell research, there are

many other ways to get stem cells. Other tissues (from the brain, bone marrow, spinal fluid, and even the nose) contain "adult" stem cells—and these have produced dozens and dozens of proven therapies. The *Journal of the American Medical Association*, for instance, has shown a "modest to significant" impact from adult stem cell research to treat multiple sclerosis, systemic lupus, system sclerosis, type I (juvenile) diabetes, rheumatoid arthritis, Crohn's disease, and cardiovascular diseases including acute heart attack damage, chronic coronary artery disease, and peripheral vascular disease. Adult stem cells have even made blind people see again. And all of this justified excitement and promise comes from readily available pluripotent stem cells (in amniotic fluid, for instance) that do not require the destruction of a single embryo. One recent development, for instance, is the creation of beating human hearts from adult stem cells. (Robin Andrews, "Beating Human Hearts Grown In Laboratory Using Stem Cells," *IFLScience!*, March 21, 2016, http://www.iflscience.com/health-and-medicine/beating-human-hearts-grown-laboratory-using-stem-cells-made-skin.). It is a shame that American politics (often related to abortion) and pursuit of research grant money drive the stem cell debate far more than what actually helps vulnerable populations.

168. Susan Donaldson James, "Down Syndrome Births Are Down in U.S.," *ABC News*, Nov. 2, 2009, http://abcnews.go.com/Health/w_ParentingResource/down-syndrome-births-drop-us-women-abort/story?id=8960803#.T1jPpPVuqSo.

169. Ruth Padawer, "The Two-Minus-One Pregnancy," *New York Times Magazine*, August 10, 2011, http://www.nytimes.com/2011/08/14/magazine/the-two-minus-one-pregnancy.html?pagewanted=all.

170. "West Coast Surrogacy Costs & Fees," *West Coast Surrogacy Inc.*, last updated 2018, https://www.westcoastsurrogacy.com/surrogate-program-for-intended-parents/surrogate-mother-cost.

171. Nilanjana S. Roy, "Protecting the Rights of Surrogate Mothers in India," *New York Times*, October 4, 2011, http://www.nytimes.com/2011/10/05/world/asia/05iht-letter05.html.

172. "Thai Surrogate Offers Clues into Japanese Man with 16 Babies," *National* (Abu Dhabi), September 3, 2014, https://www.thenational.ae/world/asia/thai-surrogate-offers-clues-into-japanese-man-with-16-babies-1.239982.

173. "India Outlawed Commercial Surrogacy—Clinics Are Finding Loopholes," October 23, 2017, https://theconversation.com/india-outlawed-commercial-surrogacy-clinics-are-finding-loopholes-81784; and Australian Associated Press, "Thailand bans commercial surrogacy," *Guardian*, February 20, 2015, https://www.theguardian.com/world/2015/feb/20/thailand-bans-commercial-surrogacy.

174. Jo Knowsley, "Surrogate Mother Says 'Sorry, But I'm Keeping Your Babies,'" *Daily Mail*, December 17, 2006, http://www.dailymail.co.uk/femail/article-423125/Surrogate-mother-says-Sorry-Im-keeping-babies.html#ixzz1oY1dulCk.

175. Tom Blackwell, "Couple Urged Surrogate Mother to Abort Fetus Because of Defect," *National Post*, October 6, 2010, https://nationalpost.com/holy-post/couple-urged-surrogate-mother-to-abort-fetus-because-of-defect.

176. Kajsa Ekis Ekman, "All Surrogacy is Exploitation – The World Should Follow Sweden's Ban," *Guardian*, February 25, 2016, https://www.theguardian.com/commentisfree/2016/feb/25/surrogacy-sweden-ban.

177. Kat Huang, "Egg Donor Ads Target Women of Ivy League," *Yale Daily News*, March 22, 2005, https://yaledailynews.com/blog/2005/03/22/egg-donor-ads-target-women-of-ivy-league/.

178. William Saletan, "The Egg Market," *Slate*, March 29, 2010, http://www.slate.com/articles/health_and_science/human_nature/2010/03/the_egg_market.html.

179. Marilee Enge, "Ad Seeks Donor Eggs For $100,000, Possible New High," *Chicago Tribune*, February 10, 2000, http://articles.chicagotribune.com/2000-02-10/news/0002100320_1_egg-donor-program-infertile-ads.

180. Anna Medaris Miller, "Should Your Travel Abroad for IVF?," *US News & World Report,* December 15, 2015, https://health.usnews.com/health-news/patient-advice/articles/2015-12-15/should-you-travel-abroad-for-ivf.

181. Paul Bentley, Sara Smyth, and Katherine Faulkner, "Crackdown on the IVF Cowboys after Probe Reveals Financial Incentives to Entice Women into Giving Away Eggs," *Daily Mail*, September 12, 2017, http://www.dailymail.co.uk/news/article-4878048/Crackdown-IVF-cowboys-probe.html?utm_content=buffere4fa4&utm_medium=social&utm_source=facebook.com&utm_campaign=buffer#ixzz4sbXvyCFm.

182. Kathleen Sloan, "Film Review: Eggsploitation," n.d., http://www.council-forresponsiblegenetics.org/genewatch/GeneWatchPage.aspx?pageId=314.

183. Jacqueline Mroz, "One Sperm Donor, 150 Offspring," *New York Times*, September 5, 2011, http://www.nytimes.com/2011/09/06/health/06donor.html?pagewanted=1&_r=1&ref=health.

184. "'I Didn't Want Children to Die': A Mother's Mission to Save Sperm Donor's 35 Kids Never Told about His Fatal, Genetic Illness," *Daily Mail*, March 7, 2012, http://www.dailymail.co.uk/news/article-2111623/Sperm-Donors-35-Kids-Never-Told-About-Fatal-Genetic-Illness.html?ito=feeds-newsxml.

185. Spain has scrapped using the terms "mother" or "father," and instead refers to progenitor A and progenitor B on their birth certificates. This is designed to avoid discrimination against LGBT couples. David Rennie, "How's Your 'Progenitor A?,'" *Telegraph*, March 7, 2006, http://www.telegraph.co.uk/news/worldnews/europe/spain/1512344/Hows-your-Progenitor-A.html.

186. Eliza Strickland, "DNA Swap Could Make Healthier Babies—With Three Genetic Parents," *Discover*, August 26, 2009, http://blogs.discovermagazine.com/80beats/2009/08/26/dna-swap-could-make-healthier-babies-with-three-genetic-parents/#.XABA__ZFyGk.

187. Jeffrey Steinberg, "Fertility Preservation," *The Fertility Institutes*, n.d., http://www.fertility-docs.com/egg_donors.phtml; and Antonio Regalado, "Eugenics 2.0: We're at the Dawn of Choosing Embryos by Health, Height, and More," *MIT Technology Review*, November 1, 2017, https://www.technologyreview.com/s/609204/eugenics-20-were-at-the-dawn-of-choosing-embryos-by-health-height-and-more/?utm_campaign=Owned+Social&utm_source=Owned+Social&utm_medium=Facebook.

188. Jane Ridley, "Mom to the Internet: Anybody Want to Trade My Girl Embryo for a Boy?," *New York Post*, November 3, 2018, https://nypost.com/2018/11/03/mom-to-the-internet-anybody-want-to-trade-my-girl-embryo-for-a-boy/.

189. Lauran Neergaard, "First Embryo Gene-Repair Holds Promise for Inherited Disease," *Associated Press*, August 2, 2017, https://apnews.com/fcf52fde924d430ca9441aa401c259ed/First-embryo-gene-repair-holds-promise-for-inherited-disease.

190. William Saletan, "Color ID," *Slate*, February 17, 2009, http://www.slate.com/articles/health_and_science/human_nature/2009/02/color_id.html.

191. Jeffrey Steinberg, "Gender Selection," *The Fertility Institutes*, n.d., http://www.fertility-docs.com/fertility_gender.phtml.

192. Clare Murphy, "Is It Wrong to Select a Deaf Embryo?," *BBC News*, March 10, 2008, http://news.bbc.co.uk/1/hi/health/7287508.stm.

193. It is important to acknowledge (1) the complexity involved when such drugs might be taken for the woman's health or to save her life, and (2) different arguments about the moral status of the fetus. Both will be addressed below and in the next chapter on abortion.

194. Inés San Martín, "Pope: No Research Justifies the Destruction of Human Embryos," *Crux*, May 18, 2017, https://cruxnow.com/vatican/2017/05/18/pope-no-research-justifies-destruction-human-embryos/.

195. *Amoris laetitia*, 18.

196. *Amoris laetitia*, 81.

197. Devin Watkins, "Pope to Pro-Life Movement: 'Politicians Should Place Defense of Life First,'" *Vatican News,* February 2, 2019, https://www.vaticannews.va/en/pope/news/2019-02/pope-francis-pro-life-movement-politicians-defend-life.html.

198. Ruth Whitbread, "Vatican Support for 'Placenta Bank,'" *BBC News,* January 1, 2001, http://news.bbc.co.uk/1/hi/sci/tech/1096133.stm.

199. Mitchell Landsberg, "Vatican Signs Deal to Collaborate on Adult Stem Cell Research," *LA Times,* October 20, 2011, http://articles.latimes.com/2011/oct/20/business/la-fi-vatican-stem-cells-20111020.

200. David P. Gushee, *The Sacredness of Human Life: Why an Ancient Biblical Vision Is Key to the World's Future* (Grand Rapids, MI: Wm. B. Eerdmans Publishing Co., 2013), 444-445.

201. Congregation for the Doctrine of the Faith, *Dignitas Personae*, Vatican Website, September 8, 2008, http://www.vatican.va/roman_curia/congregations/cfaith/documents/rc_con_cfaith_doc_20081208_dignitas-personae_en.html.

202. Helen M. Alvaré, "The Case for Regulating Collaborative Reproduction: A Children's Rights Perspective," *Harvard Journal on Legislation* 40, no. 2 (Winter 2003): 1–63.

203. Steven Jacobs, "Biologists' Consensus on 'When Life Begins,'" (working paper, *SSRN*, July 25, 2018), https://papers.ssrn.com/sol3/papers.cfm?abstract_id=3211703.

204. Congregation for the Doctrine of the Faith, *Donum Vitae*, Vatican Website, February 22, 1987, http://www.vatican.va/roman_curia/congregations/cfaith/documents/rc_con_cfaith_doc_19870222_respect-for-human-life_en.html, I:1.

205. Margie Fishman, "Delaware Couple Embraces Adoption When IVF Fails," *Delaware Online*, May 6, 2016, https://www.delawareonline.com/story/news/2016/05/06/mothers-day-del-couple-embraces-adoption-when-ivf-fails/83829210/.

206. Andrew Hough, "How Adoption for IVF Couples Could Lead to a Happier Life," *Telegraph*, April 27, 2013, https://www.telegraph.co.uk/news/health/news/10021173/How-adoption-for-IVF-couples-could-lead-to-a-happier-life.html.

207. Daniel K. Williams, *Defenders of the Unborn: The Pro-Life Movement before Roe v. Wade* (New York: Oxford University Press, 2016).

208. Though I do make new arguments in this chapter, my basic approach is laid out in much more detail in my 2015 book on a similar topic.

Charles C. Camosy, *Beyond the Abortion Wars: A Way Forward for a New Generation* (Grand Rapids, MI: Wm. B. Eerdmans Publishing Co., 2015).

209. Robert P. Jones, Daniel Cox, and Rachel Laser, "Committed to Availability, Conflicted about Morality: What the Millennial Generation Tells Us about the Future of the Abortion Debate and the Culture Wars," *PRRI*, June 9, 2011, https://www.prri.org/research/committed-to-availability-conflicted-about-morality-what-the-millennial-generation-tells-us-about-the-future-of-the-abortion-debate-and-the-culture-wars/.

210. "Roe v. Wade at 40: Most Oppose Overturning Abortion Decision," *Pew Research Center*, January 16, 2013, http://www.pewforum.org/2013/01/16/roe-v-wade-at-40/.

211. Pam Belluck, "Complex Science at Issue in Politics of Fetal Pain," *New York Times*, September 16, 2013, https://www.nytimes.com/2013/09/17/health/complex-science-at-issue-in-politics-of-fetal-pain.html.

212. Lee M. Miringoff and Barbara L. Carvalho, "Americans' Opinions on Abortion," *Marist College Institute for Public Opinion*, January 2018, https://www.kofc.org/en/resources/communications/abortion-limits-favored.pdf.

213. Aaron Blake, "Guess Who Likes the GOP'S 20-week Abortion Ban? Women." *Washington Post*, August 2, 2013, https://www.washingtonpost.com/news/the-fix/wp/2013/08/02/guess-who-likes-the-gops-20-week-abortion-ban-women/.

214. Michael J. New, "*Washington Post* Highlights Pro-Life Millennials," *National Review*, February 1, 2018, https://www.nationalreview.com/corner/abortion-millennials-washington-post-highlights-pro-life-young-people/.

215. Bradford Richardson, "Millennials Increasingly Oppose Abortion, Even If They Don't Identify as 'Pro-Life': Report," *Washington Times*, June 30, 2016, https://www.washingtontimes.com/news/2016/jun/30/millennials-increasingly-oppose-abortion-even-if-t/.

216. Rachel K. Jones, Susheela Singh, Lawrence B. Finer, and Lori F. Frohwirth, *Repeat abortion in the United States: Occasional Report* No. 29 (New York: Guttmacher Institute, 2006), https://www.guttmacher.org/sites/default/files/pdfs/pubs/2006/11/21/or29.pdf.

217. John Wilson, "Where New York's Not Proud to Lead," *New York Post*, July 1, 2010, http://www.nypost.com/p/news/opinion/opedcolumnists/where_new_york_not_proud_to_lead_236nyjSL3ZbkCV5woJqUFJ.

218. Nikita Stewart, "Baby Antonio: 5 Pounds, 12 Ounces and Homeless from Birth," *New York Times,* October 30 2018, https://www.nytimes.com/interactive/2018/10/30/nyregion/homeless-children.html?action=click&-

module=&pgtype=Homepage&fbclid=IwAR3hB2aQJlxCH0mbbOFh
L034aD-4hVpi3HuwHE7MTnQTtt6joUD_7YVbg1M.

219. Ruth Padawer, "The Two Minus One Pregnancy," *New York Times*,
August 10, 2011, http://www.nytimes.com/2011/08/14/magazine/
the-two-minus-one-pregnancy.html?pagewanted=all.

220. Caroline Mansfield, Suellen Hopfer, and Theresa M. Marteau, "Termination Rates after Prenatal Diagnosis of Down Syndrome, Spina Bifida,
Anencephaly, and Turner And Klinefelter Syndromes: A Systematic
Literature Review," *Prenatal Diagnosis* vol. 19, no. 9 (September 1999),
http://onlinelibrary.wiley.com/doi/10.1002/%28SICI%291097-
0223%28199909%2919:9%3C808::AID-PD637%3E3.0.CO;2-B/
abstract.

221. Margaret Somerville, "'Deselecting' Our Children," *Globe and Mail*,
August 22, 2011, last modified April 29, 2018, https://www.theglobean-
dmail.com/opinion/deselecting-our-children/article626406/; and Julian
Quinones and Arijeta Lajka, "'What Kind of Society Do You Want to
Live In?': Inside the Country Where Down Syndrome Is Disappearing,"
CBS News, August 14, 2017, https://www.cbsnews.com/news/down-
syndrome-iceland/?linkId=40953194.

222. Genevieve Shaw Brown, "Mom and Baby with Down Syndrome Mail
Letter to Doctor Who Suggested Abortion," *Good Morning America*,
June 7, 2016, https://www.yahoo.com/gma/mom-baby-down-syndrome-
mail-letter-doctor-suggested-185205470--abc-news-parenting.html.

223. Sarah McCammon, "U.S. Abortion Rate Falls to Lowest Level Since
Roe v. Wade," *NPR*, January 17, 2017, https://www.npr.org/sections/
thetwo-way/2017/01/17/509734620/u-s-abortion-rate-falls-to-lowest-
level-since-roe-v-wade.

224. Emily Crockett, "The Abortion Rate Is at an All-Time Low — And Better Birth Control is Largely to Thank," *Vox*, January 18, 2017, https://
www.vox.com/identities/2017/1/18/14296532/abortion-rate-lowest-
ever-because-birth-control.

225. Rebecca Wind, "About Half of U.S. Abortion Patients Report Using
Contraception in the Month They Became Pregnant," News release,
Guttmacher Institute, January 11, 2018, https://www.guttmacher.
org/news-release/2018/about-half-us-abortion-patients-report-using-
contraception-month-they-became.

226. Ross Douthat, "There is No Pro-Life Case for Planned Parenthood,"
New York Times, August 5, 2015, https://douthat.blogs.nytimes.
com/2015/08/05/there-is-no-pro-life-case-for-planned-parenthood/.

227. "Vital Signs: Trends in Use of Long-Acting Reversible Contraception
Among Teens Aged 15–19 Years Seeking Contraceptive Services —

United States, 2005–2013," Centers for Disease Control and Prevention, April 10, 2015, https://www.cdc.gov/mmwr/preview/mmwrhtml/mm6413a6.htm.

228. Charlie Camosy, "Encyclical Draws Connections Necessary to Oppose Abortion," *Catholic News Service*, April 26, 2018, https://catholic-sf.org/news/encyclical-draws-connections-necessary-to-oppose-abortion.

229. Ann Furedi, "Women are Having Abortions Because Their Contraception Doesn't Work," *Telegraph*, July 7, 2017, https://www.telegraph.co.uk/women/life/women-having-abortions-contraception-doesnt-work/.

230. Kenworthey Bilz and Janice Nadler, "Law, Moral Attitudes, And Behavioral Change," in *The Oxford Handbook of Behavioral Economics and the Law*, eds. Eyal Zamir and Doron Teichman (New York: Oxford University Press, 2014), https://www.law.northwestern.edu/faculty/fulltime/nadler/Bilz-Nadler-LawMoralAttitudesPageProofs.pdf.

231. "Pregnant Women Support Act (95-10)," Democrats for Life of America, https://www.democratsforlife.org/index.php/pregnant-women-support-act-95-10.

232. Libertad González, "The Effect of a Universal Child Benefit on Conceptions, Abortions, and Early Maternal Labor Supply," *American Economic Journal: Economic Policy* 5, 3 (August 2013): 160-88, https://www.aeaweb.org/articles?id=10.1257/pol.5.3.160.

233. Lisa Bourne, "Hungary Sees Abortion Numbers Plunge with Rise of Pro-Family Policies," *LifeSite News*, June 1, 2018, https://www.lifesitenews.com/news/hungary-sees-abortion-numbers-plunge-with-rise-of-pro-family-policies.

234. "Services," Planned Parenthood, last modified January 2014, https://www.plannedparenthood.org/files/4013/9611/7243/Planned_Parenthood_Services.pdf.

235. "Johnson: Planned Parenthood Probe a Good First Step," *Roll Call* (Washington, D.C.), October 25, 2011, http://www.rollcall.com/issues/57_48/abby_johnson_planned_parenthood_probe_good_first_step-209776-1.html.

236. This is important because federal funds go to Planned Parenthood on the condition that they not be used to provide elective abortions.

237. "False Claims and Fraud: Lawsuit Exposes Planned Parenthood Deception," Alliance Defending Freedom, March 9, 2012, http://www.adfmedia.org/%28X%281%29S%28ravdtduyoahrzeac0q2tub55%29%29/News/PRDetail/5395?AspxAutoDetectCookieSupport=1.

238. Erin Heger, "Planned Parenthood Has a History of Trying to Beat Back Labor Unions," *Rewire.News,* July 19, 2018, https://rewire.news/

article/2018/07/19/planned-parenthood-history-trying-beat-back-labor-unions/.

239. Matt Taibbi, "The Curious Case of the Planned Parenthood Union Struggle," July 18, 2018, https://www.rollingstone.com/politics/politics-news/planned-parenthood-union-700700/.

240. Natalie Kitroeff and Jessica Silver-Greenberg, "Planned Parenthood Is Accused of Mistreating Pregnant Employees," *New York Times*, December 20, 2018, https://www.nytimes.com/2018/12/20/business/planned-parenthood-pregnant-employee-discrimination-women.html.

241. Report of the Grand Jury XXIII, First District of Pennsylvania, January 14, 2011, https://cdn.cnsnews.com/documents/Gosnell,%20Grand%20Jury%20Report.pdf.

242. Linda Greenhouse, "Misconceptions," *New York Times*, January 23, 2013, http://opinionator.blogs.nytimes.com/2013/01/23/misconceptions/?_r=0.

243. Holly V. Hays, "Federal Judge Rules Indiana Abortion Law Signed by Pence Unconstitutional," *USA Today*, April 20, 2018, http://amp.usatoday.com/amp/537211002.

244. Kristen Day and Charles Camosy, "How the Democratic Platform Betrays Millions of the Party Faithful," *Los Angeles Times*, July 25, 2016, http://www.latimes.com/opinion/op-ed/la-oe-day-and-camosy-democratic-platform-abortion-20160725-snap-story.html.

245. Abortion Care Network, last modified 2018, https://www.abortioncarenetwork.org/.

246. Chloe Angyal, "Selling an Abortion Clinic Might Be Even Harder Than Running One," *Huffington Post*, August 31, 2017, last modified September 1, 2017, https://www.huffingtonpost.com/entry/independent-abortion-clinic-owners_us_59a56ffae4b0446b3b86750d.

247. *Amoris laetitia*, 83.

248. Watkins.

249. Natalie Kitroeff and Jessica Silver-Greenberg, "Pregnancy Discrimination Is Rampant Inside America's Biggest Companies," *New York Times*, June 15, 2018, https://www.nytimes.com/interactive/2018/06/15/business/pregnancy-discrimination.html?smid=tw-share.

250. Claire Cain Miller, "Americans Are Having Fewer Babies. They Told Us Why." *New York Times*, July 5, 2018, https://www.nytimes.com/2018/07/05/upshot/americans-are-having-fewer-babies-they-told-us-why.html.

251. Lyman Stone, "American Women are Having Fewer Children Than They'd Like," *New York Times*, February 13, 2018, https://www.nytimes.

com/2018/02/13/upshot/american-fertility-is-falling-short-of-what-women-want.html.

252. "Why is abortion *The UnChoice?*," Abortion is the Unchoice, last modified 2006, http://theunchoice.org/.

253. "Men Seeking Right To 'Judicial Abortions,'" *CPH Post* (Denmark), January 3, 2014, http://cphpost.dk/news/national/men-seeking-right-to-judicial-abortions.html.

254. Sara Malm, "Fathers Will Be Able to Choose a 'Legal Abortion' up until the 18th Week of Pregnancy Which Would Cut Any Lawful Responsibilities for the Child under Swedish Liberal Proposal," *Daily Mail*, March 4, 2016, http://www.dailymail.co.uk/news/article-3476888/Fathers-able-choose-legal-abortion-18th-week-pregnancy-cut-lawful-responsibilities-child-Swedish-Liberal-proposal.html.

255. Megan Hall et. al., "Associations between Intimate Partner Violence and Termination of Pregnancy: A Systematic Review and Meta-Analysis," *PLOS Medicine* vol. 11, no. 1 (January 2014), http://www.plosmedicine.org/article/info%3Adoi%2F10.1371%2Fjournal.pmed.1001581.

256. Ron Dicker, "J.J. Redick Allegedly Had 'Abortion Contract' With Ex-Girlfriend; NBA Player Denies Getting Her Pregnant," *Huffington Post*, July 25, 2013, last modified July 26, 2013. http://www.huffingtonpost.com/2013/07/25/jj-redick-abortion_n_3652293.html.

257. Maegen Chen, "It Happened to Me: Mark Hamill's Son Got Me Pregnant, and His Family Tried to Make Me Get an Abortion," *Yahoo Lifestyle*, November 21, 2016, https://www.yahoo.com/lifestyle/happened-mark-hamills-son-got-210000237.html.

258. Charles Camosy, "Why Serious Pro-Lifers Don't Want to Punish Women: What Donald Trump (And Glib Pro-Choicers) Fail to Understand About the Anti-Abortion Movement," *NY Daily News*, March 30, 2016, http://www.nydailynews.com/opinion/charles-camosy-real-pro-lifers-don-punish-women-article-1.2583258.

259. Francis, "Letter from the Holy Father Francis to the President of the Pontifical Council for the Promotion of the New Evangelization as the Extraordinary Jubilee of Mercy Approaches," Vatican Website, September 1, 2015, https://press.vatican.va/content/salastampa/it/bollettino/pubblico/2015/09/01/0637/01386.html#ing.

260. Digital image. Available from: Pinterest, https://www.pinterest.com/pin/171981279494765477/.

261. Ronnie Cohen, "Denial of Abortion Leads to Economic Hardship for Low-Income Women," *Reuters*, January 18, 2018, https://www.reuters.com/article/us-health-abortion-hardship/denial-of-abortion-leads-to-economic-hardship-for-low-income-women-idUSKBN1F731Z.

262. Amber Lapp, "Why Poor Women with Unintended Pregnancies Are Less Likely to Get Abortions," Institute for Family Studies, March 10, 2015, https://ifstudies.org/blog/why-poor-women-with-unintended-pregnancies-are-less-likely-to-get-abortions.

263. YouGov, *Huffington Post*, March 2, 2017, http://big.assets.huffingtonpost.com/tabsHPAbortion20170501.pdf.

264. Richard V. Reeves and Joanna Venator, "Sex, contraception, or abortion? Explaining class gaps in unintended childbearing," Center on Children and Families at Brookings, February 2015, http://www.brookings.edu/~/media/research/files/papers/2015/02/26-class-gaps-unintended-pregnancy/26_class_gaps_unintended_pregnancy.pdf.

265. David M. Adamson, Nancy Belden, Julie DaVanzo, and Sally Patterson, *How Americans View World Population Issues: A Survey of Public Opinion* (Santa Monica, CA: RAND, 2000), http://www.rand.org/content/dam/rand/pubs/monograph_reports/2007/MR1114.pdf.

266. Lapp.

267. Charon Gwynn, "Summary of Vital Statistics 2016: The City of New York," New York City Department of Health and Mental Hygiene, July 2018, https://www1.nyc.gov/assets/doh/downloads/pdf/vs/2016sum.pdf, 95.

268. Jason L. Riley, "Let's Talk About the Black Abortion Rate," *Wall Street Journal*, July 10, 2018, https://www.wsj.com/articles/lets-talk-about-the-black-abortion-rate-1531263697.

269. Matt Vespa, "Is Ohio's Largest Abortion Provider Targeting Black Neighborhoods in Cleveland?," *Townhall*, January 8, 2018, https://townhall.com/tipsheet/mattvespa/2018/01/08/is-ohios-largest-abortion-provider-targeting-black-neighborhoods-in-cleveland-n2431360.

270. *Box v. Planned Parenthood of Indiana and Kentucky*, 18 U.S. 483, "On Petition for Writ of Certiorari to the United States Court of Appeals for the Seventh Circuit," https://www.supremecourt.gov/DocketPDF/18/18-483/72192/20181115123021558_37089%20pdf%20Mannix.pdf

271. YouGov, *Huffington Post*, March 2, 2017, http://big.assets.huffingtonpost.com/tabsHPAbortion20170501.pdf.

272. Clare Malone and Harry Enten, "Democrats Aren't in Lockstep over Abortion — That's Why They're Fighting," *FiveThirtyEight* (New York), August 3, 2017, https://fivethirtyeight.com/features/democrats-arent-in-lockstep-over-abortion-thats-why-theyre-fighting/.

273. YouGov, *Huffington Post*, March 2, 2017, http://big.assets.huffingtonpost.com/tabsHPAbortion20170501.pdf.

274. Nina Martin, "U.S. Has the Worst Rate of Maternal Deaths in the Developed World," *NPR*, May 12, 2017, https://www.npr.org/2017/05/12/528098789/u-s-has-the-worst-rate-of-maternal-deaths-in-the-developed-world.

275. Andrea Todd, "Death By Pregnancy: Why Are So Many Moms-To-Be Dying?," *Women's Health*, October 19, 2017, https://www.womenshealthmag.com/life/a19950131/pregnant-women-dying/.

276. "Scott Peterson Trial Fast Facts," *CNN*, last modified April 15, 2018, http://www.cnn.com/2013/10/15/us/scott-peterson-trial-fast-facts/.

277. Terri LaPoint, "Bill to Protect Women from Being Tricked or Forced into Taking Abortion Pills Called Senseless by Democratic Party Chair," *Inquisitr*, May 15, 2014, http://www.inquisitr.com/1253139/bill-to-protect-women-from-being-tricked-or-forced-into-taking-abortion-pills-called-senseless-by-democratic-party-chair/.

278. Anthony Levatino, "Testimony of Anthony Levatino, MD before the Subcommittee on the Constitution and Civil Justice," U.S. House of Representatives, 2013, http://judiciary.house.gov/hearings/113th/05232013/Levatino%2005232013.pdf.

279. "Judge Permanently Blocks Indiana Law on Genetic Abnormality Abortions," *CBS News*, September 25, 2017, https://www.cbsnews.com/news/genetic-abnormality-abortions-judge-permanently-blocks-indiana-law/.

280. Sarah Terzo, "Healing for the Perpetrators: The Psychological Damage from Different Types of Killing," *Consistent Life Blog*, January 9, 2018, http://consistent-life.org/blog/index.php/2018/01/09/healing-perpetrators/.

281. "Staff," And Then There Were None, https://abortionworker.com/staff/.

282. Eric J. Lyman, "Pope: Abortion Is 'White Glove' Equivalent to Nazi Crimes," *USA Today*, June 16, 2018, https://www.usatoday.com/story/news/world/2018/06/16/pope-francis-abortion-equivalent-nazi-eugenics-crimes/707661002/.

283. JoNel Aleccia, "UW Experts Shed Light on False Positives in Prenatal Tests," *Seattle Times*, April 1, 2015, https://www.seattletimes.com/seattle-news/health/uw-experts-shed-light-on-false-positives-in-prenatal-tests/.

284. Brian G. Skotko, Susan P. Levine, and Richard Goldstein, "Self-perceptions from People with Down Syndrome," *American Journal of Medical Genetics* vol. 155, no. 10 (October 2011), http://onlinelibrary.wiley.com/doi/10.1002/ajmg.a.34235/full.

285. Amanda Prestigiacomo, "Nazi Whispers: Dutch Govt Official Tells Man with Down Syndrome How 'Expensive' He Is," *Daily Wire*, December 14, 2017, https://www.dailywire.com/news/24705/nazi-whispers-dutch-govt-official-tells-man-down-amanda-prestigiacomo.

286. Bridget Mora, "Prenatal testing and the Denial of Care," *Ethics and Medics* vol. 43, no. 2 (February 2018), https://www.ncbcenter.org/files/2415/1612/7537/EM_February2018_FINAL.pdf.

287. Renate Lindeman, "A Moral Duty to Abort," *Huffington Post*, September 21, 2017, last modified October 5, 2017, https://www.huffingtonpost.com/entry/a-moral-duty-to-abort_us_59c3a01ae4b0ffc2dedb5b3c.

288. John Pring, "My Disability Abortion Bill Could Halt Britain's Slide towards Eugenics, Says Tory Peer," *Disability News Service*, August 3, 2017, https://www.disabilitynewsservice.com/my-disability-abortion-bill-could-halt-britains-slide-towards-eugenics-says-tory-peer/.

289. "Perinatal Hospice & Palliative Care: Continuing Your Pregnancy When Your Baby's Life Is Expected to Be Brief," Perinatal Hospice and Palliative Care, last modified 2018, https://www.perinatalhospice.org/.

290. Heidi Cope, Melanie E. Garrett, Simon Gregory, and Allison Ashley-Koch, "Pregnancy Continuation and Organizational Religious Activity following Prenatal Diagnosis of a Lethal Fetal Defect Are Associated with Improved Psychological Outcome," *Prenatal Diagnosis* vol. 35, no. 8 (August 2015): 761, doi: 10.1002/pd.4603.

291. This not only includes *Beyond the Abortion Wars*, but several popular articles I've written, including "7 Reasons It Is Deeply Misleading to Claim Americans Support Roe v. Wade," *Federalist*, July 6, 2018, http://thefederalist.com/2018/07/06/7-reasons-deeply-misleading-claim-americans-support-roe-v-wade/.

292. Charles Camosy, *Peter Singer and Christian Ethics: Beyond Polarization* (Cambridge: Cambridge University Press, 2012).

293. Beata Mostafavi, "Artificial Placenta Holds Promise for Extremely Premature Infants," *Michigan Medicine* (University of Michigan), April 27, 2016, http://labblog.uofmhealth.org/health-tech/artificial-placenta-holds-promise-for-extremely-premature-infants.

294. Judith Jarvis Thomson, "A Defense of Abortion," *Philosophy & Public Affairs* vol. 1, no. 1 (Fall 1971), http://spot.colorado.edu/~heathwoo/Phil160,Fall02/thomson.htm.

295. Rachel's Vineyard, last modified 2018, http://www.rachelsvineyard.org/.

296. "Cardinal Bernardin's Message for 'Respect Life Sunday' in the USA," (originally "Deciding for Life," October 1, 1989), http://www.priestsforlife.org/magisterium/89-10-01bernadinmessage.htm.

297. I respond to some of that criticism here: "What Does It Really Mean to Speak of the Right to Life?," *Church Life Journal*, August 31, 2018, http://churchlife.nd.edu/2018/08/31/what-does-it-really-mean-to-speak-of-the-right-to-life/.

298. It should be said, however, that the two cases (pregnancy due to sexual violence and the duty to aid) differ significantly because, at the end of the day, the victim of sexual violence is the mother of the child. In a political context focused on autonomy and freedom, it is difficult to imagine such a dramatic thing happening without choice, but in fact we incur many moral obligations without our choosing—among them, our moral obligation (barring some exceptional circumstance) to care for our parents as they age.

299. John Paul II, *Evangelium vitae*, Vatican Website, March 25, 1995, http://w2.vatican.va/content/john-paul-ii/en/encyclicals/documents/hf_jp-ii_enc_25031995_evangelium-vitae.html, 41.

300. Thomas Reese, "Political Priorities of US Bishops May Surprise You," *National Catholic Reporter*, July 28, 2017, https://www.ncronline.org/blogs/faith-and-justice/political-priorities-us-bishops-may-surprise-you.

301. Jack Jenkins, "Catholic Bishops Rebuke Trump's Asylum Changes, Suggest 'Canonical Penalties,'" *RNS*, June 13, 2018, https://religionnews.com/2018/06/13/catholic-bishops-rebuke-trumps-asylum-changes-suggest-policy-is-a-life-issue/.

302. Christopher White, "Bannon Pushes Back Against Bishops over Criticism of Immigration Policy," *Crux*, June 17, 2018, https://cruxnow.com/church-in-the-usa/2018/06/17/bannon-pushes-back-against-bishops-over-criticism-of-immigration-policy/.

303. Francis, "Messages World Day of Migrants and Refugees," Vatican Website, https://w2.vatican.va/content/francesco/en/messages/migration.index.html.

304. Thomas Massaro SJ, *Mercy in Action: The Social Teachings of Pope Francis* (Lanham, MD: Rowman and Littlefield Publishing, 2018).

305. Ibid., 131-132.

306. Ibid., 121.

307. Elise Harris, "The World Needs a Merciful Response to Refugees, Pope Francis Says," *Catholic News Service*, September 17, 2016, https://www.catholicnewsagency.com/news/the-world-needs-a-merciful-response-to-refugees-pope-francis-says-44360.

308. Massaro, 128-129.

309. David Luhnow, "Latin America Is the Murder Capital of the World," *Wall Street Journal*, last modified September 20, 2018, https://www.wsj.com/articles/400-murders-a-day-the-crisis-of-latin-america-1537455390.

310. Amanda Taub, "The Awful Reason Tens of Thousands of Children are Seeking Refuge in the United States," *Vox*, June 30, 2014, https://www.vox.com/2014/6/30/5842054/violence-in-central-america-and-the-child-refugee-crisis.

311. Patrick Gothman, "I Was an American Missionary in Honduras. I Witnessed Firsthand the Violence They Endure," *America*, November 27, 2018, https://www.americamagazine.org/faith/2018/11/27/i-was-american-missionary-honduras-i-witnessed-firsthand-violence-they-endure.

312. Kathleen Naab, "Why Is Mexico the Deadliest Place to Be a Priest?," *National Catholic Register*, May 22, 2018, http://www.ncregister.com/daily-news/why-is-mexico-the-deadliest-place-to-be-a-priest.

313. Taub.

314. Suzanne Gamboa, Mariana Atencio, and Gabe Gutierrez, "Why are So Many Migrants Crossing the U.S. Border? It Often Starts with an Escape from Violence in Central America," *NBC News*, June 20, 2018, https://www.nbcnews.com/storyline/immigration-border-crisis/central-americas-violence-turmoil-keeps-driving-families-u-s-n884956.

315. Serena Marshall, "Obama Has Deported More People than Any Other President," *ABC News*, August 29, 2016, https://abcnews.go.com/Politics/obamas-deportation-policy-numbers/story?id=41715661.

316. John Burnett, "Almost 15,000 Migrant Children Now Held at Nearly Full Shelters," *NPR*, December 13, 2018, https://www.npr.org/2018/12/13/676300525/almost-15-000-migrant-children-now-held-at-nearly-full-shelters.

317. Jonathan Blitzer, "The Trump Administration Is Completely Unravelling the U.S. Asylum System," *New Yorker*, June 11, 2018, https://www.newyorker.com/news/news-desk/the-trump-administration-is-completely-unraveling-the-us-asylum-system.

318. "Sen. Bob Casey Unleashes Tweetstorm at White House," *Pittsburg Post-Gazette*, May 3, 2017, http://www.post-gazette.com/news/politics-nation/2017/05/03/Bob-Casey-Trump-Tweetstorm-immigration-Honduran-mother/stories/201705030198.

319. Ted Hesson, "Kelly Slams Sen. Casey Over Deportation Tweets," *Politico*, May 4, 2017, https://www.politico.com/story/2017/05/04/bob-casey-mother-son-deported-john-kelly-react-237986.

320. "Latin America and the Caribbean: Tax Revenues Continue to Rise Despite Low Economic Growth," OECD, March 23, 2017, http://www.oecd.org/tax/latin-america-and-the-caribbean-tax-revenues-continue-to-rise-despite-low-economic-growth.htm.

321. Laura Paddison, "These 7 Numbers Show How Global Poverty Remains a Huge Problem," *Huffington Post*, October 16, 2017, last modified December 6, 2017, https://www.huffingtonpost.com/entry/global-poverty-by-the-numbers_us_59e4d77ee4b04d1d5183787b.

322. Amy Whalley, "Why are Millions of Children Still Dying from Prevent-

able Diseases?," *Guardian*, April 27, 2016, https://www.theguardian.com/global-development/2016/apr/27/millions-children-dying-preventable-diseases-immunisation-programme.

323. Vladimir Canudas-Romo, "Life Expectancy and Poverty," *The Lancet* vol. 6, no. 8 (August 1, 2018), https://www.thelancet.com/journals/langlo/article/PIIS2214-109X(18)30327-9/fulltext.

324. Peter Dizikes, "New Study Shows Rich, Poor have Huge Mortality Gap in U.S.," *MIT News*, April 11, 2016, http://news.mit.edu/2016/study-rich-poor-huge-mortality-gap-us-0411.

325. Mike Stobbe, "U.S. Life Expectancy Will Likely Decline for Third Straight Year," *Bloomberg*, May 23, 2018, https://www.bloomberg.com/news/articles/2018-05-23/with-death-rate-up-us-life-expectancy-is-likely-down-again.

326. Maria Shriver, "The Female Face of Poverty," *The Atlantic*, January 8, 2014, https://www.theatlantic.com/business/archive/2014/01/the-female-face-of-poverty/282892/.

327. Carmen Rios, "These 5 Statistics Prove That We're Feminizing Poverty (And Keeping Women Down in the Process)," *Everyday Feminism*, June 20, 2015, https://everydayfeminism.com/2015/06/feminizing-poverty/.

328. Sarah Hassmer, "Black Women and Latina Headed Households Face High Poverty Rates," National Women's Law Center, September 13, 2017, https://nwlc.org/blog/black-women-and-latina-headed-households-face-high-poverty-rates/.

329. Joshua J. McElwee, "Launching World Day of the Poor, Francis Says 'No Christian May Disregard' Serving Them," *National Catholic Reporter*, June 13, 2017, https://www.ncronline.org/news/vatican/launching-world-day-poor-francis-says-no-christian-may-disregard-serving-them.

330. Joshua Breisblatt, "Trump's Mass Deportation Plan Is Passed by the House Judiciary Committee," *Immigration Impact* (American Immigration Council), May 26, 2017, http://immigrationimpact.com/2017/05/26/trump-mass-deportation-plan/.

331. Charles C. Camosy, "Bishop Says Deporting Migrants 'Not Unlike' Abortion," *Crux*, July 26, 2016, https://cruxnow.com/interviews/2016/07/26/camosy-interview-bp-brownsville-tx/.

332. "A Statement from Daniel Cardinal DiNardo," United States Conference of Catholic Bishops, June 13, 2018, http://www.usccb.org/news/2018/18-098.cfm.

333. Rhina Guidos, "Update: Bishops Across U.S. Condemn Separation, Detention of Children," *Catholic News Service*, June 19, 2018, http://www.catholicnews.com/services/englishnews/2018/bishops-across-us-condemn-separation-detention-of-migrant-children.cfm.

334. Francis, *Evangelii gaudium*, Vatican Website, November 24, 2013, http://w2.vatican.va/content/francesco/en/apost_exhortations/documents/papa-francesco_esortazione-ap_20131124_evangelii-gaudium.html, 53.

335. This middle paragraph cites the great fourth century Church father, Bishop Ambrose of Milan.

336. *Catechism of the Catholic Church*, Vatican Website, http://www.vatican.va/archive/ENG0015/_INDEX.HTM, 904 and 2269.

337. Second Vatican Council, *Gaudium et spes,* Vatican Website, December 7, 1965, http://www.vatican.va/archive/hist_councils/ii_vatican_council/documents/vat-ii_const_19651207_gaudium-et-spes_en.html, 138, 69.

338. Annette Bernhardt et al., *Broken Laws, Unprotected Workers: Violations of Employment and Labor Laws in American Cities*, National Employment Law Project, 2009, https://www.nelp.org/wp-content/uploads/2015/03/BrokenLawsReport2009.pdf.

339. Michael Grabell, "Exploitation and Abuse at the Chicken Plant," *New Yorker*, May 8, 2017, https://www.newyorker.com/magazine/2017/05/08/exploitation-and-abuse-at-the-chicken-plant.

340. Sally Kohn, "Exploiting Poverty Caused the Financial Crisis," *Huffington Post*, October 19, 2008, last modified May 25, 2011, https://www.huffingtonpost.com/sally-kohn/exploiting-poverty-caused_b_127401.html.

341. Thomas B. Edsall, "Making Money off the Poor," *New York Times*, September 17, 2013, https://opinionator.blogs.nytimes.com/2013/09/17/making-money-off-the-poor/?mtrref=www.google.com&gwh=58D65881F1D655C6DACDFED2501FA641&gwt=pay&assetType=opinion.

342. "Pope Francis Calls Migrants 'An Opportunity for Human Growth,'" *Crux*, August 14, 2017, https://cruxnow.com/vatican/2017/08/14/pope-francis-calls-migrants-opportunity-human-growth/.

343. Manny Fernandez, "Pope Francis Visits U.S. – Mexico Border," *New York Times*, February 17, 2016, https://www.nytimes.com/live/pope-francis-at-us-mexico-border/.

344. *Evangelium vitae*, 41.

345. Thomas and Dominicans. English Province, *Summa Theologica*, 3057, II:II, Q66, Art 7.

346. "Climate Change Could Force Over 140 Million to Migrate Within Countries by 2050: World Bank Report" (press release), World Bank, March 19, 2018, https://www.worldbank.org/en/news/press-release/2018/03/19/climate-change-could-force-over-140-million-to-migrate-within-countries-by-2050-world-bank-report.

347. Daniel Nikbakht and Sheena McKenzie, "The Yemen War Is the World's Worst Humanitarian Crisis, UN Says," *CNN*, April 3, 2018, https://www.

cnn.com/2018/04/03/middleeast/yemen-worlds-worst-humanitarian-crisis-un-intl/index.html.

348. Nicholas Kristof, "Be Outraged by America's Role in Yemen's Misery," *New York Times*, September 26, 2018, https://www.nytimes.com/2018/09/26/opinion/yemen-united-states-united-nations.html.

349. Jeff Faux, "How US Foreign Policy Helped Create the Immigration Crisis," *Nation*, October 18, 2017, https://www.thenation.com/article/how-us-foreign-policy-helped-create-the-immigration-crisis/.

350. Jorge Ramos, "The Migrant Caravan Isn't Causing the Border Crisis. Trump Is," *Time*, November 29, 2018, http://time.com/5466781/migrant-caravan-trump-border-crisis/.

351. Susannah George, "US Again Slashing Number of Refugees It Will Accept," *Associated Press*, September 18, 2018, https://apnews.com/db40014c014b45f88b28f0e135a7c24d.

352. Charles Mathewes and Evan Sandsmark, "Being Rich Wrecks Your Soul. We Used to Know That." *Washington Post*, July 28, 2017, https://www.washingtonpost.com/outlook/being-rich-wrecks-your-soul-we-used-to-know-that/2017/07/28/7d3e2b90-5ab3-11e7-9fc6-c7ef4bc58d13_story.html?utm_term=.af366b537fd7.

353. The Notorious B.I.G., "Mo' Money Mo' Problems Lyrics," Genius, n.d., https://genius.com/The-notorious-big-mo-money-mo-problems-lyrics.

354. Meera Jagannathan, "Study Reveals More Money Totally Causes More Problems," *New York Post*, April 17, 2018, https://nypost.com/2018/04/17/study-reveals-more-money-totally-causes-more-problems/?utm_campaign=SocialFlow&utm_source=NYPTwitter&utm_medium=SocialFlow.

355. Catey Hill, "The Dark Reasons So Many Rich People are Miserable Human Beings," *MarketWatch*, February 22, 2018, https://moneyish.com/splurge/the-dark-reasons-so-many-rich-people-are-miserable-human-beings/.

356. Matt Bruenig, "Who Was Poor in 2016 and Why Our System Keeps Failing Them," People's Policy Project, September 12, 2017, https://peoplespolicyproject.org/2017/09/12/who-was-in-poverty-in-2016/.

357. Elizabeth Bruenig, "If the Poor Must Work to Earn Every Dollar, Shouldn't the Rich?," The Washington Post, January 5, 2018 https://www.washingtonpost.com/opinions/if-the-poor-must-work-to-earn-every-dollar-shouldnt-the-rich/2018/01/05/c36d9a10-f243-11e7-b390-a36dc3fa2842_story.html?utm_term=.1c9e21e9ed68.

358. Elizabeth Bruenig, "The Undeserving Poor: A Very Tiny History," Medium (blog), January 6, 2018, https://medium.com/@ebruenig/the-undeserving-poor-a-very-tiny-history-96c3b9141e13.

359. *Amoris laetitia*, 186.

360. If the reader would like more information on the complexity of this tension, I explore it in more detail in chapter 4 of *Peter Singer and Christian Ethics*.

361. *Laudato si'*, 128.

362. Arthur O. Lovejoy, *The Great Chain of Being: A Study of the History of an Idea* (Cambridge, MA: Harvard University Press, 1936).

363. *Catechism of the Catholic Church*, Vatican Website, http://www.vatican.va/archive/ENG0015/_INDEX.HTM, 2416, 2418.

364. *Laudato si'*, 128.

365. Christopher Joyce, "Climate Report Warns of Extreme Weather, Displacement of Millions without Action," *NPR*, October 8, 2018, https://www.npr.org/2018/10/08/655360909/grim-forecast-from-u-n-on-global-climate-change.

366. John Paul II, "Peace with God the Creator, Peace with All of Creation" (World Day of Peace Message), Vatican Website, January 1, 1990, http://w2.vatican.va/content/john-paul-ii/en/messages/peace/documents/hf_jp-ii_mes_19891208_xxiii-world-day-for-peace.html, IV.

367. Benedict XVI, "Address of His Holiness Benedict XVI to H.E. Mr Noel Fahey, New Ambassador of Ireland to the Holy See," Vatican Website, September 15, 2007, https://w2.vatican.va/content/benedict-xvi/en/speeches/2007/september/documents/hf_ben-xvi_spe_20070915_ambassador-ireland.html.

368. *Laudato si'*, 24.

369. Inés San Martín, "Turkson: Pro-life cause and concern for environment are 'inseparable,'" *Crux*, September 1, 2017, https://cruxnow.com/interviews/2017/09/01/turkson-pro-life-cause-concern-environment-inseparable/.

370. These examples have come from David Clough's new book, *On Animals: Volume II: Theological Ethics* (Edinburgh: T&T Clark, 2018) and my book *For Love of Animals: Christian Ethics, Consistent Action* (Cincinnati, OH: Franciscan Media, 2013).

371. Susan Kopp and Charles Camosy, "Animals 2.0: A Veterinarian and a Theologian Survey a Brave New World of Biotechnology," *America*, May 13, 2015, https://www.americamagazine.org/issue/animals-20.

372. *Dirty Jobs*, season 4, episode 13, "Turkey Inseminator," performed by Mike Rowe, aired May 12, 2008, on Discovery Channel, https://www.tvguide.com/tvshows/dirty-jobs/episode-13-season-4/turkey-inseminator/279523/.

373. *Laudato si'*, 11.

374. "Ag-gag Laws," https://www.sourcewatch.org/index.php/Ag-gag_laws.

375. Scott Weathers, Sophie Hermanns, and Mark Bittman, "Health Leaders Must Focus on the Threats from Factory Farms," *New York Times*, May 21, 2017, https://www.nytimes.com/2017/05/21/opinion/who-factory-farming-meat-industry-.html.

376. Damian Carrington, "Huge Reduction in Meat-Eating 'Essential' to Avoid Climate Breakdown," *Guardian*, October 10, 2018, https://amp. theguardian.com/environment/2018/oct/10/huge-reduction-in-meat-eating-essential-to-avoid-climate-breakdown?CMP=share_btn_tw&__twitter_impression=true.

377. *Laudato si'*, 25.

378. Ibid., 16.

379. Ibid., 59.

380. Benedict XVI, *Caritas in veritate*, June 29, 2009, http://w2.vatican. va/content/benedict-xvi/en/encyclicals/documents/hf_ben-xvi_enc_20090629_caritas-in-veritate.html, 51.

381. John Paul II, *Centesimus annus*, Vatican Website, May 1, 1991, http:// w2.vatican.va/content/john-paul-ii/en/encyclicals/documents/hf_jp-ii_enc_01051991_centesimus-annus.html, 36.

382. Ashitha Nagesh, "The Harrowing Psychological Toll of Slaughterhouse Work," *Metro*, December 31, 2017, https://metro.co.uk/2017/12/31/how-killing-animals-everyday-leaves-slaughterhouse-workers-trauma-tised-7175087/.

383. Ibid.

384. Amy J. Fitzgerald, Linda Kalof, and Thomas Dietz, "Slaughterhouses and Increased Crime Rates: An Empirical Analysis of the Spillover From 'The Jungle' Into the Surrounding Community," *Organization & Environment* 22, no. 2 (June 2009): 158–84, http://journals.sagepub. com/doi/abs/10.1177/1086026609338164.

385. Michael Grabell, "Exploitation and Abuse at the Chicken Plant," *New Yorker*, May 8, 2017, https://www.newyorker.com/maga-zine/2017/05/08/exploitation-and-abuse-at-the-chicken-plant.

386. Ibid.

387. Roy Lagarde, "Whatever We Do to Nature Comes Back to Us – Cardinal Tagle," *CBCP News*, September 1, 2017, http://cbcpnews.net/cbcpnews/whatever-we-do-to-nature-comes-back-to-us-cardinal-tagle/.

388. *Laudato si'*, 205.

389. Colin Ellard, "Stress and the City," *Psychology Today*, August 21, 2012, https://www.psychologytoday.com/us/blog/mind-wandering/201208/stress-and-the-city.

390. Adam Boult, "Being Around Trees Makes You Less Stressed – Study," *Tele-*

graph, May 6, 2016, https://www.telegraph.co.uk/science/2016/05/06/
being-around-trees-makes-you-less-stressed--study/.

391. Ephrat Livni, "The Japanese Practice of 'Forest Bathing' is Scientifically
Proven to Improve Your Health," *Quartz,* October 12, 2016, https://
qz.com/804022/health-benefits-japanese-forest-bathing/.

392. Auslan Cramb, "Jogging in Forest Twice as Good as Trip to Gym for
Mental Health," *Telegraph,* June 20, 2012, https://www.telegraph.co.uk/
news/health/news/9344129/Jogging-in-forest-twice-as-good-as-trip-to-
gym-for-mental-health.html.

393. Severin Carrell, "Scottish GPs to Begin Prescribing Rambling and Birdwatching, *Guardian,* October 4, 2019, https://www.theguardian.com/
uk-news/2018/oct/05/scottish-gps-nhs-begin-prescribing-rambling-
birdwatching.

394. Steven Feldman, "Alleviating Anxiety, Stress and Depression with the
Pet Effect," Anxiety and Depression Association of America, n.d.,
https://adaa.org/learn-from-us/from-the-experts/blog-posts/consumer/
alleviating-anxiety-stress-and-depression-pet.

395. Hal Herzog, "Do Psychiatric Service Dogs Really Help Veterans with
PTSD?," *Psychology Today,* February 15, 2018, https://www.psychology-
today.com/us/blog/animals-and-us/201802/do-psychiatric-service-dogs-
really-help-veterans-ptsd.

396. Jacquie Brennan, "Service Animals and Emotional Support Animals,"
ed. Vinh Nguyen, ADA National Network, 2014, https://adata.org/
publication/service-animals-booklet.

397. *Laudato si',* 233.

398. *Catechism,* 340, 344.

399. *Caritas in veritate,* 50.

400. *Laudato si',* 112.

401. *Caritas in veritate,* 48.

402. *Laudato si',* 159.

403. Ibid., 122, 123.

404. Jennifer Ludden, "Should We Be Having Kids in the Age of
Climate Change?," *NPR,* August 18, 2016, https://www.npr.
org/2016/08/18/479349760/should-we-be-having-kids-in-the-age-of-
climate-change.

405. "World Population in 2300," United Nations (Proceedings of the United
Nations Expert Meeting on World Population in 2300, New York, 2004),
http://www.un.org/esa/population/publications/longrange2/longrange2.
htm, 1.

406. David Roberts, "I'm an Environmental Journalist, But I Never Write
About Overpopulation. Here's Why," *Vox,* September 2017, last modi-

fied November 29, 2018, https://www.vox.com/energy-and-environ-ment/2017/9/26/16356524/the-population-question.

407. Jennifer Chevinsky, "Fertility Rates Drop to Lowest Level Measured in the US, Says the CDC," *ABC News*, August 9, 2016, http://abcnews. go.com/Health/fertility-rates-drop-lowest-level-measured-us-cdc/ story?id=41233697.

408. Wendy Koch, "This Chart Shows How U.S. Carbon Emissions Are Ris-ing—Again," *National Geographic*, April 21, 2015, http://news.nation-algeographic.com/energy/2015/04/150421-US-carbon-emissions-rise/.

409. *Laudato si'*, 50.

410. "Extreme Carbon Inequality" (media briefing), OXFAM, December 2, 2015, https://www.oxfam.org/sites/www.oxfam.org/files/file_attach-ments/mb-extreme-carbon-inequality-021215-en.pdf.

411. Mary Eberstadt, "Pro-Animal, Pro-Life," *First Things*, June 2009, https:// www.firstthings.com/article/2009/06/pro-animal-pro-life.

412. Elizabeth Bristow, "Evangelical Coalition Releases Statement on Respon-sible Care for Animals," Ethics and Religious Liberty Commission of the Southern Baptist Convention, press release (September 28, 2015), https://erlc.com/resource-library/press-releases/evangelical-coalition-releases-statement-on-responsible-care-for-animals.

413. Catholic News Service, "Pope Francis: Euthanasia is a Triumph of Selfishness, Not Compassion," *Catholic Herald*, June 11, 2016, http:// www.catholicherald.co.uk/news/2016/06/11/pope-francis-euthanasia-is-triumph-of-selfishness-not-compassion/.

414. Much of the following history comes from chapter 2 of my book *Peter Singer and Christian Ethics: Beyond Polarization* (Cambridge, UK: Cam-bridge University Press, 2012).

415. Peter Singer, *Rethinking Life and Death: The Collapse of Our Traditional Ethics* (New York: St. Martin's Griffin, 1994), 25.

416. "Delimiting Death," Editorial, *Nature* 461: 570 (October 1, 2009), http://www.nature.com/nature/journal/v461/n7264/full/461570a.html.

417. Stephen Drake, "Maryland: Using a 'PVS' Diagnosis to Justify Organ Harvesting without Consent," Not Dead Yet: The Resistance, February 21, 2012, http://notdeadyet.org/2012/02/maryland-using-pvs-diagnosis-to-justify.html.

418. Raymond Hoffenberg et al., "Should Organs from Patients in Perma-nent Vegetative State Be Used for Transplantation?," *The Lancet* vol. 350, no. 9078 (November 1, 1997): 1320-1321, http://www.academia. edu/12276686/Should_organs_from_patients_in_permanent_vegeta-tive_state_be_used_for_transplantation.

419. "Oregon's Death with Dignity Act—2014," Oregon Public Health Division, February 2015, http://public.health.oregon.gov/ProviderPartnerResources/EvaluationResearch/DeathwithDignityAct/Documents/year17.pdf.

420. Madeline Li et al., "Medical Assistance in Dying — Implementing a Hospital-Based Program in Canada," *New England Journal of Medicine* Vol. 376, No. 21 (May 25, 2017), https://www.nejm.org/doi/full/10.1056/NEJMms1700606.

421. Jessica Nutik Zitter, "Should I Help My Patients Die?," *New York Times*, August 5, 2017, https://www.nytimes.com/2017/08/05/opinion/sunday/dying-doctors-palliative-medicine.html.

422. Chrisstopher de Bellaigue, "Death on Demand: Has Euthanasia Gone Too Far?," *Guardian,* January 18, 2019, https://www.theguardian.com/news/2019/jan/18/death-on-demand-has-euthanasia-gone-too-far-netherlands-assisted-dying?CMP=Share_iOSApp_Other.

423. Wesley J. Smith, "Dutch MDs 'Treat' Sex Abuse Victim with Euthanasia," *National Review*, May 11, 2016, http://www.nationalreview.com/corner/435237/dutch-mds-treat-sex-abuse-victim-euthanasia?d4DSEsjol6A3TriY.01.

424. Michael Cook, "A Peek Behind Belgium's Euthanasia Curtain," *MercatorNet*, February 8, 2016, http://www.mercatornet.com/careful/view/a-peek-behind-belgiums-euthanasia-curtain/17572.

425. Emma Elliott Freire, "Netherlands Considers Euthanasia for Healthy People, Doctors Say Things Are 'Getting Out of Hand,'" *Federalist,* June 30, 2017, http://thefederalist.com/2017/06/30/netherlands-considers-euthanasia-healthy/.

426. Daniel Boffey, "'Any Taboo Has Gone': Netherlands Sees Rise in Demand or Euthanasia," *Guardian*, November 9, 2017, https://amp.theguardian.com/world/2017/nov/09/any-taboo-has-gone-netherlands-sees-rise-in-demand-for-euthanasia.

427. "Facts and Figures," Alzheimer's Association, 2018, https://www.alz.org/alzheimers-dementia/facts-figures#prevalence.

428. Simon Caldwell, "Dutch Euthanasia Regulator Quits Over Dementia Killings," *Catholic Herald*, January 23, 2018, http://catholicherald.co.uk/news/2018/01/23/dutch-euthanasia-regulator-quits-over-dementia-killings/.

429. Associated Press, "Dutch Probe 'Appalling' Euthanasia of Dementia Patient," WTOP, April 20, 2018, https://wtop.com/national/2018/04/dutch-probe-appalling-euthanasia-of-dementia-patient/.

430. Maria Cheng, "Death of Dementia Patient Stirs Belgium Euthanasia

Fears," *Medical Press*, February 16, 2018, https://medicalxpress.com/news/2018-02-death-dementia-patient-belgium-euthanasia.html.

431. Rob Kuznia, "In Oregon, Pushing to Give Patients with Degenerative Diseases the Right to Die," *Washington Post*, March 11, 2018, https://www.washingtonpost.com/national/in-oregon-pushing-to-give-patients-with-degenerative-diseases-the-right-to-die/2018/03/11/3b6a2362-230e-11e8-94da-ebf9d112159c_story.html?utm_term=.f2bc2b87fd1c.

432. Charles Lane, "Children Are Being Euthanized In Belgium," *Washington Post*, August 6, 2018, https://www.washingtonpost.com/amphtml/opinions/children-are-being-euthanized-in-belgium/2018/08/06/9473bac2-9988-11e8-b60b-1c897f17e185_story.html?__twitter_impression=true.

433. Laura Secorun Palet, "Roller Coaster of Death," *OZY*, September 2, 2015, https://www.ozy.com/flashback/roller-coaster-of-death/37275.

434. Ken Murray, "How Doctors Die," *Zocalo Public Square*, November 30, 2011, http://www.zocalopublicsquare.org/2011/11/30/how-doctors-die/ideas/nexus/.

435. John Wyatt, "End-of-life Decisions, Quality of Life and The Newborn," *Acta Pædiatrica* vol. 96, no. 6 (May 24, 2007), http://onlinelibrary.wiley.com/doi/10.1111/j.1651-2227.2007.00349.x/abstract.

436. Carlo V. Bellieni and Giuseppe Buonocuore, "Flaws in the Assessment of the Best Interests of the Newborn," *Acta Pædiatrica* vol. 98, no. 4 (March 6, 2009), http://onlinelibrary.wiley.com/doi/10.1111/j.1651-2227.2008.01185.x/full.

437. Linda Thrasybule, "Heart patients prefer longevity over quality of life," *Reuters*, November 25, 2011, https://www.reuters.com/article/us-heart-patients-longevity/heart-patients-prefer-longevity-over-quality-of-life-idUSTRE7AO1UR20111126.

438. Kim Painter, "Disabled N.J. Girl Thrives, Inspires after Transplant," *USA Today*, October 5, 2013, https://www.usatoday.com/story/news/nation/2013/10/05/disabled-transplant-amelia-rivera/2917989/.

439. Nancy Flanders, "'Slow Code': Outraged Parents Say Doctors Delay Care for Kids with Disabilities," *LiveAction*, August 5, 2018, https://www.liveaction.org/news/doctors-slow-code-disabilities-kids/.

440. J. Randall Curtis, "Is There an Epidemic of Burnout and Post-traumatic Stress in Critical Care Clinicians?," *American Journal of Respiratory and Critical Care Medicine* vol. 175, no. 7 (April 1, 2007), https://www.atsjournals.org/doi/full/10.1164/rccm.200702-194ED.

441. Kenneth R. Stevens Jr., "Emotional and Psychological Effects of Physician-Assisted Suicide and Euthanasia on Participating Physicians," *Issues*

in Law and Medicine vol. 21, no. 3 (Spring 2006), https://www.ncbi. nlm.nih.gov/pubmed/16676767.

442. Rowena Mason, "Assisted Dying Bill Overwhelmingly Rejected by MPs," *Guardian*, September 12, 2015, https://www.theguardian.com/ society/2015/sep/11/mps-begin-debate-assisted-dying-bill.

443. *AMA Principles of Medical Ethics*, "Code of Medical Ethics Opinion 5.7," American Medical Association, 2016, https://www.ama-assn.org/ delivering-care/physician-assisted-suicide.

444. Richard Doerflinger, "The Effect of Legalizing Assisted Suicide on Pallia-tive Care and Suicide Rates: A Response to Compassion and Choices," Charlotte Lozier Institute, March 3, 2017, https://lozierinstitute.org/ the-effect-of-legalizing-assisted-suicide-on-palliative-care-and-suicide-rates/#_ftnref8.

445. Jennifer Kim, "Physician Assisted Suicide's Demographic Divide," *Brown Political Review*, November 29, 2015, http://www.brownpoliticalreview. org/2015/11/physician-assisted-suicides-demographic-divide/.

446. Charles Camosy, "Euthanasia, Abortion and Academic Discourse on Racial Justice," *Catholic Moral Theology* (blog), September 7, 2014, https://catholicmoraltheology.com/euthanasia-abortion-and-academic-discourse-on-racial-justice/.

447. Kim.

448. Ben Mattlin, "People with Disabilities Often Fear They're a Burden. That's Why Legal Assisted Suicide Scares Me," *Vox*, September 21, 2017, https://www.vox.com/first-person/2017/9/21/16307868/assisted-suicide-disabilities-legal.

449. Jamie Hale, "We're Told We Are a Burden. No Wonder Disabled People Fear Assisted Suicide," *Guardian*, June 1, 2018, https://www.theguard-ian.com/commentisfree/2018/jun/01/disabled-people-assisted-dying-safeguards-pressure.

450. Janet Adamy and Paul Overberg, "The Loneliest Generation: Americans, More than Ever, Are Aging Alone," *Wall Street Journal*, December 11, 2018, https://www.wsj.com/articles/the-loneliest-generation-americans-more-than-ever-are-aging-alone-11544541134.

451. Lucia Silecchia, "Elderly at Special Risk in a 'Throwaway Culture,'" *Crux*, June 15, 2017, https://cruxnow.com/global-church/2017/06/15/ elderly-special-risk-throwaway-culture/.

452. *Amoris laetitia*, 191.

453. Bradford Richardson, "Insurance Companies Denied Treatment to Pa-tients, Offered to Pay for Assisted Suicide, Doctor Claims," *Washington Times*, May 31, 2017, https://www.washingtontimes.com/news/2017/ may/31/insurance-companies-denied-treatment-to-patients-o/.

454. "Chronically Ill Man Releases Audio of Hospital Staff Offering Assisted Death," *CTV News*, August 2, 2018, https://www.ctvnews.ca/health/chronically-ill-man-releases-audio-of-hospital-staff-offering-assisted-death-1.4038841#_gus&_gucid=&_gup=twitter&_gsc=0o3DwBh.

455. Ibid.

456. Charles Collins, "Euthanasia Stems from Reducing Life to 'Efficiency and Productivity,' Pope Says," *Crux*, January 26, 2018, https://cruxnow.com/vatican/2018/01/26/euthanasia-stems-reducing-life-efficiency-productivity-pope-says/.

457. Melinda Henneberger, "Doctor-Assisted Suicide is Contagious, Too. Why Aren't We Sounding the Alarm?," *Kansas City Star*, June 21, 2018, http://amp.kansascity.com/opinion/opn-columns-blogs/melinda-henneberger/article213548244.html?__twitter_impression=true.

458. John Hardwig, "Is there a Duty to Die?," *Hastings Center Report* 27, no. 2 (1997): 36.

459. Geoff Bartlett, "Mother Says Doctor Brought Up Assisted Suicide Option as Sick Daughter was Within Earshot," *CBC News*, July 24, 2017, https://www.cbc.ca/news/canada/newfoundland-labrador/doctor-suggested-assisted-suicide-daughter-mother-elson-1.4218669.

460. Kevin J. Jones, "Conscientious Objection in Assisted Suicide Cases under Threat in Ontario," *Crux*, August 18, 2017, https://cruxnow.com/global-church/2017/08/18/conscientious-objection-assisted-suicide-cases-threat-ontario/.

461. Peter Stockland, "Assisted Dying Was Supposed to Be an Option. To Some Patients, It Looks Like the Only One," *Maclean's*, June 22, 2018, https://www.macleans.ca/society/assisted-dying-was-supposed-to-be-an-option-to-some-patients-it-looks-like-the-only-one/.

462. Anna Keating, "Addressing the American Suicide Contagion," *Church Life Journal*, August 3, 2018, http://churchlife.nd.edu/2018/08/03/addressing-the-american-suicide-contagion/.

463. Amanda Lenhart, "In the Midst of a Coming Elder Care Shortage, the Case for Robot Caregivers," *Slate*, November 21, 2017, https://slate.com/human-interest/2017/11/robot-caregivers-why-more-americans-think-robots-could-do-as-well-as-people-or-even-better.html.

464. Camosy, *Peter Singer and Christian Ethics*.

465. Michael Specter, "The Dangerous Philosopher," *New Yorker*, September 6, 1999, http://archives.newyorker.com/?i=1999-09-06#folio=CV1.

466. Karen Weintraub, "Man Partly Wakes From 15-Year Vegetative State— What It Means," *National Geographic*, September 25, 2017, https://news.nationalgeographic.com/2017/09/vegetative-state-vagus-nerve-stimulation-health-science/?utm_source=Facebook&utm_medium=Social&utm_

content=link_fb20170925news-vegetativeman&utm_campaign=Cont ent&sf116553291=1.

467. Adrian Owen, "How Science Found a Way to Help Coma Patients Communicate," *Guardian*, September 5, 2017, https://www.theguardian.com/news/2017/sep/05/how-science-found-a-way-to-help-coma-patients-communicate; and Aimee Swartz, "Brain Imaging Scans Show Some Vegetative Patients Are Living on the Edge of Consciousness," *Newsweek*, April 26, 2016, https://www.newsweek.com/2016/05/06/ vegetative-state-consciousness-brain-imaging-452747.html.

468. Joseph J. Fins, "Bring Them Back," ed. Pam Weintraub, *Aeon*, May 10, 2016, https://aeon.co/essays/thousands-of-patients-diagnosed-as-vegetative-are-actually-aware?utm_source=Aeon+Newsletter&utm_campaign=f3c11e932f-Daily_Newsletter_10_May_20165_10_2016&utm_medium=email&utm_term=0_411a82e59d-f3c11e932f-68910097%27.

469. Rachel Grace Son and Susan M. Setta, "Frequency of Use of the Religious Exemption in New Jersey Cases of Determination of Brain Death," *BMC Medical Ethics* vol. 19, no. 76 (August 14, 2018), https://www.ncbi.nlm.nih.gov/pmc/articles/PMC6092846/.

470. Congregation for the Doctrine of the Faith, "Declaration on Euthanasia," Vatican Website, May 5, 1980, http://www.vatican.va/roman_curia/ congregations/cfaith/documents/rc_con_cfaith_doc_19800505_euthanasia_en.html , II.

471. Charles Camosy, *Too Expensive to Treat? Finitude, Tragedy, and the Neonatal ICU* (Grand Rapids, MI: Wm. B. Eerdmans Publishing Co., 2010).

472. Kenneth A. Briggs, "Bernardin Asks Catholics to Fight Both Nuclear Arms and Abortion," *New York Times*, December 7, 1983, https://www.nytimes.com/1983/12/07/us/bernardin-asks-catholics-to-fight-both-nuclear-arms-and-abortion.html.

473. EWTN News, "Pope Benedict: End the Death Penalty," *National Catholic Register*, November 30, 2011, http://www.ncregister.com/daily-news/ pope-benedict-end-the-death-penalty; and "Pope Benedict XVI: 'Put an End to the Pointless Slaughters of War and Do Not Forget the Mistakes of the Past!,'" *Catholic News Agency*, July 22, 2007, https://www.catholic-newsagency.com/news/pope_benedict_xvi_put_an_end_to_the_pointless_slaughters_of_war_and_do_not_forget_the_mistakes_of_the_past.

474. Inés San Martín, "Pope Francis Changes Teaching on Death Penalty, It's 'Inadmissible,'" *Crux*, August 2, 2018, https://cruxnow.com/vatican/2018/08/02/pope-francis-changes-teaching-on-death-penalty-its-inadmissible/.

475. Andrea Gagliarducci, "What Does the Church Really Teach About Nuclear War?," *Catholic News Agency*, November 17, 2017, https://www.catholicnewsagency.com/news/what-does-the-church-really-teach-about-nuclear-war-23759.

476. Brian Fraga, "Church Rejects Morality of Nuclear Weapons," *Our Sunday Visitor Newsweekly* (Huntington, IN), January 10, 2018, https://www.osv.com/OSVNewsweekly/Story/TabId/2672/ArtMID/13567/ArticleID/23969/Church-rejects-morality-of-nuclear-weapons.aspx.

477. Catholic News Service, "Pope Francis: The Possession of Nuclear Weapons Should Be Firmly Condemned," *Catholic Herald*, November 11, 2017, https://catholicherald.co.uk/news/2017/11/11/pope-francis-the-possession-of-nuclear-weapons-should-be-firmly-condemned/.

478. "Highest to Lowest - Prison Population Rate," *World Prison Brief*, last modified November 2018, http://www.prisonstudies.org/highest-to-lowest/prison_population_rate?field_region_taxonomy_tid=All.

479. Thomas L. Friedman, "Foreign Affairs Big Mac I," *New York Times*, December 8, 1996, https://www.nytimes.com/1996/12/08/opinion/foreign-affairs-big-mac-i.html.

480. Tom O'Connor, "U.S. Has Spent Six Trillion Dollars on Wars That Killed Half a Million People Since 9/11, Report Says," *Newsweek*, November 14, 2018, https://www.newsweek.com/us-spent-six-trillion-wars-killed-half-million-1215588.

481. Azmat Khan and Anand Gopal, "The Uncounted," *New York Times Magazine*, November 16, 2017, https://www.nytimes.com/interactive/2017/11/16/magazine/uncounted-civilian-casualties-iraq-airstrikes.html?smid=tw-share.

482. "Kids were Playing Outside as Coalition Strike 'Directly Targeted' Raqqa Civilians – Witness to RT," *RT*, August 23, 2017, last modified August 24, 2017, https://www.rt.com/news/400626-syria-kids-coaltion-airstrike/.

483. Dave Philipps, "Decorated Navy SEAL Is Accused of War Crimes in Iraq," *New York Times*, November 15, 2018, https://www.nytimes.com/2018/11/15/us/navy-seal-edward-gallagher-isis.html?smid=fb-nytimes&smtyp=cur.

484. Liz Sly and Mustafa Salim, "ISIS is Making a Comeback in Iraq Just Months After Baghdad Declared Victory," *Washington Post*, July 17, 2018, https://www.washingtonpost.com/world/isis-is-making-a-comeback-in-iraq-less-than-a-year-after-baghdad-declared-victory/2018/07/17/9aac54a6-892c-11e8-9d59-dccc2c0cabcf_story.html?noredirect=on&utm_term=.ef5719864799.

485. Niall McCarthy, "The U.S. Never Dropped as Many Bombs on Afghanistan as It Did in 2018 [Infographic]," *Forbes*, November 13, 2018, https://www.forbes.com/sites/niallmccarthy/2018/11/13/the-u-s-never-dropped-as-many-bombs-on-afghanistan-as-it-did-in-2018-infographic/#7e4af0a12fae.

486. Melissa Dalton, Hijab Shah, and Timothy Robbins, "U.S. Support for Saudi Military Operations in Yemen," Center for Strategic and International Studies, March 23, 2018, https://www.csis.org/analysis/us-support-saudi-military-operations-yemen.

487. David D. Kirkpatrick and Carlotta Gall, "Audio Offers Gruesome Details of Jamal Khashoggi Killing, Turkish Official Says," *New York Times*, October 17, 2018, https://www.nytimes.com/2018/10/17/world/europe/turkey-saudi-khashoggi-dismember.html.

488. Haley Britzky, "An estimated 85,000 children have died of starvation in Yemen," *Axios*, November 21, 2017, https://www.axios.com/yemen-civil-war-children-died-starvation-72bbcaa8-07fa-41d5-bf3b-eb6e272cb3e4.html.

489. Rooj Alwazir, "Yemenis Seek Justice in Wedding Drone Strike," *Al Jazeera*, May 21, 2014, https://www.aljazeera.com/indepth/features/2014/01/yemenis-seek-justice-wedding-drone-strike-201418135352298935.html.

490. Devin Dwyer, "Obama: Nobel Peace Prize Winner Becomes Drone Warrior-in-Chief," *ABC News*, May 29, 2012, https://abcnews.go.com/Politics/Blotter/obama-drone-warrior-chief/story?id=16451227.

491. Spencer Ackerman, "Trump Ramped Up Drone Strikes in America's Shadow Wars," *Daily Beast*, November 25, 2018, https://www.thedailybeast.com/trump-ramped-up-drone-strikes-in-americas-shadow-wars?source=twitter&via=desktop.

492. Kara Fox, "North Korea Tested Its Longest-Ranging Missile Ever. Now What?," *CNN*, August 1, 2017, https://www.cnn.com/2017/07/31/asia/north-korea-missile-test-catchup/index.html.

493. Daniel R. DePetris, "Forget North Korea: Pakistan Might Be the Real Nuclear Threat," *National Interest*, August 2, 2018, https://nationalinterest.org/blog/buzz/forget-north-korea-pakistan-might-be-real-nuclear-threat-27647.

494. Seymour M. Hersh, "Defending the Arsenal," *New Yorker*, November 16, 2009, https://www.newyorker.com/magazine/2009/11/16/defending-the-arsenal.

495. John Maguire, "Pakistan Again Supporting Terrorists," *Real Clear Politics*, November 30, 2018, https://www.realclearpolitics.com/articles/2018/11/30/pakistan_again_supporting_terrorists_138790.html.

496. Mikhail Gorbachev, "Mikhail Gorbachev: A New Nuclear Arms Race Has Begun," *New York Times*, October 25, 2018, https://www.nytimes. com/2018/10/25/opinion/mikhail-gorbachev-inf-treaty-trump-nuclear-arms.html.

497. Jenny Starrs, "The Modern Nuclear Arsenal: A Nuclear Weapons Expert Describes a New Kind of Cold War," *Washington Post*, August 24, 2018, https://www.washingtonpost.com/news/checkpoint/wp/2018/08/24/ the-modern-nuclear-arsenal-a-nuclear-weapons-expert-describes-a-new-kind-of-cold-war/?utm_term=.1e2899c689e6.

498. Stephen Chen, "China Steps Up Pace in New Nuclear Arms Race with U.S. and Russia as Experts Warn of Rising Risk of Conflict," *Politico*, May 28, 2018, https://www.politico.com/story/2018/05/28/china-nuclear-arms-race-610028.

499. "National Statistics on the Death Penalty and Race," Death Penalty Information Center, last modified December 14, 2018, https://death-penaltyinfo.org/race-death-row-inmates-executed-1976#defend.

500. "Studies: Victims' Social Status Plays Influential Role in Death Cases," Death Penalty Information Center, n.d., https://deathpenaltyinfo.org/ studies-victims-social-status-plays-influential-role-death-cases.

501. "National Statistics," Death Penalty Information Center.

502. "Studies: Disparities in Legal Representation in Harris County, Texas," Death Penalty Information Center, n.d., https://deathpenaltyinfo.org/ studies-disparities-legal-representation-harris-county-texas.

503. "Prominent, Diverse Voices Call for Supreme Court to Once Again Stop Bobby James Moore's Execution," Death Penalty Information Center, 2018, https://deathpenaltyinfo.org/category/categories/issues/ intellectual-disability.

504. "Death Penalty Cost," Amnesty International, n.d., https://www.am-nestyusa.org/issues/death-penalty/death-penalty-facts/death-penalty-cost/.

505. "DNA Exonerations in the United States," Innocence Project, 2018, https://www.innocenceproject.org/dna-exonerations-in-the-united-states/.

506. V.v.B., "Why Support for the Death Penalty is Rising Again in America," *Economist*, August 24, 2018, https://www.economist.com/the-economist-explains/2018/08/24/why-support-for-the-death-penalty-is-rising-again-in-america.

507. Ibid.

508. "Lawyers Call for Investigation of 'Horrifying' Arkansas Execution After Witnesses Report 'Coughing, Convulsing,'" Death Penalty Information Center, https://deathpenaltyinfo.org/node/6752.

509. Associated Press, "Second Tennessee Prisoner on Death Row Chooses Electric Chair for Execution," *NBC News*, November 26, 2018, https://www.nbcnews.com/storyline/lethal-injection/second-tennessee-prisoner-death-row-chooses-electric-chair-execution-n940341.

510. Joseph P. Williams, "The Return of the Firing Squad," *US News & World Report*, March 3, 2017, https://www.usnews.com/news/the-report/articles/2017-03-03/the-firing-squad-is-making-a-comeback-in-death-penalty-cases.

511. The following facts come from "Criminal Justice Facts," The Sentencing Project, last modified 2017, https://www.sentencingproject.org/criminal-justice-facts/.

512. "Criminal Justice Fact Sheet," National Association for the Advancement of Colored People, last modified 2018, https://www.naacp.org/criminal-justice-fact-sheet/.

513. "Incarceration, Substance Abuse, and Addiction," The Center for Prisoner Health and Human Rights, n.d., https://www.prisonerhealth.org/educational-resources/factsheets-2/incarceration-substance-abuse-and-addiction/.

514. E. Fuller Torrey et al., "The Treatment of Persons with Mental Illness in Prisons and Jails: A State Survey," Treatment Advocacy Center, https://www.treatmentadvocacycenter.org/storage/documents/treatment-behind-bars/treatment-behind-bars.pdf.

515. "Jail Inmates in 2016," Bureau of Justice Statistics, February 2018, https://www.bjs.gov/content/pub/pdf/ji16_sum.pdf.

516. George Williams SJ, "Review: 'Refuge in Hell' is a Dante-esque Journey into Our Prison System," *America*, November 16, 2018, https://www.americamagazine.org/arts-culture/2018/11/16/review-refuge-hell-dante-esque-journey-our-prison-system.

517. JD Flynn, "'Heat Is a Human Right'—Power Restored to Brooklyn Jail after Week without Heat and Lights," *Catholic News* Agency, February 4, 2019, https://www.catholicnewsagency.com/news/heat-is-a-human-right--power-restored-to-brooklyn-jail-after-week-without-heat-and-lights-47177.

518. Ronald D. Lemmert, *Refuge in Hell: Finding God in Sing Sing* (Maryknoll: Orbis Books, 2018).

519. Scottie Andrew, "Prison Employees Face Same Rates of PTSD as War Veterans, New Research Claims," *Newsweek*, July 13, 2018, https://www.newsweek.com/prison-workers-face-high-rates-ptsd-study-says-1024273.

520. Dasha Lisitsina, "'Prison Guards Can Never Be Weak': The Hidden PTSD Crisis in America's Jails," *Guardian*, May 20, 2015, https://

www.theguardian.com/us-news/2015/may/20/corrections-officers-ptsd-american-prisons.

521. Shane Claiborne, "The Latest Botched Execution Shows There's No Good Way to Kill Someone," *Sojourners*, November 17, 2017, https://sojo.net/articles/latest-botched-execution-shows-there-s-no-good-way-kill-someone.

522. Robert Walsh, "He Killed 140 Men in the Electric Chair. Then He Took His Own Life," *Narratively*, March 1, 2017, https://narratively.com/he-killed-140-men-in-the-electric-chair-then-he-took-his-own-life/.

523. Linda Collins, "Op-ed: My Husband Supervised Ohio Executions for 5 Years. It Changed His Life," *WCPO Cincinnati*, July 21, 2017, https://www.wcpo.com/news/opinion/op-ed-my-husband-supervised-ohio-executions-for-5-years-it-changed-his-life.

524. *AMA Principles of Medical Ethics*, "Code of Medical Ethics Opinion 9.7.3," American Medical Association, 2016, https://www.ama-assn.org/delivering-care/ethics/capital-punishment.

525. Tom Vanden Brook, "Suicide Kills More U.S. Troops than ISIL in Middle East," *USA Today*, December 29, 2016, https://www.usatoday.com/story/news/nation/2016/12/29/suicide-kills-more-us-troops-than-isil-middle-east/95961038/.

526. Eyal Press, "The Wounds of the Drone Warrior," *New York Times*, June 13, 2018, https://www.nytimes.com/2018/06/13/magazine/veterans-ptsd-drone-warrior-wounds.html.

527. Micaiah David Dutt, "Confessions of a Catechumen and Ex-Marine," Orthodoxy in Dialogue, August 11, 2018, https://orthodoxyindialogue.com/2018/08/11/confessions-of-a-catechumen-and-ex-marine-by-micaiah-david-dutt/.

528. "Children in Syria Suffer from 'Human Devastation Syndrome,'" *TRT World*, March 3, 2017, https://www.trtworld.com/mea/un-report-says-children-in-syria-suffer-mental-health-problems-308871.

529. "How Do Our Words Dehumanize?," Rehumanize International, last modified 2018, https://www.rehumanizeintl.org/badwords.

530. "Pope Francis: Powerful People Don't Want Peace because they Profit from War," The Ring of Fire Network, May 13, 2015, https://trofire.com/2015/05/13/pope-francis-powerful-people-dont-want-peace-because-they-profit-from-war/.

531. John W. Whitehead, "Jailing Americans for Profit: The Rise of the Prison Industrial Complex," *Huffington Post*, April 10, 2012, last modified June 10, 2012, https://www.huffingtonpost.com/john-w-whitehead/prison-privatization_b_1414467.html.

532. Joe Weisenthal, "This Investor Presentation for a Private Prison is One

of the Creepiest Presentations We've Ever Seen," *Business Insider*, March 12, 2012, http://www.businessinsider.com/the-private-prison-business-2012-3#ixzz1pZb7JybJ.

533. Eric Schlosser, "The Prison-Industrial Complex," *The Atlantic*, December 1998, https://www.theatlantic.com/magazine/archive/1998/12/the-prison-industrial-complex/304669/.

534. Katie Mulvaney, "Brown U. Student Leader: More African-American Men in Prison System Now than Were Enslaved in 1850," *Politifact*, Ecember 7, 2014, https://www.politifact.com/rhode-island/statements/2014/dec/07/diego-arene-morley/brown-u-student-leader-more-african-american-men-p/.

535. Sarah Shemkus, "Beyond Cheap Labor: Can Prison Work Programs Benefit Inmates?," *Guardian*, December 9, 2015, https://www.theguardian.com/sustainable-business/2015/dec/09/prison-work-program-ohsa-whole-foods-inmate-labor-incarceration.

536. "The Disgrace of America's Prison-Industrial Complex," *National Post*, PressReader, March 23, 2013, https://www.pressreader.com/canada/national-post-national-edition/20130323/281801396410269.

537. G.E.M. Anscombe, "Mr. Truman's Degree," Oxford, 1958, http://www.ifac.univ-nantes.fr/IMG/pdf/Anscombe-truman.pdf.

538. Dutt.

539. "How It Works," Crossroads Prison Ministries, n.d., https://cpministries.org/mentorship-program/how-it-works/.

540. Alexandra Bowman, "Georgetown Launches Inmate Re-Entry and Education Program," *Hoya* (Georgetown University), November 30, 2018, http://www.thehoya.com/georgetown-launches-inmate-re-entry-education-program/?fbclid=IwAR2Nt7zu0FtO5GcbmvGtJF6_xrq4UlAy98fz7vSbOAPQS77wjHhILgi-oG8.

541. Jack Wellman, "Creating a Prison or Jail Ministry," *Patheos*, August 7, 2014, https://www.patheos.com/blogs/christiancrier/2014/08/07/creating-a-prison-or-jail-ministry/.

542. "Write a Prisoner…Change a Life," WriteAPrisoner.com, last modified 2018, https://writeaprisoner.com/.

543. "7 Helpful Programs for Children of Incarcerated Parents," Connect-Network, October 4, 2016, https://web.connectnetwork.com/programs-for-children-of-incarcerated-parents/.

544. "VA Voluntary Service," U.S. Department of Veterans Affairs, last modified December 4, 2018, https://www.volunteer.va.gov/.

545. Ingrid Herrera-Yee, "5 Ways You Can Support Veterans' Mental Health" (blog), National Alliance on Mental Illness, November 10, 2015, https://

www.nami.org/Blogs/NAMI-Blog/November-2015/5-Ways-You-Can-Support-Veterans%E2%80%99-Mental-Health.

546. Ward Wilson, "The Bomb Didn't Beat Japan ... Stalin Did," *Foreign Policy*, May 30, 2013, https://foreignpolicy.com/2013/05/30/the-bomb-didnt-beat-japan-stalin-did/.

547. Gar Alperovitz, "Did America Have to Drop the Bomb? Not to End the War, but Truman Wanted to Intimidate Russia," *Washington Post*, August 4, 1985, https://www.washingtonpost.com/archive/opinions/1985/08/04/did-america-have-to-drop-the-bombnot-to-end-the-war-but-truman-wanted-to-intimidate-russia/46105dff-8594-4f6c-b6d7-ef1b6cb6530d/?utm_term=.c19d4b7c6510.

548. John Finnis, "The Church Could Teach that Capital Punishment is Inherently Wrong," *Public Discourse*, August 23, 2018, https://www.thepublicdiscourse.com/2018/08/39401/.

549. Pius XII, "Discours du Pape Pie XII aux Participants au Congrès International D'histopathologie du Système Nerveux," Vatican Website, September 14, 1952, https://w2.vatican.va/content/pius-xii/fr/speeches/1952/documents/hf_p-xii_spe_19520914_istopatologia.html.

550. "Nuova Redazione del n. 2267 del Catechismo della Chiesa Cattolica sulla Pena di Morte – Rescriptum 'ex Audentia SS.mi,'" Vatican Website, August 2, 2018, http://press.vatican.va/content/salastampa/it/bollettino/pubblico/2018/08/02/0556/01209.html#IN.

551. Christopher O. Tollefsen, "Doubting Thomas (Aquinas) on Private and Public Killing," *Public Discourse*, November 14, 2017, https://www.thepublicdiscourse.com/2017/11/20396/.

552. David Bentley Hart, "Christians & the Death Penalty," *Commonweal*, November 16, 2017, https://www.commonwealmagazine.org/christians-death-penalty?utm_source=Main+Reader+List&utm_campaign=3073842e96-EMAIL_CAMPAIGN_2017_03_16&utm_medium=email&utm_term=0_407bf353a2-3073842e96-91263797.

553. John Paul II, *Evangelium vitae*, Vatican Website, March 25, 1995, http://w2.vatican.va/content/john-paul-ii/en/encyclicals/documents/hf_jp-ii_enc_25031995_evangelium-vitae.html.

554. "Deterrence: States Without the Death Penalty Have Had Consistently Lower Murder Rates," Death Penalty Information Center, last modified 2016, https://deathpenaltyinfo.org/deterrence-states-without-death-penalty-have-had-consistently-lower-murder-rates.

555. "Criminal Justice Facts," The Sentencing Project.

556. Daniel K. Williams, *Defenders of the Unborn: The Pro-Life Movement before Roe v. Wade* (New York: Oxford University Press, 2016).

557. Jean M. Twenge and W. Keith Campbell, "Associations between Screen Time and Lower Psychological Well-Being Among Children and Adolescents: Evidence from a Population-Based Study," *Preventive Medicine Reports* vol. 12 (December 2018): 271-283, https://www.sciencedirect.com/science/article/pii/S2211335518301827.

558. Jean M. Twenge, "Have Smartphones Destroyed a Generation?," *The Atlantic*, September 2017, https://www.theatlantic.com/magazine/archive/2017/09/has-the-smartphone-destroyed-a-generation/534198/.

559. Anderson Cooper, "What is "Brain Hacking"? Tech Insiders on Why You Should Care," *CBS News*, June 11, 2017, https://www.cbsnews.com/news/what-is-brain-hacking-tech-insiders-on-why-you-should-care/.

560. Christopher Bergland, "Cortisol: Why the "Stress Hormone" is Public Enemy No. 1," *Psychology Today*, January 22, 2013, https://www.psychologytoday.com/us/blog/the-athletes-way/201301/cortisol-why-the-stress-hormone-is-public-enemy-no-1.

561. Ben Sasse, *Them: Why We Hate Each Other--and How to Heal* (New York: St. Martin's Press, 2018).

562. Kate Snow and Cynthia McFadden, "Generation at Risk: America's Youngest Facing Mental Health Crisis," *NBC News*, December 10, 2017, last modified December 11, 2017, https://www.nbcnews.com/health/kids-health/generation-risk-america-s-youngest-facing-mental-health-crisis-n827836.

563. Jane E. Brody, "The Surprising Effects of Loneliness on Health," *New York Times*, December 11, 2017, https://www.nytimes.com/2017/12/11/well/mind/how-loneliness-affects-our-health.html.

564. Erin Blakemore, "Neuroscientist Thinks One Way to Fight Opioid Addiction is to Tackle Loneliness," *Washington Post*, December 1, 2018, https://www.washingtonpost.com/amphtml/national/health-science/neuroscientist-thinks-one-way-to-fight-opioid-addiction-is-to-tackle-loneliness/2018/11/30/8f651440-f33d-11e8-80d0-f7e1948d55f4_story.html?__twitter_impression=true.

565. Lenny Bernstein, "U.S. Life Expectancy Declines Again, a Dismal Trend Not Seen Since World War I," *Washington Post*, November 29, 2018, https://www.washingtonpost.com/amphtml/national/health-science/us-life-expectancy-declines-again-a-dismal-trend-not-seen-since-world-war-i/2018/11/28/ae58bc8c-f28c-11e8-bc79-68604ed88993_story.html?utm_term=.7732c81efd06&wpisrc=nl_rainbow&wpmm=1&__twitter_impression=true.

566. Emma Green, "National Politics Has Taken Over America," *The Atlantic*, November 5, 2018, https://www.theatlantic.com/amp/article/574885/?__twitter_impression=true.

567. Arthur C. Brooks, "How Loneliness Is Tearing America Apart," *New York Times*, November 23, 2018, https://www.nytimes.com/2018/11/23/opinion/loneliness-political-polarization.html.

568. Zack Beauchamp, "The Midterm Elections Revealed that America is in a Cold Civil War," *Vox*, November 7, 2018, https://www.vox.com/midterm-elections/2018/11/7/18068486/midterm-election-2018-results-race-surburb.

569. Sabrina Tavernise, "These Americans are Done with Politics," *New York Times*, November 17, 2018, https://www.nytimes.com/2018/11/17/sunday-review/elections-partisanship-exhausted-majority.html.

570. In some ways, the current pro-life movement—insofar as it is fixated on national politics in this way—is both a victim and perpetrator of this culture. And this provides yet another reason the CLE is so important. It doesn't hurt us, but rather makes us stronger. Maybe the most damaging critique of the movement is that we are hyper-focused on using politics as a way of protecting the prenatal child by law. This is a good goal, and one which I've spent a lot of personal time supporting, but it is a disaster when it becomes a singular focus for the movement. Especially given the history of the pro-life movement, the CLE isn't an example of mission creep. It is returning to our (far healthier) roots.

571. Georgetown CST, Twitter Post, October 15, 2017, 4:25pm, https://twitter.com/GUcstpubliclife/status/919660578230108160.

572. Francis, *Evangelii gaudium*, Vatican Website, November 24, 2013, http://w2.vatican.va/content/francesco/en/apost_exhortations/documents/papa-francesco_esortazione-ap_20131124_evangelii-gaudium.html, 88.

573. "Pope: Franciscan 'Littleness' is a Place of Encounter," *Vatican News*, November 23, 2017, https://www.vaticannews.va/en/pope/news/2017-11/pope--franciscan--littleness--is-a-place-of-encounter.html.

574. John L. Allen, Jr., "Christ Child Is with Refugees, Child Soldiers and Abortion Victims, Pope Says," *Crux*, December 24, 2016, https://cruxnow.com/vatican/2016/12/24/christ-child-refugees-child-soldiers-abortion-victims-pope-says/.

575. David Scales, "Making Health Social: Friends and Family as Part of the Health Care Team," *Harvard Health Publishing*, March 15, 2017, https://www.health.harvard.edu/blog/making-health-social-bringing-friends-family-onto-health-care-team-2017031511282.

576. The first studies done on this were by Leon Festinger in the 1950s when he studied the psychological responses to incorrect predictions about the end of the world. See Leon Festinger, Henry W. Riecken, and Stanley Schachter, *When Prophecy Fails: A Social and Psychological Study of a*

Modern Group that Predicted the End of the World (Minneapolis: University of Minnesota Press, 1956).

577. This insight is one of several which might lead us to consider the act displayed on this book's cover as ambiguous when it comes to a genuine culture of encounter and hospitality.

578. Francis, *Amoris laetitia*, Vatican Website, March 19, 2016, https://w2.vatican.va/content/dam/francesco/pdf/apost_exhortations/documents/papa-francesco_esortazione-ap_20160319_amoris-laetitia_en.pdf, 118. Francis is quoting Martin Luther King, Jr.'s "'Loving Your Enemies': Sermon Delivered at Dexter Avenue Baptist Church" (sermon, Dexter Avenue Baptist Church, Montgomery, AL, November 17, 1957), Martin Luther King Jr. Papers Project, http://okra.stanford.edu/transcription/document_images/Vol04Scans/315_17-Nov-1957_Loving%20Your%20Enemies.pdf.

New City Press

New City Press is one of more than 20 publishing houses sponsored by the Focolare, a movement founded by Chiara Lubich to help bring about the realization of Jesus' prayer: "That all may be one" (John 17:21). In view of that goal, New City Press publishes books and resources that enrich the lives of people and help all to strive toward the unity of the entire human family. We are a member of the Association of Catholic Publishers.

www.newcitypress.com
202 Comforter Blvd.
Hyde Park, New York

Periodicals
Living City Magazine
www.livingcitymagazine.com

Scan to join our mailing list
for discounts and promotions
or go to www.newcitypress.com
and click on "join our email list."